THE SOLAR RETURN
or
VARSHAPHAL

By the same authors:

- ASPECTS IN VEDIC ASTROLOGY
- ASTROLOGICAL SECRETS OF FRIENDSHIP, LOVE AND MARRIAGE
- ASTROLOGY AND YOU
- BODY READING
- NUMEROLOGY FOR ALL
- PALMISTRY FOR ALL
- PREDICTIVE ASTROLOGY OF THE HINDUS
- अंकविद्या (ज्योतिष)
- जातक-पारिजात (२ भाग)
- जातकादेश मार्ग-चन्द्रिका
- फलदीपिका (भावार्थबोधिनी)
- भारतीय लग्न-सारिणी
- त्रिफला (ज्योतिष)
- सुगम ज्योतिष प्रवेशिका
- हस्तरेखा विज्ञान

THE SOLAR RETURN

or

Varshaphal

The Tajik System of the Year

GOPESH KUMAR OJHA
ASHUTOSH OJHA

MOTILAL BANARSIDASS PUBLISHERS
PRIVATE LIMITED • DELHI

First Edition: Delhi, 2005

ISBN: 81-208-2656-6 (Cloth)
ISBN: 81-208-2674-4 (Paper)

MOTILAL BANARSIDASS
41 U.A. Bungalow Road, Jawahar Nagar, Delhi 110 007
8 Mahalaxmi Chamber, 22 Bhulabhai Desai Road, Mumbai 400 026
236, 9th Main III Block, Jayanagar, Bangalore 560 011
203 Royapettah High Road, Mylapore, Chennai 600 004
Sanas Plaza, 1302 Baji Rao Road, Pune 411 002
8 Camac Street, Kolkata 700 017
Ashok Rajpath, Patna 800 004
Chowk, Varanasi 221 001

Printed in India
BY JAINENDRA PRAKASH JAIN AT SHRI JAINENDRA PRESS,
A-45 NARAINA, PHASE-I, NEW DELHI 110 028
AND PUBLISHED BY NARENDRA PRAKASH JAIN FOR
MOTILAL BANARSIDASS PUBLISHERS PRIVATE LIMITED,
BUNGALOW ROAD, DELHI 110 007

CONTENTS

CHAPTERS

LIST OF TABLES AND CHARTS

TABLES

CHARTS

Om Adipurushaya Namah

PREFACE

प्रणवो धनुः शरो ह्यात्मा ब्रह्म तल्लक्ष्यमुच्यते।
अप्रमत्तेन वेद्धव्यं शरवत्तन्मयो भवेत॥

(मुण्डकोपनिषत् २:४)

Without ego the 'ATMA' in the shape of arrow on the bow 'OM' should be aimed to hit the bull's eye in the form of 'BRAHMA'. Just as a well directed arrow enters into the aim and attains invisibility and oneness, in the same manner with this practice 'ATMA' is unified with 'BRAHMA' and merges into HIM.

Astrology comprises of many branches viz., the horoscope erected for the birth time, Mundane Astrology, Medical Astrology, Horary Astrology, Varshaphal or the Solar Returns Horoscopes and many more branches. Although our main purpose is to deal with the method and interpretation of the Solar Return charts yet what are these other branches of Astrology. Horoscope at birth is called the nativity or the Birth Chart or Janma Lagnam; Mundane Astrology deals with the Horoscope of Countries: Medical Astrology is concerned with the disease and medical sciences in general; the best time to pick up herbal plants and prepare medicine, selection of Doctors, time of administration of medicine or the right time for physical operations i.e., surgery. Horary Astrology takes into account the Chart erected for the time (without prior appointment, i.e., at random) of meeting with an Astrologer of the time of asking a question (in person).

The purpose of Astrology for a layman is to know the

future. How expectant and attentive a person becomes when he opens up his palms to be read or his horosocope is about to be examined by a fortuneteller? The look which he throws is a mixture of hope, pride and beseeching and has no parallel.

The main interest is not only in knowing the events but as to when and how these will materialize. For this purpose, there are various methods in Astrology. From the Natal chart (birth chart) the timing of events is arrived at with the help of various kinds of Dashas, antardashas, natural years of planets and most importantly from the Transits.

Horary Astrology also called Prasna Kundali is another excellent method which makes it easier to arrive at the timing of events as well as it describes in details the manner and description of persons who will be helpful or those who will put obstacles in the realization of a goal.

This branch of Astrology is based on the principle of from *known to unknown*. The belief is that events are so synchronized in life that only at a particular time they take shape and so a person when he goes to meet an Astrolger carries with him the essence of his stars. This meeting is a random meeting without prior appointment. The Astrologers erect a chart for the time of meeting and this chart tells us all about the past, present and future of the visitor. Some expert Astrologers can even tell the question of the person without being told about it and the answer is also correct to the dot.

In this regard the majority of the astrologers agree that the chart should be erected for the time when the astrologer sees the client and not when he goes to see him or when he asks his questions. All related matters pertaining to the client viz., his questions, his walk of life, his surroundings will unfold themselves—accurate and fast. This brings us to the Solar return horoscopes. What is a solar return and in what manner it works, what are its advantages etc. All this is thoroughly discussed in the introduction and then in the main book. Here, we would like to indicate that all the principles and methods used in the judgement of a Solar Return chart applies in toto to Horary Astrology.

The present book *'The Solar Return'* comprises the subject matter developed by *'Yavanacharya'*. Acharya means Guru and Guru of the *'yavanas'*. The word *'Yavana'* was used for the Persians and Arabs—The people from the west (Arabia & Persia) who attacked India a number of times and that made the scholars seek Asylum in Tibet with their monumental works—to save and preserve the sancitity of these books of Mantra Shastra, Spiritualism, Astrology etc.

However, in the early 3000 B.C. India was attacked by the *'Shakya'* dynasty from the East and then the scholars turned to the West to seek Asylum—The lesser evil so to say. And it was there that the system of the solar revolution was perfected. The various names of the yogas viz., Itthashal, Ikkabal, Israf etc. indicate the root, the origin of this subject. These words are used in Persian.

The chief subject matter of this book is the solar revolution, the return* of the Sun to the same sign, degree, minute, seconds that it had at the time and date of birth. A chart is erected for that date and time (as well as the place of birth of the native) and then due consideration is given to this horoscope (Varsh lagnam). It is our strong belief that this subject will be easily learned by a person with even moderate abilities and he can master the basic difficulties with a few days' of study. It may be well understood and reduced to constant practice in less than four months. 'Practice makes a man perfect' and the more we practice it, the more closer to perfection we will be. The total perfection exists only in theory and not in reality, still no heights are denied if one wants to become perfect.

The advantage of mastering this book is that you become proficient in one and the second one will come to you on its own. You know the system of the Solar return and you will also know Horary Astrology. All principles of the Solar Return applies to Horary Astrology.

* N.B. : The Sun does not move. It is the time taken by the Earth in the Ecliptic which is used by the term—The return of the 'Sun'.

We would like to add here that Horary Astrology is very useful in case:

1. The date and time of birth is unknown.
2. Closer inspection of the whereabouts and matters related to a third party.
3. To know the question of the visitor without being told about it.
4. If a proposition of any type is made to an individual, and he is anxious and therefore uncertain whether to accede to it or not, let him note the hour and minute when the proposition was first made and his solutions will come. He will in a few minutes, arrive at the right decisions. The Ascendant, the planet there in, the lord of the Ascendant will describe the party making the offer — his character and his capabilities and this will enable the inquirer to arrive at a conclusion.

We would further like to point out as to when Horary Astrology fails:

1. When someone wants to get an enquiry on telephone.
2. The inquirer goes to the Astrologer empty handed or in an arrogant manner.
3. The Astrologer either does not know the subject matter or is a conman in the 'grab' of a professional to grind his wheel.

The present book is simple, easy to understand and does not rely on rigorous mathematical calculations. For easy references we have given various tables which will work like ready-reckoners. The different yogas have been well illustrated by example charts. The Tripati Chakra links the Nativity and the Solar Return chart. The results are accurate. The Varsh langa viz., the Solar Return chart is in fact a *magnified version of the events to take shape in the year.* From this we can also cast:

(A) Monthly Horoscopes, (B) Daily Horoscopes, and (C) Lunar Horoscopes.

Monthly Horoscopes are cast when the Sun enters into the next sign of the Zodiac from the one which it occupied at birth. For example, let us say that Sun at birth was in Virgo 7° – 8' – 30". In order to calculate the second month we should see when Sun moves to Libra 7 deg. 8 min. 30 sec. For the 3rd month, Sun in Scorpio 7 dig. 8 min. 30 secs. and so on. These horoscopes of the months are interpreted in correlation with (*i*) the birth chart and (*ii*) The Solar Return chart.

What is indicated in the Solar Return charts will materialize only if it is also indicated in the Nativity and what is indicated in the charts for the months will take shape if it is indicated in the nativity as well as in the annual chart or monthly charts for after all these are only the magnified versions of the events indicated in the original Nativity.

In addition to the horoscopes of the months, it is possible to cast daily and hourly horoscopes. By adding the daily motion of the Sun in a month's chart, we will get the daily horoscopes and by adding the 24th portion of the Sun's daily motion, we get the hourly charts, viz., if the motion of Sun is 60 minutes in 24 hours then add 2.5 minutes in the motion of Sun for each hour.

In general we take the average daily motion of Sun as 1 degree or 60 minutes. If the Sun is in Virgo in 7 deg. 8 min. 30 Secs. Then the horoscope for the next day will be when Sun is in Virgo 8 deg. 8 min. 30 secs. Add one degree for each day and 2.5 minutes for each hour. We should keep on changing the year as well according to the Solar Return charts.

Example:

Date of Birth	17.08.1974
Completed years	20
Beginning of 21st year	17.08.1994

The chart for the first day of the first month will be the same as that of the solar return chart for the year.

For the second day it will be for 18.8.1994; for 3rd day 19.8.1994; for 4th day 20.8.1994 and so on. In this monthly chart, all months constitues 30 days each.

Another method is to use each house of the monthly chart as to represent two and a half days viz., The first house, the first two and a half days, the second house for the next two and a half days (upto the 5th day) and so on..

The lunar months are calculated when the moon comes to the same degree, minute, secs. etc. that it occupied at birth. The change is in the Zodiacal signs as in the case of the Solar monthly horoscope. The year also changes. The way to interpret is the same as for the year chart. In order to know as to when the event will take shape, the difference between the degree of two planets in orbs who are the applying to each other (Itthasal) or (Israf) separating will indicate the months, weeks or days according as they are in fixed, dual, or moveable signs respectively. In the monthly charts the events will be known by multiplying the difference in the degrees by 2.5 (2 and ½) as to the day, hours and minutes according to the placement of planets in the fixed, dual, or moveable signs respectively.

The science of Astrology is fascinating, accurate and fast. It gives an insight into the future which no other science can do, i.e., as to what will happen after 30 years or 75 years? What disease or calamities will fall to a Nation or an Individual? One who is well prepared is stronger and worth more than 32 combined.

In India *Horoscope* is Cast as soon as a child is born and many stories are around as to what this child will do or achieve in life by the sages who looked at his chart.

To conclude the matter now let us state that 'Ignorance is Bliss' but knowledge of the future is much better. The theory of karma enuciates that "what you sow so shall you reap" but the intensity of the destiny is three fold:

1. What has to be will be—one who is born has to go some day.
2. Certain things however can be totally eliminated—by prayers, by good deeds, by the blessing of others.

3. Certain things can be modified by control on ones mind, which cames by meditation, by prayers, and also by taking steps to be prepared for the coming shadows.

'Fatalism' is a frame of mind behind which the weak, the lazy and those who want to find a lame excuse hide themselves for their inactions.

'Aham Brahmasmi'. I am Brahma—The creator and I can achieve everything. Learned readers! believe in yourself—let confidence ooz out of every pore and success is yours.

Authors

ASHUTOSH OJHA
H.No. 1952, Sector IV,
Urban Estate, Gurgaon (Haryana)
aojha@vsnl.com

INTRODUCTION

Sri Ganeshaya Namah

I touch the holy feet of the cluster of Light who is mentioned in the *Upanishads,* in Nirguna Swarupa, and also mentioned as the other half of Brahma in Sagunarupa, with the cherry-red lips and a veena, in the form of Saraswati.

The present book is based on knowledge passed down by the old masters over the past few thousand years. Its purpose is to bring to light some of the ancient principles of the Jyotish Shastra. These principles were transmitted by the word of mouth from the sages to their disciples. Some of them have been lost through the centuries; others have been retained in particular families, sometimes fully intact but sometimes incomplete. (In India, it is traditional for the father to act as spiritual master to the son. This is why, in so many astrological texts from South India, the Ninth house, ordinarily regarded as the house of the guru, is called the house of the father. In North India, the Tenth is the house of the father, though the Ninth must also be taken into account if the father acts as guru to his son).

This book deals with the technique of Solar Returns. Chapters I through III deal with the calculation of the Solar Return chart, the house divisions, aspects, and attributes of the signs and planets, and with the Lord of the year. Chapters IV through VI deal with Muntha, with the sixteen yogas (very important for arriving at conclusions regarding Solar Returns), the sensitive points or Sahamas, and with a special technique called the Tripataki Chakra. Chapter VII deals with the timing of events and Chapters VIII onwords through are concerned with interpretation and delineation.

Jyotish, the science of astrology, is more than 5000 years old. Its ultimate origins can be traced to India, where it is called the "eyes of the Vedas", indicating that it should be regarded as the most important branch of Vedic knowledge. The Solar Return chart which is the subject of this book gives very accurate and precise information about the events which will take place during any particular solar year. It provides a magnified view of the year in question.

The Solar Return chart is called Varsha Kundali (i.e., "annual chart") in Sanskrit. It should not be confused with the "progressed horoscope" as defined in Western Astrology; it refers to the Solar Return pure and simple. Its purpose is to supplement any predications based on the natal chart. The technique of Solar Returns would seem to have originated with the Chaldeans, who attached great importance to it and directed their energies only toward such pursuits as boded success during the coming year. The *De Revolutionibus Nativatum,* ascribed to Hermes, states:

> The Babylonians, Persians, Indians and Egyptians, both kings and private persons, undertook nothing in any year without examining their revolutions, and if they found the year good they set to work; otherwise they refrained. The kings examined the nativities of their generals and observed their revolutions, and if they found that for one of them the return indicated power and victory, they sent him agianst the enemy; otherwise they left him aside. And they observed the genitures not only of their generals but of ambassadors, to see if their anniversaries (solar returns) indicated a successful result. If they signified prosperity they sent for them but if not they appointed instead others whose anniversaries did presage success. In the same manner, kings and citizens chose food, drink, medicine; bought, sold and did everything according to their returns; and they used these things and left aside those likely to be hurtful that year. They deduced from their own nativities and those of others and acted

accordingly. Men wishing to beget a son observed their wives' revolutions as well as their own, and if both signified procreation they cohabited with them; otherwise they looked for other women whose nativities did signify the birth of a son. So the study of revolution is very useful and expedient... (*).

This raises the fundamental question of fate vs. free will. The psychological and philosophical implications of this question have such wide ramifications that it is not possible even to address the essentials of it here. But let us simply state that the entire foundation of astrology rests upon the cornerstone of "the compulsion of the stars", which may be marginally checked or modified due to our actions and environment, but which can never be completely wiped out.

To revert to the main topic of this book, we must now ask: what date is to be employed for erecting the Solar Return chart?

The principle is that the Solar Return chart should be cast for the exact time when the sun *returns* (due to the earth's revolution around the sun) to the same longitude (sign, degree, minute and second) which it occupied at the time of one's birth. This happens approximately on one's birthday according to the Gregorian Calendar—sometimes a day earlier or later.

In India, both the radix or natal chart and the Solar Return chart are computed in terms of *sidereal* coordinates. During the last few decades a number of Western astrologers have switched their allegiance to the sidereal zodiac, primarily because the signs of the sidereal zodiac (called the "zodiac of the constellations" by some Western astrologers) maintain an unaltered relationship with the fixed stars, whereas the tropical zodiac, due to both the precession of the equinoxes and nutation, keeps receding year after year and cannot continue to align itself with the fixed stars and constellations. Those interested

---

* Bouche Leclerc, *L'Astrologie Grecque*, Paris 1899.

in pursuing the matter further may consult the works of Westerners such as Cyril Fagan, Llewellyn George, Donald A. Bradley, Alten Garth, and George Cecil Nixon.

One important point which has a practical bearing on the erection of the Solar Return chart, however, is that many of the above-mentioned scholars compute the longitudes of the sidereal zodiac by assigning a value to Spica (a fixed star known as Chitra in Sanskrit) which is slightly different from that used in India. Thus, many Western siderealists affirm that the value of the precession of the equinoxes and nutation on January 1, 1960, was 24 degrees, 16' 54", while according to Hindu astrologers who follow the correction of N.C. Lahiri, it was 23 degrees, 17' 54"—a difference of some 59 minutes. There are a few astrologers in India who support a correction (Sanskrit: ayanamsha) which is at variance with that of Lahiri, but these are in the definite minority. An abridged table giving the correctional values is provided in an appendix. Though the rate of precession is not uniform from year to year, a very workable correction can be worked out for a date intermediate between any two given years simply by using the rule of three.

Readers who do not have a sidereal or Hindu birth chart will have to convert their Western charts, otherwise all references to the radix will be off the mark. For the Solar Returns as well, all tropical positions must be converted to their sidereal equivalents by deducting the appropriate ayanamsha for the date in question. Another issue which will be discussed in its proper place is house division: common Western house system such as Placidus, Campanus or Regiomontanus will not work here; it will be necessary to use a particular variant of the Western Porphyry house system as practiced in India.

A working knowledge of astrology—and of Hindu astrology in particular—is assumed in these pages, wherein we are principally concerned with the differences between the *natal* and *Tajik* (i.e., Solar Return) systems. Those who are unfamiliar with the rudiments of Vedic astrology for them we start from the beginning.

I

How do We Proceed to Calculate?

We need the date, time and place of birth to start with. We also need to know the name of the person.

Here, we start with the data of Mr. Ambirsh Sharma who was born on May 1st 1979 at 06.15 a.m. at New Delhi, India. We need his Solar Return chart fo the 24th Year. The Solar Return chart is dependent for interpretation on the birth chart, so we shall first calculate his Birth Chart.

(a) Birth chart will include the calculation of Ascendant, cusps of houses and their midpoints, Longitudes of planets, Mahadashas, Navansha etc.

(b) We shall then calculate the commencement of his 24th year, i.e., 23 years completed which will be in May 2002 at a certain hour.

(c) We shall then calculate for the purpose of illustration the Rising Sign at the time of commencement of the year and the following:

- (*i*) Longitudes [Int. II]
- (*ii*) Mudda Dashas [CH.I]
- (*iii*) The Lord of the year [CH. III]
- (*iv*) Planetary Joys [CH. I]
- (*v*) Some Sensitive points [CH. IV]
- (*vi*) Muntha's placement [CH. I]
- (*vii*) Tripataki Chakra etc. [CH. VI]

How to find the Ascendant or Lagna for Mr. Ambrish?

In the calculation of the Ascending degree at the Eastren Horizon (as seen from birth place), accuracy is needed. We attach the greatest importance to the locality (where a person is born). It is so because at the same standard time, the Ascending degree at different cities in a country will be different.

We should therefore convert the Standard Time in this case I.S.T., to the Local Mean Time (in short L.M.T.) of New Delhi which is needed for the calculation of the Ascendant.*

We should ascertain the Longitude at which the standard time of a country is kept. For this we look at the time difference between the Greenwich Mean Time (which is for 0 degree longitude) and the I.S.T. This difference is 5 Hours 30 minutes. By allowing 4 minutes for each degree of longitude we find that the I.S.T. is kept for 82 degrees 30 minutes. [(82° – 30') × 4 = 330 minutes)].

(a) *Conversion of Standard Time to LMT*

For calculation of Ascendant, Local Mean Time is used.

The I.S.T. is for	82° - 30' East
Longitude of New Delhi*	77° - 13' East
Difference	5° - 17'

This (5° - 17') at the rate of 4 minutes per degree gives us 21 minutes 8 seconds which is the difference between the standard time and the local time. Sun rises earlier in the East and as the Longitude of I.S.T. is East of New Delhi so we will reduce 21 minutes 8 seconds from the Standard Time of birth. If it is West of I.S.T. then we add, to convert into the L.M.T.

	Hrs.	*Min.*	*Secs.*
I.S.T. at birth	06	15	00
Difference	– 00	21	08
Local Mean Time	05	53	52

Sidereal time of birth at preceding noon on birth date from the 'Table of Ascendants' by N.C. Lahiri, page no. 2

Sid. time at Noon on 30 April 1979	02	30	59	(P.2)
Correction for the year 1979	– 00	00	32	(P.4)
Remainder	02	30	27	

* For all purposes, the majority opinion of old masers is to use the place of birth for calculating the solar return charts irrespective of the place where he/she is residing at the time of commencement of the New solar year.

The Longitude of New Delhi is 77 degrees 13 minutes East and the Latitude is 28 degrees 39 minutes North.

The sidereal time for preceding Noon, i.e., on 30th April 1979 has been calculated as 02 hrs. 30 min. 27 sec.

To find R.A.M.C.

(Next) Process

	Hrs.		*Mnts.*		*Secs.*
(*i*) Sid. Time at preceding Noon	02	–	30	–	27
(*ii*) Add local Mean time elapsed since Noon which is 12.00+ (5-53-52) i.e.	+17	–	53	–	52
(*iii*) Add increase in sid. time @10 secs. per hour from Noon which is 179 secs, i.e.,	00	–	02	–	59
Total	20	–	27	–	18

This 'Total' is called the Sidereal time at birth or Right Ascension of the Meridian Cusp which here is 20 Hrs. 27 Mnts. 18 Secs.

(b) *Calculation of the Ascendant*

Now we need the table of Ascendants again and here we use the table of Ascendant (Niraryan Basis) by N.C. Lahiri. The Latitude of the birth place is 28° 39' North.

Referring to the *Table of Ascendants* we find that on page 48 Delhi's Latitude is 28° 39' North.

Going through the columns of Sidereal time and looking up for RAMC which is 20 hrs. 27 mnts. 18 secs.

Sid. Time	*Ascendant*			
	S	*D*	*Mnts.*	*Secs.*
20 Hrs. 28 Mnts. 0 Secs.	0	26	26	00
20 Hrs. 24 Mnts. 0 Secs.	0	25	15	00
By subtracting for 4 mnts. or for 240 Secs. it is		01 –	11 –	00
			71 mnts.	

By rule of three we find for 42 secs. (which is the difference between 20 hrs. 28 mnts. 00 secs. and RAMC i.e., (71 ÷ 240 × 42) = 12 mnts.

So the Ascedant is	0–26°–26'–00"
	– 0– 0°–12'–00"
or Aries 26°–14'–0"	0–26°–14'–00"

(c) *Calculation of the Meridian Cusp.*

We shall now calculate the Meridian Cusp for RAMC.

On page 8, in the Table of Ascendants we find that for 20 hrs. 28 mins. 00 secs. It is

	Si.	*Deg.*	*Mins.*	*Secs.*
20 hrs. 28 mins.	9	– 11	– 39	– 00
For 20 hrs. 24 mins.	9	– 10	– 41	– 00
Deducting for 4' or 240 secs.		00 –	58	– 00

By rule of three we find for 42 secs. 58/240 × 42=10 Minutes

The Meridian	9	– 11	– 39	– 00
Cusp is	–0	–0	– 10	– 0
M.C.	9	–11°	– 29'	– 00"

We need the Ascendant and the meridian cusp in order to calculate the cusps of houses and their midpoints in the birth chart.

(d) *Cusp of houses and their mid points:*

Now we proceed to calculate the cusps and midpoints of the house by using the Ascendant and the Meridian Cusp.

	Si.	*Deg.*	*Mins.*	*Secs.*
Cusp of the Ascendant Or the First house	0	– 26	– 14	– 00
Cusp of the 10th house	9	– 11	– 29	– 00
Subtract	3	14	45	00
The difference between the two by deduction is	3 signs 14 degrees 45 minutes			

This 3 signs 14 degrees 45 minutes is the difference between the cusp of the 1st and 10th houses. This difference when divided by 6, (3 cusps + 3 midpoints) will give us the difference between one house and its midpoint and also between the midpoint and the other house.

Si.	*Deg.*	*Mins.*	*Secs.*
3	– 14	– 45	– 00

So one-sixth division is equal to 17° – 27'-30". By adding this one-sixth division in the cusp of the 10th house and again in the resultant sum again and again. We shall get the cusp of the XI and XII houses as well as their midpoints, i.e., the intersections of houses.

	Si.	*Deg.*	*Mins.*	*Secs.*
Cusp of the X house	9	– 11 –	29 –	00
By adding	+0	– 17 –	27 –	30
X house ends XI begins	9	– 28 –	56 –	30
Add again	0	– 17 –	27 –	30
Cusp of XI house	10	– 16 –	24 –	00
Add again	0	– 17 –	27 –	30
XI house end XII begins	11	– 3 –	51 –	30
Add again	0	– 17 –	27 –	30
Cusp of XII house	11	– 21 –	19 –	00
Add again	0	– 17 –	27 –	30
XII house ends I begins	0	– 8 –	46 –	30
Add again	0	– 17 –	27 –	30
Cusp of the I house	0	– 26 –	14 –	00

After the above calculation of the cusp of 10th, 11th and 12th houses and the midpoints between these, the calculations of the cusps of the other houses and their mid points is easy:

	Si.	*Deg.*	*Mins.*	*Secs.*
(a) Thus, midpoint between XII	0	8	46	30
and I Add I Sign	– 1	0	0	0
Midpoint between I and II	1	– 8 –	46 –	30
Cusp of the XII	11	– 21 –	19 –	0
(b) Add 2 signs	2	– 0 –	0 –	0
Cusp of the II house (13) or	1	– 21 –	19 –	0
(c) Midpoint between XI				
And XII	11	– 3 –	51 –	30
Add 3 sings	3	– 0 –	0 –	0
Midpoint between II&III (14) or	2	– 3 –	51 –	30

(d) Cusp of XI	10 – 16	– 24	–	0
Add 4 signs	4 – 0	– 0	–	0
Cusp of 3rd house	14(2) – 16	– 24	–	0
(e) Midpoint between XI & X	9 – 28	– 56	–	30
Add 5 signs	5 – 0	– 0	–	0
Midpoint between 3rd & 4th	14 or (2) – 28	– 56	–	30
Cusp of X house	9 – 11	– 29	–	00
Add 6 signs	6 – 0	– 0	–	0
Cusp of the 4th house	15 or (3)– 11	– 29	–	0

We write this in the following format:

Cusp of house

	X	*Midpoint*	*XI*	*Midpoint*	*XII*	*Midpoint*
Si	9	9	10	11	11	0
D	11	28	16	3	21	8
M	29	56	24	51	19	46
S	00	30	00	30	00	30

	I	*Midpoint*	*II*	*Midpoint*	*III*	*Midpoint*
Si	0	1	1	2	2	2
D	26	8	21	3	16	28
M	14	46	19	51	24	56
S	00	30	00	30	00	30

	IV
Si	3
D	11
M	29
S	00

By adding 6 sign to each of the above cusps of X, XI, XII, I, II and III houses as well as to all the six midpoints we get the remaining cusps of IV, V, VI, VII, VIII and IX houses and we also get their corresponding midpoints. Please note that *'Si'* stands for signs; *'D'* stands for degrees; *'M'* stands for Minutes and *'S'* stands for seconds. Now by adding 6 signs, we get the remaining cusps of houses and their midpoints.

	IV	*Midpoint*	*V*	*Midpoint*	*VI*	*Midpoint*
Si	3	3	4	4	5	5
D	11	28	16	3	21	8
M	29	56	24	51	19	46
S	00	30	00	30	00	30

	VII	*Midpoint*	*VIII*	*Midpoint*	*IX*	*Midpoint*
Si	6	7	7	8	8	8
D	26	8	21	3	16	28
M	14	46	19	51	24	56
S	00	30	00	30	00	30

The advantage of working out the cusps of the houses and their midpoints is that planets are strongest when they are nearer to the cusp of the houses and they keep on showing less and less effect as they move closer to the midpoints.

Before proceeding to the calculations of the longitudes of planets let me point out that this system of house division is as per the Keshaviyya and Shripati Jataka Paddhatis. This system is also followed in Western Astrology and known by Porphyry's systems of house division.

How to Calculate the Longitudes of Planets

In these calculations, we are concerned with Sun and Moon which are the Luminaries but for practical purpose are called 'Planets' in Astrology. The other planets we use are Mars, Mercury, Jupiter, Venus, and Saturn.

Besides these seven planets Rahu and Ketu are also used in the traditional Hindu Astrology. Rahu and Ketu are shadow planets. Rahu is the northern node of Moon and Ketu is the Southern node of Moon. They always move backwards and always maintain a difference of 180 degrees between them.

The twelve signs of the Zodiac are Aries, Taurus, Gemini, Cancer, Leo, Virgo, Libra, Scorpio, Sagittarius, Capricorn, Aquarious and Pisces. The signs are the same in the Western, Hindu or Tajik Systems.

We shall limit our calculations to the seven planets as well as to Rahu and Ketu. Consideration for Uranus, Neptune and Pluto are not taken because their light did not come to Earth when Hindu Astrology and Tajik came into being.

Calculation

For the purpose of calculation we need the Ephemeris of the year of birth. In the illustration, the year of birth is 1979. We shall open up any ephemeries for 1979. Here, the ephemeries [condensed ephemeries 1971 to 1981] by N.C. Lahiri, page no. 60, gives the position of planets for 1st May 1979 at 5.30 a.m.

In the calculation of Ascendant, *Local Mean Time of the birth* is used whereas we use the *Standard Time of Birth for Calculating the Longitudes of Planets.*

	hrs.	mins.	secs.	IST
The time of birth is	06	15	00	
Position given in the Ephemeries is for	05	30	00	IST
Time elapsed until birth took place	00	45	00	

(i.e., 45 minutes)

We shall start with the calculation of Longitude of Saturn.

Planet-Saturn

	Si	*D*	*M*	*Daily Motion*
Position in the Ephemeris at 5.30 a.m.	4^s	13°	34'	0 0' 30"R
Motion of Saturn for 24 hrs. or 1440 minutes	0-30"			
Motion for 45 minutes	$\frac{30}{1440}$ x45			=1" app.

The ephemeris tells us that Saturn is retrograde, so we reduce the longitude at 5.30 a.m. by 1" and we get 4^s – 13° – 33' – 59" (R). (R) indicates that the planet was in retrograde Motion.

Position of the other Planets

Planet	*At 5.30 a.m.* si d m s	*Motion in 24 hrs.* d m s	*Motion in 45'* m s
Jupiter	3–07–24–00	0–06–30	00–12
Mars	11–24–55–00	0–46–00	01–26
Sun	00–16–28–00	0–58–30	01–50
Venus	11–15–52–00	1–12–30	02–12
Mercury	11–21–11–00	1–24–30	02–38
Rahu	04–21–18–00	0–3–11	00–06
Ketu	10-21–18-00	0–3–11	00–06
Moon	02–11–02–00	12–21–00	23–10

We will now add (or subtract) the motion in 45 minutes from the longitudes of planets at 5.30 a.m.

	Si	*Deg.*	*Mnts.*	*Secs.*
Longitude of Jupiter at 5.30 a.m.	3	7	24	00
Add motion in 45 mnts.			00	12
Position at birth	3	7	24	12
Long. of Mars	11	24	25	00
Add		00	01	26
Position at birth	11	24	26	26
Long. of Sun	00	16	28	00
Add		00	01	50
Position at Birth	00	16	29	50
Long. of Venus	11	15	52	00
Add		00	02	16
Position at Birth	11	15	54	16
Long. of Mercury	11	21	11	00
Add		00	02	42
Position at Birth	11	21	13	42
Long. of Rahu	04	21	18	00
Subtract		00	00	06
Position at Birth	04	21	17	54
Long. of Ketu	10	21	18	00
Subtract		00	00	06
Position at Birth	10	21	17	54
Long. of Moon	02	11	02	00
Add			23	10
Position at Birth	02	11	25	10

Table of Longitudes & Daily Motion of Planets

We have with us the Ascendant, M.C., Longitude of planets, daily motion of Planets and we shall write them in the following format:

Planet	*Longitude*	*Daily Motion*
	si d m s	*d m s*
Sun	00–16–29–50	00–58–30
Moon	02–11–25–10	12–32–00
Mars	11–24–26–26	00–46–00
Mercury	11–21–13–42	01–24–30
Jupiter	03–07–24–12	00–06–30
Venus	11-15–54-16	01–12–30
Saturn	04-13–33-59R	00–00–30
Rahu	04-21–17–54	00–03–11
Ketu	10-21–17-54	00–03–11
Ascendant	00-26–14-00	
M.C.	09-11–29-00	

After writing them as above we shall place them in the traditional chart prevalent in most parts of Northern India. To make a chart (a) draw a rectangle, (b) draw lines by joining the opposite corners (diagonals) and (c) make another rectangle inside the first rectangle by joining the mid-points on each of the four lines to their adjacent points. We have now the complete chart.

Next step:

We place the number of the Ascendant in this case Aries, at the top centre.

The sidereal Longitude of the Ascendant is 0 – 26 – 14 – 00 which means that 12 signs (0 signs) are complete so 1 is put in the top centre. The number is a symbol for Aries. The other signs follow in the anti-clockwise direction.

Traditional Chart

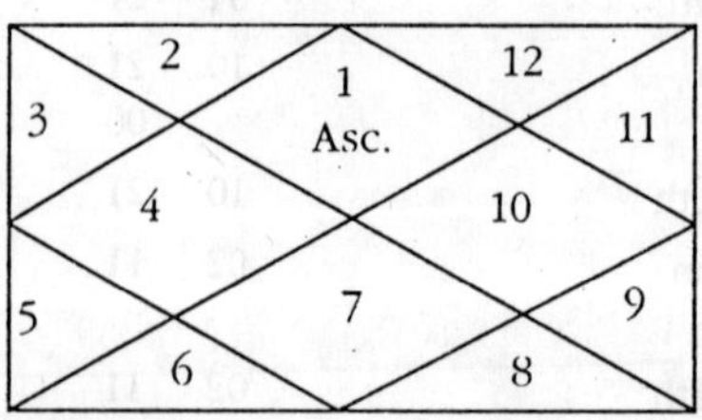

The remaining numbers which represents other signs are put in anti-clockwise manner viz., 2 for Taurus, 3 for Gemini, 4 for Cancer and so on.

We have the Longitudes of planets and we will put the planets in their respective signs. We shall also place the M.C. (X house) in Capricorn. See the chart given below:

Birth Chart

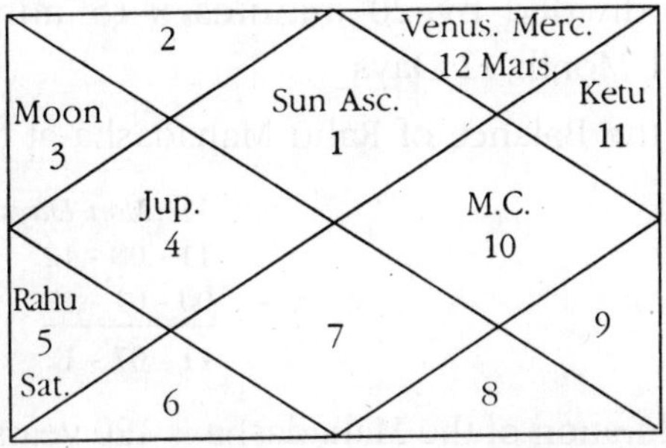

The position of Planets as given in the above chart are as follows:

Sun is in Aries in the I house (Ascendant is the first house) and Sun is exalted: Moon is in Gemini in the 3rd house: Jupiter is in cancer in the 4th house and is exalted: Saturn and Rahu are in Leo in the 5th house: Meridian cusp is in Capricorn in the 10th house: Ketu is in Aquarius in the 11th hosue: Venus, Mercury, and Mars are in Pisces in the 12th house, Venus is exalted and Mercury is debilitated.

Calculation of the Mahadashas

We shall now calculate the Mahadashas at birth for the native whose chart is erected.

The mahadasha is based on the longitude of Moon at birth and here the Moon is in Gemini at 11 degrees 25 minutes and 10 seconds.

We look up in the table (see appendix) which gives the balance of Mahadashas at birth.

The longitude of Moon in Gemini	*Yrs. Mon. Days*
gives Rahu Mahadasha	
For 11 degrees 20 minutes	11 - 08 - 12
For 11 degrees 40 minutes	11 - 03 - 00
So for 20 minutes	00 - 05 - 12

By rule of three, we find the Dasha for 5'10" which is the difference in the longitude of Moon at birth and the Longitude for which the dasha balance is given in the Table.

(5m 12d) divided by 20 minutes × (5 minutes 10 seconds)=1 Month 12 Days.

Therefore the Balance of Rahu Mahadasha at birth is

	Yrs. Mon. Days
	11 - 08 - 12
–	00 - 01 - 12
	11 - 07 - 12

The total duration of the Mahadasha is 120 years and these are called Vimshottari Mahadashas. These dashas occur in cyclic order beginning with that of

Planet	*Duration*
Sun	6 years
Moon	10 years
Mars	7 years
Rahu	18 years
Jupiter	16 years
Saturn	19 years
Mercury	17 years
Ketu	7 years
Venus	20 years

In the above balance of Rahu is 11 yrs. 7 months. In Hindu Astrology this is called the *Bhogya dasha*. The total duration of Rahu is 18 years and so the native has already passed through 6 years 5 months in his previous life. (18 yrs.) – (11 yrs. 7 months). This is called the *Bhukta Dasha*, i.e., the one which elapsed before birth took place.

The following table gives the mahadasha:

Table of Mahadashas

	Duration Y. M. D.	*Till the age of* Y. M. D.
Balance of Rahu at birth	11 -7 - 0	11 - 7 - 0
Jupiter	16	27 - 7 - 0
Saturn	19	46 - 7 - 0
Mercury	17	63 - 7 - 0
Ketu	7	70 - 7 - 0
Venus	20	90 - 7 - 0
Sun	6	and so on.

The centre Pillor on which the interpretation in Hindu Astrology rests is the *Mahadashas* and *Antardashas*. The Mahadashas are of Long durations and so these are divided into Antardashas (nine in number). An antardasha is again divided into *Pratyantara dashas*.

Appendix II will enable us to look at the Antardashas which will be as follows:

Antardashas in that of Jupiter Mahadasha

	Start at Y M D	*Duration* Y M D	*Until the age of* Y M D
Jup. in Jup.	11 - 7 - 0	2 - 1 - 12	13 - 8 - 18
Saturn in Jup.	13 - 8 - 18	2 - 6 - 12	16 - 3 - 00
Merc. in Jup.	16 - 3 - 00	2 - 3 - 6	18 - 6 - 6
Ketu in Jup.	18 - 6 - 6	0 - 11 - 6	19 - 5 - 12
and so on			

Similarly, the Pratyantara dashas are also calculated. It should be noted that the first Antardasha or Pratyantardasha will be of the same planet whose dasha or Antar is in vogue and the others follow in the same cyclic order.

Sub-Divisions *

Another important factor of the Hindu Astrology is the calculation of Sub-Divisions. These are used mainly to gauge

* See Ch. I

the strength of a planet. These are called Navamsha (9th part); Shashtiamsha (6th part): Dreshkana (Decanate); Trìnshansha, Hora etc. Here, we are mostly concerned with the navamsha which is called the heart of a horoscope.

Navamsha Calculation

Each sign of the Zodiac is divided into 9 equal parts of 3 degrees and 20 minutes and so we get 108 divisions in 12 signs. See Table No. III. Ch. I which gives the Navamsha of the Ascendant and planets at a glance:

To illustrate, Moon is in Gemini 11° – 25' – 10". The first column gives the spread out of the degrees and minutes so look in the first column fourth row – (10° – 00' to 13° – 20'). Now we look in the fourth row for the sign Gemini and the Navamsha is 'Capricorn'. Similarly, the Ascendant is 0–26° 14'–00" and in the same manner in the 8th row, second column we have the Navamsha of the Ascendant as 'Scorpio'. Similarly, we look to the Navamsha of all the remaining planets and put them in the following table.

Planet	*Navamsha*
Sun	Leo
Moon	Capricorn
Mars	Aquarius
Mercury	Capricorn
Jupiter	Virgo
Saturn	Leo
Rahu	Libra
Ketu	Aries
Ascendant	Scorpio
M.C.	Aries

We have tried to find out the Navamsha of planets as Navamsha in the Hindu System indicates the inner strength of planets. The Navamsha chart is attached with the same importance similar to the heart in a human body. The Navansha also indicates the type of spouse, one will get in life. With the Navamsha position of Ascendant and all planets with us, we place them in the chart as follows:

Scorpio in the I house (Ascendant); Venus in the I; Moon and Mercury in the 3rd., Mars in the 4th; Ketu in the 6th; Sun and Saturn in the 10th, Jup. in the 11th; Rahu in the 12th. Please see the chart given below.

Navamsha Chart

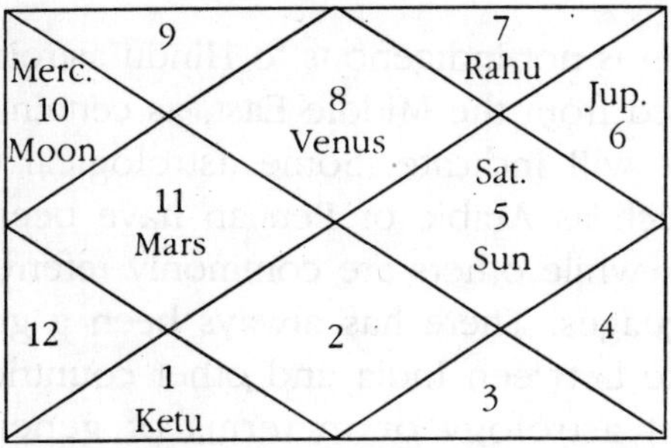

Now we have erected a horoscope in the traditional Hindu system.

We have also calculated the following:

1. Ascendant
2. Longitude of planets
3. Cusp of the houses and their midpoints
4. Mahadashas - Antardashas
5. Navamsha chart

We are sure that if the readers devote six to eight weeks to practice the above calculation by calculating thirty different horoscopes, they will master the technique well enough. The calculations are simple and in order to make it easier we have provided ready recknors and tables.

II

The next in line is that with the birth chart ready, we shall proceeds to find the 24th year (i.e., 23 years completed) for the native whose horoscope is under consideration. But before we proceed with the mathematical part we would like to point out as to what is a *Solar Return*.

What is a Solar Return?

When the sun, in its revolution, reaches the exact degree, minute and second it occupied at the time of one's birth, a chart is cast for the exact time of the sun's return. This is called the Solar Return chart or Varsha Kundali (annual chart). Predictions for the year ahead are made on the basis of this chart.

This system is not indigenous to Hindu astrology but has been imported from the Middle East, as certain terms used in this book will indicate. Some astrological terms from languages such as Arabic or Persian have been translated into Sanskrit, while others are commonly referred to in the original languages. There has always been a great deal of give and take between India and other countries, whether in the art of astrology or in terms of general cultural interchange. During medieval times, the technique of Solar Returns was so permanently grafted onto Hindu astrology that today it is considered as much a part of the Vedic astrological package as anything else. A great number of works on *Solar Returns* were written during medieval times, and the Hindu mind-quick and intelligent to imbibe and absorb new systems—took to it readily. *Some notable works on the subject, all of them in Sanskrit,* are:

- Tajik Sar
- Tajikalankar
- Yoga Sudhanidhi
- Tajik Ratnamala
- Muktavali
- Tajik Nil Kanthi
- Hayan Sundar
- Hilaj Deepika
- Tajik Sarvaswa Sar
- Tajik Bhushan
- Tajik Tilak
- Jirna Tajik
- Hayan Ratna

But it is not our purpose to catalogue every work written on the subject during the last few centuries; the names given above are illustrative rather than exhaustive. Our main point here is that this system, though originally imported from the Middle East, is now completely assimilated to Hindu astrology.

Readers may have been struck by the word *tajik* occuring in several of these works. The Sanskrit word *jatak* means "born", "produced", "ceremony performed after the birth of a child", "astrological calculationas for nativity", and so on. Hence some of the classical Sanskrti works have titles such as *Jataka Parijata, Jatakalankar,* and *Jatakabharana*. The Sanskrti *jataka* has, by metathesis, become *tajika* when used in connection with the Solar Return.

Let us begin with the erection of the Solar Return chart. As stated earlier, the principle is that the chart is to be cast for the exact time when the sun returns to the logitude it ocupied at the time of birth. This happens more or less on one's birthday each year.

The *Surya Siddhanta,* a monumental work on Hindu astronomy written in Sanskrit about two thousand years ago, states that the sidereal year covers 365 days, 15 ghatis, 31 palas, and 30 vipalas(*). Astrologers in India add this increase for each year elapsed since the subject's birth and erect the Solar Return chart on this basis.

Modern astronomical instruments, however, indicate that the earth now takes about three minutes less than the interval cited above in order to complete its full orbit. It may be that when the *Surya Siddhanta* was written the period of a sidereal year as specified therein may have been correct. Vashishtha and other ancient astrological savants affirmed, many centuries ago, that over very long periods of time some fluctuation is noticeable in the earth's motion. It should not be regarded as unusual if the earth now completes its orbits a few minutes sooner, whether because of a slight narrowing

* 60 vipalas = 1 pala; 60 palas = 1 ghati; 1 ghati = 24 minutes

of the orbit or due to faster motion which may be attributed to any number of causes not yet identified.

Normailly, a difference of three minutes per year would be too small to create a matter of concern, but when we erect a Solar Return chart (also called the annual chart, Varshaphala, or Varsha Kundali) for a person in, by way of example, his forty-first year then the difference in time interval to be added to the birth time would amount to 40×3=120 minutes or two hours—a difference large enough to give incorrect house cusps and possibly even an incorrect Ascendant. Therefore, this is an important point. The modern value of the sidereal year is 365.2563628 days or 365 days, 6 hours, 9 minutes, 9.7 seconds. Since 52 weeks is comprised of 364 days, we must add to the birthdate (expressed as a day of the week; see below) 1 day, 6 hours, 9 minutes, 9.7 seconds, for each year elapsed since birth; we shall arrive at the day and exact time when the sun will be at the same longitude it occupied at birth.

Mathematically expert persons may, by their own methods, arrive at the exact day and time when the sun, in any year, will have the same longitude as in the birth chart or radix. But for lay readers we give below a table of increase for each year which, when added to the birthday and time will give the exact time of the sun's return to its radical place. The table simply shows the product of 1 day, 6 hours, 9 minutes and 9.745 seconds multiplied by the number of years elapsed. In order to find out what time interval should be added to the birthday and time for, let us say, the 43rd annual chart (42 years elapsed), we must add the figures for 2 years and 40 years in order to get the sum 3 days, 18 hours, 24 minutes and 48 seconds.

We give below a table which gives the commencement of the Solar Return Time. With the help of the table we will be able to quickly get the time and day of the commencement of any year.

We should add the figure below for completed years to the day and time of birth which will give the day and time of the new year.

Table 1

(Time of Varshapravesh)
Solar Return (Varshpravesh)

The moment in each year when the nirayana or sidereal longitude of the Sun becomes equal to the longitude of Sun at the time of birth of the native is the moment of Solar return or *Varsapravesh*.

Year	*d*	*h*	*m*	*Year*	*d*	*h*	*m*	*Year*	*d*	*h*	*m*
1	1	6	9.2	41	2	12	15.7	81	3	18	22.1
2	2	12	18.3	42	3	18	24.8	82	5	0	31.3
3	3	18	27.5	43	5	0	34.0	83	6	6	40.5
4	5	0	36.6	44	6	6	43.1	84	0	12	49.6
5	6	6	45.8	45	0	12	52.3	85	1	18	58.8
6	0	12	55.0	46	1	19	1.5	86	3	1	8.0
7	1	19	4.1	47	3	1	10.6	87	4	7	17.1
8	3	1	13.3	48	4	7	19.8	88	5	13	26.3
9	4	7	22.5	49	5	13	29.0	89	6	19	35.4
10	5	13	31.6	50	6	19	38.1	90	1	1	44.6
11	6	19	40.8	51	1	1	47.3	91	2	7	53.8
12	1	1	49.9	52	2	7	56.4	92	3	14	2.9
13	2	7	59.1	53	3	14	5.6	93	4	20	12.1
14	3	14	8.3	54	4	20	14.8	94	6	2	21.3
15	4	20	17.4	55	6	2	23.9	95	0	8	30.4
16	6	2	26.6	56	0	8	33.1	96	1	14	39.6
17	0	8	35.8	57	1	14	42.3	97	2	20	48.7
18	1	14	44.9	58	2	20	51.4	98	4	2	57.9
19	2	20	54.1	59	4	3	0.6	99	5	2	7.1
20	4	3	3.2	60	5	9	9.7	100	6	15	16.2
21	5	9	12.4	61	6	15	18.9	101	0	21	25.4
22	6	15	21.6	62	0	21	28.1	102	2	3	34.5
23	0	21	30.7	63	2	3	37.2	103	3	9	43.7
24	2	3	39.9	64	3	9	46.4	104	4	15	52.8
25	3	9	49.1	65	4	15	55.6	105	5	22	2.0
26	4	15	58.2	66	5	22	4.7	106	0	4	11.2
27	5	22	7.4	67	0	4	13.9	107	1	10	20.3
28	0	4	16.5	68	1	10	23.0	108	2	16	29.5
29	1	10	25.7	69	2	16	32.2	109	3	22	38.7
30	2	16	34.9	70	3	16	41.4	110	5	4	47.8
31	3	22	44.0	71	5	4	50.5	111	6	10	57.0
32	5	4	53.2	72	6	10	59.7	112	0	17	6.1
33	6	11	2.4	73	0	17	8.9	113	1	23	15.3
34	0	17	11.5	74	1	23	18.0	114	3	5	24.5
35	1	23	20.7	75	3	5	27.2	115	4	11	33.6
36	3	5	29.8	76	4	11	36.3	116	5	17	42.8
37	4	11	39.0	77	5	17	45.5	117	6	23	52.0
38	5	17	48.2	78	6	23	54.7	118	1	6	1.1
39	6	23	57.3	79	1	6	3.8	119	2	12	10.3
40	1	6	6.5	80	2	12	13.0	120	3	18	19.4

Take from the above figure the completed years and add them to the day and time of birth.

The result gives the day of week and the time of *Varsapravesh*. The English date for the table below may differ by a few minutes from that obtained from equality of longitudes of the Sun at the two epochs, this being due to the perturbations of Sun's longitude caused by the planets. Actually calculation of equality of the longitude of Sun will give the exact time of *Varsapravesh*.

Calculation of the Solar Return Chart

The day and date of birth of the native Mr. Ambrish is

Tuesday 1st May 1979		
Place of Birth	New Delhi	
	Longitude	77-13 East
	Latitude	28-39 North

Standard time of birth is 06.15 hrs. (a.m.)

In order to arrive at what time Sun in its revolution comes to the same sign, degree, minutes and seconds in the year 2002, i.e., when the native completed his 23rd years of age (2002-1979=23) and entered into his 24th year. We shall consult the above table given above [Solar Return or Varshaphal].

Method of Calculation of the Time of Solar Return

(A) Finding the time of Solar Return

Write down the day, followed by the hours, minutes, and seconds of birth as shown below:

	Day	Hours	Minutes	Seconds
	Tuesday	06 –	15 –	00
From the above table of Solar Return, take the figures given against completed years which is 23 years, and add		21 –	30.7 –	00
	Tuesday	27 –	45.7	

As 27 hours are more than 24 so we take 24 out of it and increase the day from Tuesday to Wednesday. The time of commencement of the 24th year would be Wednesday 03.46 (a.m.).

In the ephemeris* of the year 2002, page 22 (Wednesday) is on 1st May therefore the 24th year will commence on 1st May 2002 at 03.46 a.m. at New Delhi.

With these details we shall revert to the method we discussed in the calculation of the brith chart on page nos. 6 to 15 .

Rising Sign for the Solar Return Chart

	Hrs.	*Mins.*	*Secs.*
The I.S.T. of the New year	03	- 46	- 00 (a.m.)
Correction for L.M.T.	00	- 21	- 08
L.M.T. of the New Year	03	- 24	- 52 (a.m.)
The Sidereal Time at noon on the Preceding day (30th April 2002)	02	- 32	- 10
Add the time time elapsed since the preceding Noon to the beginning of the year	15	- 24	- 52
Correction @10 secs., per hour	+ 00	- 02	- 34
R.A.M.C	17	- 59	- 36

In the above work out we have not done any correction for the year because we are using the ephemeris of the year 2002 itself.

Now we look in the 'Table of the Ascendant' on page 48, and we find that the Ascendant is 11 signs 6 degrees 51 minutes and 00 seconds.

M.C. is 8 signs 06 degrees 55 minutes and 00 seconds.

We would like to point out again the we had calculated the Ascendant and the M.C. on the basis of the Local Mean Time of birth. However, the Longitudes are always calculated on the *Standard Time*.

---

* Ephemeries by N.C. Lahiri for the year 2002

Calculation of the Longitudes

Here, the I.S.T. of the commencement of the New Year is 03.46 (a.m.)

The method of calculation is already explained earlier.

In the present instance the position of planets at 05.30 on page no. 22 and 23 is given for 1st May 2002.

	Hrs.		Mins.		Secs.
Position for	05	–	30	–	00 (a.m.)
The time of the New Year is	03	–	46	–	00
Difference in the above two	01	–	44	–	00

We shall as in earlier case find the daily motion of all the planets and then see as to the motion in 1 Hour and 44 Minutes. As the time of birth is before 5.30 a.m., so we shall reduce the motion so obtained by subtracting unless the planets are retrograde and then we shall add in the longitudes of planets given for 5.30.

On 1st May except Rahu and Ketu all the Planets are direct in motion.

Planet	Daily Motion	Motion in 01.44 hrs	Position at 5.30	Position at 03.46
	deg.–m–sec.	m.–Sec.	si–d–m–sec.	si–d–m–sec.
Sun	00–58–15	04 – 13	0–16–33–54	0–16–29–41
Moon	13–34–36	30 – 40	8–07–45–54	8–07–15–14
Mars	00–40–00	02 – 53	1–17–49–00	1–17–46–07
Mercury	01–15–00	05 – 25	1–06–59–00	1–06–53–35
Jupiter	00–10–00	00 – 42	2–17–03–00	2–17–02–53
Venus	01–13–00	05 – 16	1–12–30–00	1–12–24–44
Saturn	00–07–00	00 – 51	1–19–37–00	1–19–36–09
Rahu	00–03–00	00 – 13	1–26–07–00	1–26–07–13
Ketu	00–03–00	00 – 13	7–26–07–00	7–26–07–13

After the Ascendant of the year and planetary longitude are worked out, we draw the chart and place the planet in the respective signs.

Longitude of Planets for the Year

Planets	Si	–	Deg.	–	Mins.	–	Secs.
Sun	0	–	16	–	29	–	41
Moon	8	–	7	–	15	–	14
Mars	1	–	17	–	46	–	7
Mercury	1	–	6	–	53	–	35
Jupiter	2	–	17	–	2	–	53
Venus	1	–	12	–	24	–	44
Saturn	1	–	19	–	36	–	9
Rahu	1	–	26	–	7	–	13
Ketu	7	–	26	–	7	–	13
Asc	11	–	6	–	51	–	00
MC	8	–	6	–	55	–	00

The Solar Return Chart (24th year)

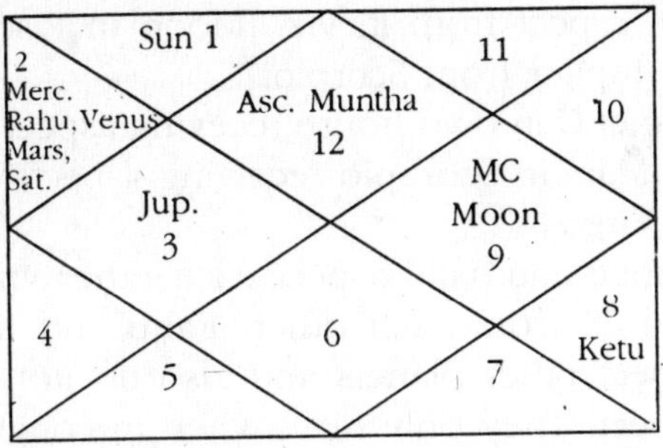

Sun in Aries in the 2nd house; Moon in Sagittarius in the 10th house; Ketu in Scorpio in the 9th house; Jupiter in Gemini in the 4th house; Mars, Mercury, Venus, Saturn and Rahu in Taurus in the 3rd house. The above are the position of planets at the time of the beginning of 24th year.

Aspects:

In the Solar Return charts aspects are measured in different manner vis-á-vis in the aspect in the Natal chart. We give the two different manners of Aspects and this should not be mixed together.

Aspects in Natal (or Birth chart)/Tajik.

Aspects in the Natal chart is two fold.

1. Aspects between planets:
   a. All Planets aspect the 7th house or the planets placed therein.
   b. Jupiter also aspects the 5th and 9th houses from it.
   c. Mars aspects the 4th and 8th houses as well,
   d. And Saturn also fully aspects the 3rd and the 10th house from it.

2. The Second type of aspects in Hindu Astrology is the 'Sambandh' between the planets, i.e., *relationship*
   e. Exchange of houses between two planets viz., Moon in the house of Mars and Mars goes to the house of Moon. (8 and 4) or (1 and 4).
   f. Planet A in the house of Planets B and receivng a full aspect from it, viz., Moon in Pisces aspected by Jupiter from Scorpio.
   g. Planet C in own house receving aspect from Planet D, Mars in Scoropio receiving aspects from Saturn in Virgo.
   h. Planets mutually aspect each other viz., in the 1st and 7th from each other. Rahu and Ketu do not aspect other planets and also do not recieve any aspect. They only react when in conjunction with other planets.

The question arises as to why so much importance is attached to Aspects* or relationships between planets?

The answer is simple. The aspects join together two forces of equal power which when operating in unison brings forth strong results.

Secondly, the aspect between two or more planets make it convenient to interpret. The results between the sub period of planet 'A' in the major period of planet B if they are related or not related will be good or bad respectively. The rulership of a house is important when making judgement, if the Sambandh or relationship between two planets is good or otherwise.

---

* See 'Aspects in Vedic Astrology' by the Authors.

With the purpose of making it more clear any aspect (full) or Sambandh with the lord of the 8th house or with the lord of the 11th house drastically reduces the good effects. Look into the birth chart on page 15. Jupiter is exalted and it aspects Mars, Mercury, and Venus in Pisces. Pisces is ruled by Jupiter so the Antardashas of Mars, Mercury and Venus in the Mahadasha of Jupiter will be good and vice versa.

Please note that Jupiter does not have any 'sambandh' with Saturn and as such, the antardasha of Saturn in that of Jupiter will be troublesome. Jupiter is the lord of the 9th house (a trine) and Saturn rules the 10th house (an angle) —so this period would be much worse than it would have been if the planets would rule other houses. The reason is that if one of the planetes whose Mahadasha-antardashas are in the offing, rules an angle and the other planet a trine and they are related than that period would be extremely good but if they have no 'Samabandha' than it would be the worst.

In the context of the Sambandha we had also stated that a relationship with the lord of the 8th or 11th house reduces the good effects.

This is so because the 8th house is the 12th from the 9th (fortunes) and it indicates loss of fortunes. It is also called the 'Chidrasthana' in Sanskrit which means a 'Hole' - an outlet for the fortunes. In the same way the 11th house is the 8th houses from the 4th and as 4th house rules Happiness and mother, the 8th from it signifies the destruction of the above.

In any horoscope the association of the lords of the 8th or 11th house will destroy the biggest Rajayoga. The learned readers should also note that this law will become null and void if any planet simultaneously with rulership of the 8th or 11th also owns an angle (1,4,7*, or 10) or a trine (5 or 9) viz., for Cancer rising, Venus rules the 11th as well as 4th; for Gemini Ascendant Saturn rules the 8th and 9th simultaneously and as such they will not destroy by their association. Similarly Mars and Saturn for Aries rising; Jupiter for Leo rising; Venus for Libra rising; and Mercury for Aquarius rising natives will not destroy by their association.

---

* The rulership of the 7th house although an angle is not considered good (as it is "Marak Sthana"), if any planet simultaneously rules the 8th as well, as is the case for cancer rising nativity.

On the other hand, the union of any planet with the lord of the 1, 5th, 9th is always good and if it is between the lord of a trine (1, 5, 9) and a Kendra (1, 4, 7, 10), it is wonderful. *First house is both a trine and a Kendra.*

Note: **There is an exception. The association of lord of the 11th is bad. However, if the lord of the 11th house conjoins with the lords of the 1st and 2nd simultaneously then it is one of the best yogas for wealth.

The above methods of aspects should be used only for interpretation of a natal chart.

Aspects in Solar Return chart and Western Astrology are similar.

This is so because in the Western Astrology or the Solar Returns, different type of aspects are used.

1. **Friendly Aspects:** If planets are in the 3rd, 5th, 9th and 11th from each other, these are called
   a. Sextile - Sixty degree aspect (3rd & 11th)
   b. Trine - One hundred and twenty degree (5th & 9th)
2. **Unfriendly or inimical aspects:** If planets are in the 4th, 7th, 10th from each other, these are
   c. Square - Ninety degree aspects (3rd & 10th)
   d. Opposition-One hundred and eighty degree aspect. (1st and 7th from each other).

Conjunctions: If Planets are posited in the same house then they are said to be in conjunction. Whether these conjunction are malefic or benefic will depend upon the nature of planets. This is in the Western Astrology and in the Solar Return charts. In Western method conjunctions are powerful if within Orbs. The closer the planets the more powerful they become.

In the natal chart or birth chart, the benefic or malefic effects of conjunction will depend upon the lordship of the houses of Planets, i.e., houses which the planets own. It will also depend upon the placement of planets in a particular house. The planets are conjunct even if they are far apart but in the same sign viz., Venus in 1 degree will be in conjunction with Sun in the 29th degree in the same sign.

We have the Ascendant, 10th house, and the Longitudes of the planets. With the help of the Table of Navamsha (See Table No. III, Ch. I) we shall work out the navamsha for the Solar Return chart and then place them in the Navamsha chart of the year.

Longitudes of Planets and their Navamsha (Year Chart)

Planets	*Longitude* *si - d - m - s*	*Navamsha*
Sun	00–16–29–41	Leo
Moon	08–07–15–14	Gemini
Mars	01–17–46– 7	Gemini
Mercury	01–06–53–35	Pisces
Jupiter	02–17–02–53	Pisces
Venus	01–12–24–44	Aries
Saturn	01–19–36–09	Gemini
Rahu	01–26–07–13	Leo
Ketu	07–26–07–13	Aquarius
Ascendant	11–06–51–00	Virgo
M.C. (X house)	08–06–55–00	Gemini

Navamsha Chart (of the Year)

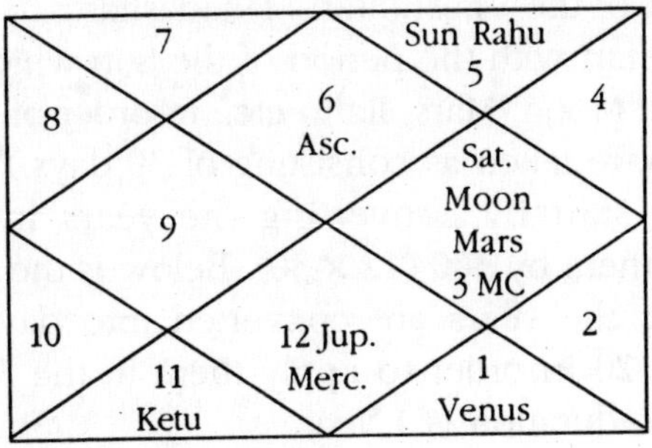

The Navamsha of the Ascendant is Virgo, so Virgo (or no. 6) goes to the top centre. The other signs follow anticlock-wise. Then other planets are put according to the Navamsha they are in viz. Sun, Rahu in Leo; Moon, Mars, Saturn in Gemini, Venus in Aries; Mercury, Jupiter is Pisces, and Ketu is Aquarius.

We have erected a chart for the Navamsha. It is similar to the birth chart. The difference is that the planets that we place in it are for the year 2002, i.e., these will rule from 1st May 2002 till 1st May 2003. On 1st May 2003 another Solar Return will occur and another Chart will be erected for the 25th Year and then for the 26th year in May 2004, 27th year in May 2005 and so on.

As soon as a new Solar year starts the new chart will take precendence over the old chart and it takes the pride of place together with the Nativity.

Mudda Dashas

This brings us to the Dashas and Antardashas. Can we apply the Vimshottari Mahadashas in the Varsha Charts that we use for the birth chart? The answer is yes but with some modifications.

The duration of the Vimshottari Mahadashas is 120 years whereas the duration of the Solar Return chart is only one year. How can or can we fit in a cycle of 120 years into a period of 1 year viz. 12 months? Yes we can do it. In order to do it the cycle of Mahadashas of planets are divided by 120, resulting in a smaller period of some days and Months. This 120 we have used as one year is the 120th part of the full duration of the Vimshottari Mahadashas.

We shall start with the period of the Sun which is 6 years and then the Moon, Mars, Rahu etc., in order of the Dashas. (All months are taken as consisting of 30 days.)

We shall start by converting the years into days by multiplying them by 360 (12 × 30). Below is the table of the Dashas after the years are converted into days and then divided by 120 in order to apply them in the Solar Return charts whose duration is 1 year.

Calculation of Mudda Dashas

Planets	*Duration in Vimshottari years*	*Process as suggested*		*Days*	*M - D*
Sun	6	6 × 360 divided by 120	=	18	0 - 18
Moon	10	10 × 360 divided by 120	=	30	1 - 00
Mars	7	7 × 360 divided by 120	=	21	0 - 21
Rahu	18	18 × 360 divided by 120	=	54	1 - 24
Jupiter	16	16 × 360 divided by 120	=	48	1 - 18
Saturn	19	19 × 360 divided by 120	=	57	1 - 27
Mercury	17	17 × 360 divided by 120	=	51	1 - 21
Ketu	7	7 × 360 divided by 120	=	21	0 - 21
Venus	20	20 × 360 divided by 120	=	60	2 - 00

The total is 360 days. However, as the full year is of 365 days so when changing over month at the end of one dasha, we shall use the months as uniformly consisting of 30 days and not of 28, 29 or 31 days. This will enable us to synchronize the Dashas to the extent of 12 months.

This smaller Dashas used for the year are called *Mudda Dashas* and their duration is on one year.

Another popular system of Dashas in the Solar Return chart is called the *Hinansha-Patyansha Dasha System*.

In this system the full period of one year (here 360 days) is divided in between the 7 planets and the Ascendant.

Method of Calculating the Hinansha-Patyansha

We start by writing the logitudes of planets and Ascendants in ascendng order, i.e., the planet or ascendant whichever has the least degree, minutes, and seconds will be written in the first place; the second place will be given to the planet or ascendant which has more degrees than the first one but less than that of the remaining 6 and then the third one follows and so on. In this manner all the 8 (planets and Ascendant) are written out one after the other.

In this we do not take the signs that planets and Ascendant are in. We ignore these as we are concerned with the longitudes, minutes, and seconds on which the Hinansha and Patyansha dashas are based.

The second important thing here is that Rahu and Ketu are not considered for this dasha, Rahu and Ketu show the effect similar to that of Saturn. According to many old masters Ketu shows effect like that of Mars.

Next Process

In the first place we write the lowest Patyansha. Next we write the difference in the Longitude of first and second; then second and third, then third and fourth, then fourth and fifth, and so on until all the 8 are written out. The 360 days will be proportionately divided between the 8 of them viz. the lowest patyansha and the differences between 1 and 2; 2 and 3; 3 and 4; 4 and 5; 5 and 6; 6 and 7; 7 and 8. These dashas will be 8 in numbers.

Duration of the Dashas

We shall discuss the duration of the dashas elaborately at a subsequent chapter, 'The Timing of the Events'. Here we shall take up the calculation of the Dashas for *the exmple Birth chart which will also be the Solar Return chart for the first year of the native.*

Let us work out the Hinansha Patyansha dasha for the first year of the native on the basis of the chart given earlier on page no. 15.

Hinansha Patyansha Table

In the first column we write the planet, then in the second column Planetary Longitudes, in the third column degrees and minutes converted into minutes, in the 4th column the patyanshas.

I *Planet*	II *si - d - m - s*	III *degrees converted Into minutes*	IV *Patyansha*
Jupiter	03-07-24-12	444	444
Moon	02-11-25-10	685	241
Saturn	04-13-23-59	803	118
Venus	11-15-54-16	954	151

Sun	·00-16-29-50	989	35
Mercury	11-21-13-42	1273	284
Mars	11-24-26-26	1466	193
Ascendant	00-26-14-00	1574	108

The total of these 8 Patyanshas will always be equal to highest degree minutes and seconds. In this case it is 1574.

Duration of the Dashas will be calculated according to the following formula;

360 × (Patyansha of a planet) ÷

(the sum total of the Patyansha), = duration of dasha of the planet

We will work out the complete dasha as shown below:

Dasha of Planets			*days*
Jupiter	360 × 444 ÷ 1574	= 101.55	= 102
Moon	360 × 241 ÷ 1574	= 55.12	= 55
Saturn	360 × 118 ÷ 1574	= 26.98	= 27
Venus	360 × 151 ÷ 1574	= 34.53	= 35
Sun	360 × 35 ÷ 1574	= 8.00	= 08
Mercury	360 × 284 ÷ 1574	= 64.95	= 65
Mars	360 × 193 ÷ 1574	= 44.14	= 44
Ascendant	360 × 108 ÷ 1574	= 24.70	= 25
	1574		361

Special Note:

(i) If two or more planets are in the same degree, minutes, and seconds then the planet which is strongest of them, its dasha will come before that of others.

(j) However, if two planets are of equal strength as well then the first priority is given to the one which is slower in motion.

(k) If the degrees and the strength of the Ascendant and a planet are equal then the lord of the Ascendant should be considered instead of the Ascendant.

Antardasha in Hinansha Patyansha

We shall use the following;

Method

(Duration of Dasha of a planet in which the antars are needed) divided by highest Patyansha × (Patyansha of the planet whose antar is needed) = The Antardashas.

Example of Antardashas in the Dasha of Jupiter:
Duration of Jupiter dasha = 102 days
Highest Patyansha
Or total of all patyanshas = 1574
102 divided by 1574 = .064803

Antardashas in Jupiter Dasha

Jupiter in Jupiter	.064803 × 444	=	28.77 (Days)
Moon	.064803 × 241	=	15.61
Saturn	.064803 × 118	=	07.64
Venus	.064803 × 151	=	09.79
Sun	.064803 × 035	=	02.26
Mercury	.064803 × 284	=	18.40
Mars	.064803 × 193	=	12.51
Ascendant	.064803 × 108	=	07.00

The readers can work out the antardashas of other Planets as shown above.

In order to elaborate it more another example is given in the chapter of *The Timing of Events*. The readers should work out the Hinansha Patyansha of the Example Solar Return of Mr. Ambrish for his 24th Year with the method explained above. We give below the Data of the Planets and Ascendant in Ascending order.

Longitudes of Planets in Ascending Order (24th Year)

Planet	*Longitudes* *si - d - m - s*	*Degrees converted in to minutes*	*Patyansha*
Ascendant	11-06-51-00	411	411
Mercury	01-06-53-35	413	2
Moon	08-07-25-14	435	22
Venus	01-12-24-33	744	309

Sun	00-16-29-41	989	245
Jupiter	2-17-2-53	1022	33
Mars	01-17-46-07	1066	44
Saturn	01-19-36-09	1176	110

Here we have ignored the Minutes of Planets when converting the Longitudes into minutes. The signs are also not taken into consideration.

We shall use the Forumula for the Dashas of Planets in this year.

(No. of days divided by the total of Patyansha) × Patyansha of the Planet

Here the days are = 360

Total of patyansha = 1176

Now we work out the duration of the dashas with the formula given above.

Planet	*Process*			*Dashas in Days*
Ascendant	360 / 1176 × 411	=	125.816	126
Mercury	360 / 1176 × 2	=	0.7999	1
Moon	360 / 1176 × 22	=	8.796	9
Venus	360 / 1176 × 309	=	94.591	95
Sun	360 / 1176 × 245	=	74.999	75
Jupiter	360 / 1176 × 33	=	10.102	10
Mars	360 / 1176 × 44	=	13.469	13
Saturn	360 / 1176 × 110	=	33.673	34

We write the dashas in the following format

Hinansha Patyansha Dashas of the 24th year

Planet	*Duration Days*	*(Ending Time)* *Date Month Year*	*From 1.05.2002*
Ascendant	126	04 - 09 - 2002	
Mercury	1	05 - 09 - 2002	
Moon	9	14 - 09 - 2002	
Venus	95	17 - 12 - 2002	
Sun	75	03 - 03 - 2003	
Jupiter	10	13 - 03 - 2003	
Mars	13	26 - 03 - 2003	
Saturn	34	30 - 04 - 2003	

In the above table the First column is the Planet whose dasha is considered, in the second column the duration of the Dashas in Days in the third column is the ending time of the Dashas. It is also mentioned that the dashas start with the start of the 24th year on 1 May 2003. When converting decimals into full numbers we made minor adjustments. We had also taken the exact days in the months when giving the ending time of the Dashas.

Calculation of the Solar Return Months and Days

When the Sun in its revolution (Transit) comes back to the same sign degree, minutes and seconds, which it had at birth then a Solar Return year commences. We have earlier illustrated the method to calculate the time of the Solar Return year.

By adding one signs to the sign of the Sun, we get the second month. By adding one more sign, we get the third month and so on. The degrees, minutes and seconds are the same. These are not changed.

By adding one — one degree exactly into the each degree of the Sun, we get the daily horoscopes. The process may look a little tedious but if the time of birth is exact (as is the case in most cases) then amazing results can come from these charts.

In order to arrive at the time of the commencement of the monthly year, we will use the rule of three.

Now we refer to the Longitude of Sun in the Solar Return chart and find that the Sun was

	Si	*Deg.*	*Mints.*	*Secs.*
1 May 2002	0 –	16 –	29 –	41
add 1 sign	+ 1			
	1 –	16 –	29 –	41

So we should find the time when Sun attains 1 Sign 16 degrees 29 mints. 41 seconds, i.e., Sun moves one sign forward to Taurus.

We look into the Lahiri's Ephemeries on page 24.

On 1 June 2002	*Si*		*Deg.*		*Mints.*		*Secs.*
Sun is	1	–	16	–	27	–	16
We have Sun for the Second month	1	–	16	–	29	–	41
	0	–	0	–	2	–	25

We should find the time taken by Sun in moving 2 minutes 25 seconds. The motion of Sun for 24 hrs. is 57' – 30" on first June. By rule of three or 24/57' – 30" × 2'25" or 24/3450 × 145 = 1 hour 0 mints. 31 secs.) by adding this to the 5-30 a.m. we get 06 hrs 30 mnts 31 secs, which is the time of the beginning of second month.

In similar manner by adding 1 – 1 degree we get the chart for second day, 3rd day and so on.

The degree of Sun for the 2nd month 24th year is 1 – 16 – 29 – 41. This will also be the chart for the 1st day of the 2nd month of 24th year.

By adding one degree to the above we get 1 – 17 – 29 – 41 so we calculate the 2nd day when the Sun attains 17° – 29' – 41" in Taurus which will be on 2nd June 2002.

As the motion of Sun is not uniform and it varies so we will deduct the Longitude, mints. Secs. of 2nd June from that of the 3rd June in order to arrive at the daily motion of Sun on 2nd June.

	H – M – S	
Longitude at	05 – 30 – 00	1 – 16 – 27 –16
Add	01 – 00 – 31	
Long. of the Sun at	06 – 30 – 31	1 – 16 – 29 – 41

The time of the New (Second) Solar month is 6 – 30 – 31 am I.S.T.

We shall do the necessary calculation for 1 June 2002, at 6 hrs. 30 mints. 31 secs. at New Delhi. The method of calculating a chart is already illustrated under the following heading in the Introduction.

1. How to calculate Birth chart?
2. How to calculate the Solar Return chart?

The following chart is for the second month of 24th year.

Chart - 2nd month (24th year)

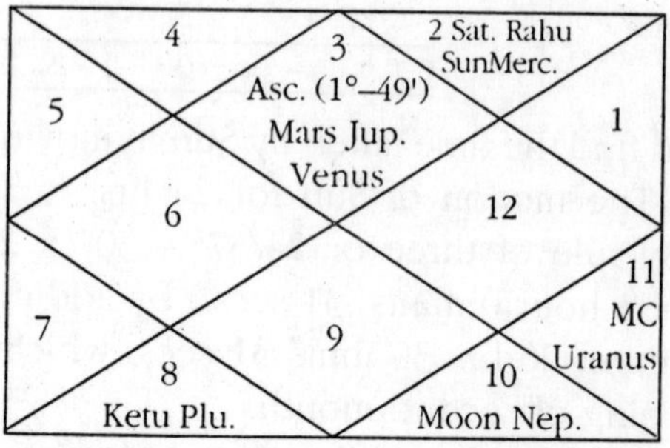

3rd June at 5.30 am Sun is	1 – 18 – 22 – 15
2nd June at 5.30 am Sun is	1 – 17 – 24 – 46
	0 – 00 – 57 – 29

So the motion of Sun in 24 hrs. is 0° – 57' – 29". We will work by rule of three as to how much time Sun takes to move from 1 – 17° – 24' – 46" to 1 – 17° – 29' – 41" when the motion is 57' – 29" in 24 hrs. or a distance of 4' – 55". We shall arrive at the time of commencement of the month and then we calculate the chart for the day.

In chapter III, we have indicated how to select the lord of the year. This will be done first by calculating Panchavargyabala, i.e., the five type of strength of the planets entitiled to compete for the lord of the year.

The five planets entitled for this are:

1. Lord of the Ascendant in the Solar Return chart
2. Lord of the Ascendant in Natal chart
3. The dispositer of Muntha
4. Trirashapti
5. The dispositer of Sun if the Solar Return is during day time and if the birth time is at night then the dispositer of Moon in the Varsh Lagnam.

The method of selection is well illustrated in Chapter III.

We would like to mention that the five types of strength in the chart are:

1. Graha bala
2. Hadda bala
3. Dreshkana bala
4. Navamsha bala
5. Uchcha bala

These are called the Panchavargyabala of Planets: This is a mathematical method and one of the surest ways of measuring the exact strength of a planet.

Another method to decide the strength of a planet is its distance from the cusp of a house.

We shall next take up the House Division in a Solar Return chart.

House Division

Every sign has 30 degrees but the spread out of every house is not the same. Some signs are bigger and others are comparatively smaller. The spread out of the house depends upon the Latitude of Place of birth. In the Northern Hemisphere (if we move Northwards) the duration of a house will be much bigger. At times many Zodiacal Signs will fall in one house and comparatively some houses will become very small.

Various methods of House Divisions exist. These are:

1. Ptolemaic System or *modus equalis viz*:, Equal House Division where all house are of 30 degrees each.
2. Porphyry's or Current House division
3. Placidius or Semi Arc system
4. Regiomantanus system of House division and
5. Campanus.

However, in the Tajik system the house Division followed goes by the name of the Keshaviyya and Shripati Jataka Paddhatis. This is the same as is followed in the Western System of Astrology and goes by the name of 'Prophyry' system.

In all the above systems the Ascendants and the M.C. is the same.

In a subsequent chapter the system is illustrated.

Muntha

Muntha* is an imaginary but very important factor in the Solar Return chart. Muntha literally means that which 'churns'. Every year it** moves from the sign in the Ascendant to the next sign viz., from the 1st house to the second then from 2nd to the third, 3rd from the 4th and so on in a manner that in 12 years it completes a full circle and in the 13th year it is again in the Ascendant.

For example if a person has Sagittarius rising at birth his Muntha would go to Capricorn in the 2nd year, i.e., after the completion of the 1st year, than to Aquarius in the third year and so on. The next step would be to place Muntha in the same Zodiacal sign in the year chart to *which it has moved to in the birth chart* during the year under consideration. If Muntha is well placed in the Solar Return chart and is associated with benefics and / or with its dispositer than the full year will be good. The degree of Muntha would be the same as that of the Lagna (Ascedant) in the Natal chart.

In the example chart calculated for Mr. Ambrish, Muntha in the 24th year goes to Pisces in the 12th house and so in the Solar Return chart for the 24th Year, it is placed in Pisces which is the first house in the Year chart. the effects of Muntha is dealt with in Chapter no. IV.

Orbs (Deeptansha) of Planets

Planets (i) when their longitudes are the same and (ii) they aspect each other then their relationship is the most powerful. The main condition is that they should have aspect. The Aspect her is the Aspect according to the Tajik or Western

---

* Muntha is also called 'Intiha'

** The motion of Muntha is 5 minutes every day, i.e., in one month it moves 2 degrees and 30 minutes and in 1 year it covers 1 sign.

system of Astrology viz. their placement should be in the 1, 3, 4, 5, 7, 9, 10, 11th from each other. 'Orb' in Sanskrit means 'Mandal', The circle. The nearer the planets are, their lights on each other will be as intense. The distance will reduce the illumination. The planets throw the light all around them in a spherical manner. *This distance to which their lights extend with intensity is called the 'Deeptansha or Orbs of Planets.*

The orbs of Sun, Moon, Mars, Mercury, Jupiter, Venus, and Saturn are respectively 15, 12, 8, 7, 9, 7 and 9 degrees.

Planets within 2 degree orb show immediate and very intense effects. Beyond the orbs mentioned above, the planets when and if they come within orbs in future transits before they chane sign will show effect. If however any of the planets involved moves over to another sign before coming in orbs or completing the exact conjunction with the other planet, then it will not be able to show any effects.

In the matter of aspects the left aspect is comparatively stronger, i.e., from the 10th house to the 4th house etc. Planets when they are placed in one house show strongest effect; The aspect from one's placement to the 3rd, 4th, 5th places is the left aspect and it is comparatively more powerful than the right aspect viz. on the 11th, 10th, and 9th.

Planets within orbs show full effect before and after the degrees. In other degrees but in the same sign their effect is reduced in proporation to the distance between them.

Tripataki Chakram

In the Solar Return chart it is necessary to see if Moon has Vedh (obstruction) with a planet. Secondly if the lord of the Year or the Ascendant lord or other planets are obstructed in the chart. For this a diagram with the three flags called 'Tripataki Chakram' is made to see at a glance palnets and Moon getting Vedh. The main Planet considered here is the Moon because it is not only the satellite of the earth but is also the Planet which has control on the emotional nature of a person. The Vedh is caused in the following manner:

Planet posited in House	*Vedh from*	*Planet Posited in House*	*Vedh from*
1	4, 7, 10	7	10,1,4
2	3, 6, 9	8	9, 12, 3
3	8, 11, 2	9	2, 5, 8
4	7, 10, 1	10	1, 4, 7
5	6, 9, 12	11	12, 3, 6
6	11, 2, 5	12	5, 8, 11

Effects of the Vedh

Vedh by Rahu, Ketu, Mars and Saturn is bad, the vedh by benefics is good. This is discussed in chapter no. VI.

Mudda Dashas (or mugda dasha) Method of Easier Calculation

We have discussed Mudda dashas earlier. The method to calculate it is as follows;

Add the completed number Years with the Number of the Constellation of Moon at birth (also called birth star or Janma Nakshatra) subtract 2 from it. Divide the number that we get with the above process by 9. The remainder will give the beginning of the Mudda dasha of the planet for the year.

If the remainder is 1, 2, 3, 4, 5, 6, 7, 8 or 0 the mudda dasha will start with that of the Sun, Moon, Mars, Rahu, Jupiter, Saturn, Mercury, Ketu, or Venus respectively.

II Table of Mudda Dasha — Beginning

Remainder	1	2	3	4	5	6	7	8	0
Dasha starts with	Sun	Moon	Mars	Rahu	Jup.	Sat.	Merc.	Ketu	Venus

Saham

'Saham' is a Sanskrit word which means 'together with'. In Astrology it stands for the different combination of the longitudes of the Sun, Moon, Ascendant, and Planets in various ways which would give the sensitive points by which we can know about the matters, relatives, issues of a native. The names of the Sahams called Sensitive Points are self explaining words.

First we should calculate the *Sahams* in the nativity and than the sahams in the Solar Return or the horary charts. However, in the Horary charts or the Solar Return only those Sahams which are strong in birth chart will show full and good results. These sahams, their strength and weakness, how to calculate them, are all discussed in chapter no. IV.

This also indicates the timings. The most important Saham of all the *Sahamas* is the 'Punya Saham'. It is called 'Pars Fortuna' in the Western Astrology.

If the birth is during the day time, then subtract the longitudes of Sun from the Longitude of Moon and add the Longitude of the Ascendant viz., (M – S + L) in order to get the Punya Saham.

However, if the birth is at night then subtract the longitude of Moon from the longitude of Sun and add the Longitude of the Ascendant viz., (S – M + L). Here, S is the Sun, M is the Moon, L is the Ascendant.

The Sixteen Yogas (the Shodasha Yogas)

In Horary astrology and the Solar Return charts an important component or if we are frank, the most important method to see if a work will be fruitful or other wise, where the help will come in the accomplishment of the goal, or what obstacles can occur or which are the factors which can cause destruction when the work or function is about to take place, or the duration of success is short and is followed by calamities etc. one and all will be seen through these Sixteen Yogas dealt in chapter no V.

These results are arrived at by looking at the aspects that the planets in the Chart forms and also when they are in orbs to show the full results. The realization or frustration will depend upon the type of the Yoga. The timings of accomplishment in the horary charts and Solar returns will also be arrived at from these yogas.

The yogas have the Persian names as this section of Astrology developed in Persia. For example the word 'Itthashal' which means application, i.e., if a planet faster in motion applies to a slower moving planet and both the planets are in aspect and also within Orbs in the chart then their would be accomplishment. However, if the planets within orbs are separating then it is called 'Israf', i.e., either the goal is already realized before the chart was erected or their would be frustration. Another Yoga is called the 'Nakta Yoga'. It gives an idea as to the Agency through which the goal will be realized.

The main thing here is that one of the planets involved should be the lord of the year or the lord of the Solar Return chart. They should also aspect the Ascendant and the house which indicates the work. For example if it is a question related to wife then the 1st house and the seventh house should be aspected by the planets for the easier realization of the matter.

Illustration of Itthashal yoga

Look to the Solar Return chart for the 24 years of Mr. Ambrish.

Illustration
Asc. Lord-Sun

Jupiter is in Gemini	(17° – 02' – 53")
Moon is in Sagittarius	(07° – 15' – 14")
Sun is in Aries	(16° – 29' – 41")

Jupiter is the ruler of the 1st house.
Moon is the ruler of the 5th house.
Sun is the ruler of the 6th house.

Here, the application between Moon and Jupiter (Orb 10°) is an indication of accomplishment of education. Both planets are benefics. They aspect each other and are posited in the angles and as such aspect the lagna. Another factor that gives full support here is that Sun is 16° – 29' – 41" in Aries. Moon applies to Sun who gathers energy from the Moon and transmit it to Jupiter. There is also an application directly between Sun and Jupiter (Lord of the 6th house and I house). The indication is that the native can get a good work. Looking into the background that the native is a student the Itthashal between Jupiter and Moon (+ Sun) indicates success in studies, competition or work.

A question may arise that Jupiter is about to complete an Itthashal with Sun (Orb 33 minutes only) and as such will not be able to meet with an obligation when Moon forms an exact aspet with it. For that we should notice that all the planets are benefics. Jupiter here is also the Munthapati and Moon here indicates an additional factor. These planets so synchronise that accomplishment has to be effective.

We now conclude the Introduction with the remark that, we have bifurcated the introduction (I and II) in order to cover up the calculation of the birth chart viz., Longitudes of Planets; Navamsha, Mahadashas etc. in the I part: The second part has been devoted solely to the Solar Return viz. finding the time of the commencement of a Solar year, longitudes, Navamsha, Dashas particularly — Hinansha-Patyansha Dasha, Orbs of Planets Muntha, mudda Dashas, illustration of Itthashal yoga etc.

The XIII chapter is devoted to some interesting question generally being asked about jobs, promotion, recovery of lost things. Will I be able to marry a particular person? From what direction the marriage partner would be? This is a book worth reading and then it should be used with a view to improve one's judgement in arriving at better decisions. For example if one knows as to what could be expected in the year then one can concentrate on those matters and save his time and energy. Secondly, from horary horoscopes clear cut answer to day to day questions will come. The chapter V of the sixteen years should be applied to Horary questions to get proper replies.

We are sure that an appropriate use of the subject matter of the book will enlighten the learned readers.

CHAPTER I

JOYS AND SUBDIVISIONS

The present Chapter I should be read as addenda to the Introduction. It deals with the Calculation of another nativity, the Solar Return Chart, followed by the subject not covered in the introduction viz., Placement of Muntha, the formula to calculate the Mudda dasha and actual Illustration. It is followed by calculating the Joys of Planets, house divisions., all the subdivisions of planets. Table III is given, for ready references to locate the Navamsha.

Calculation of a Birth Chart

Let us work out another example of Solar Return for the fifth year of a boy born at New Delhi on the 4th April 1974 at 3.43 p.m. (15.43) in the afternoon. Here we will follow the conventional method of using 1, 2, 3, 4, 5, 6 and 7 (0) for Sunday, Monday, Tuesday, Wednesday, Thursday, Friday, and Saturday respectively.

We shall need the horoscope at birth and so will use the data viz., 4th April 1974. 3.43 p.m. at New Delhi.

We shall calculate the nativity with the method explained before:

The precession of the Equinoxes at birth was 23°–30'–07"

Place of birth	New Delhi
Latitude	28.39 North
Longitude	77.13 East
I.S.T. at birth	15 – 43 – 00 p.m.
Converting into L.M.T.	– 00 – 21 – 08
Local Mean time of birth	15 – 21 – 52

Let us calculate the Rising sign for the above L.M.T.

	Hrs.	*Mnts.*	*Secs.*
Sidereal time for the preceding Noon on the birth date	00	– 48	– 28
Correction for the year	00	– 00	– 18
Add L.M.T. from noon	03	– 21	– 52
Acceleration @ 10 secs. per hour	00	– 00	– 33
R.A.M.C.	04	– 11	– 11

On page 48, 'Table of Ascendants' by N.C. Lahiri. The rising sign for the above R.A.M.C. is 4 signs 13 degrees 8 minutes 23 seconds.

Meridian cusp (p.8) 1 sign 11 degrees 45 minutes 23 seconds.

The Longitudes of planets are calculated for the Standard Time of Birth.

The Longitudes and Navamsha of planets are as follows:

Planets	*Longitudes* S. D. M. S.	*Navamshas**
Sun	11 – 20 – 45 – 54	Capricorn
Moon	04 – 18 – 35 – 43	Virgo
Mars	01 – 27 – 07 – 18	Virgo
Mercury	10 – 25 – 38 – 51	Taurus
Jupiter	10 – 12 – 33 – 01	Capricorn
Venus	10 – 04 – 18 – 00	Scorpio
Saturn	02 – 05 – 39 – 27	Scorpio
Rahu	07 – 29 – 28 – 15	Pisces
Ketu	01 – 29 – 28 – 15	Virgo
Ascendant	04 – 13 – 08 – 23	Cancer
M.C.	01 – 11 – 45 – 23	Aries

Balance of Venus Mahadasha at birth 12 years 01 month 08 days.

After the calculation of the birth chart we proceed to calculate the Solar Return chart for the fifth year of the horoscope mentioned below.

* See Table III.

Birth Chart

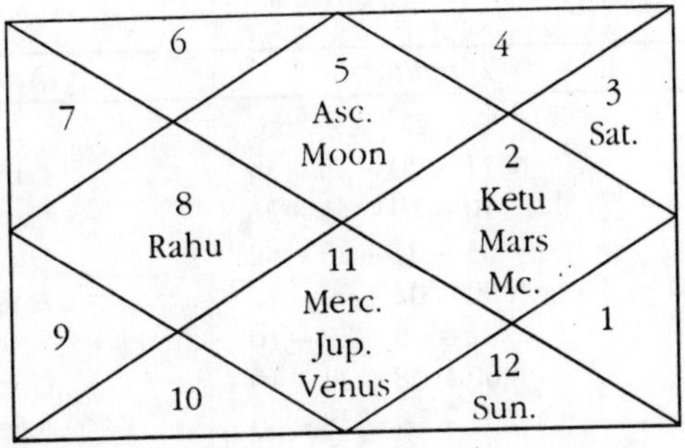

Finding the Time of the Commencement of a Year

The day and at time of birth will be written at the top: then we add the figure for the 4 completed years from the table no. I The resultant data will give us the day and time when the Sun comes back to the same position that it occupied at birth and this will be the commencement of the Fifth year of Birth.

	Day	Hrs.	Mints.	Secs.
Day and time of birth	5*	15	43	00
Completed years 4, so add	5	00	36	39
Total	10	16	19	39

10 is more than the 7 days of the week and so we subtract 7 from it and we get 3rd day or Tuesday at 16 Hours 19 Minutes and 39 Secs. as the time of commencement of the Solar Return for the fifth year.

In the Ephemeris, we find that in the year 1978 when the child is 4 years old Tuesday falls on 4th April 1978 and so we do our calculation for the above date at New Delhi for 4.19.39 p.m. or say 4.20 p.m.

The procedure for calculations of the Rising sign, M.C. and the Longitudes of Planets will be the same as we had illustrated for the Calculation of the Birth chart.

* See note 1 at the end of the chapter.

The position of Planets and their Navamshas for the fifth year of the Solar Return are as follows:

Planet	*Longitudes*	*Navamsha*
	S. D. M. S.	
Sun	11 – 20 – 45 – 54	Capricorn
Moon	10 – 10 – 43 – 25	Capricorn
Mars	03 – 04 – 25 – 52	Leo
Mercury	00 – 02 – 09 – 22	Aries
Jupiter	02 – 05 – 27 – 16	Scorpio
Venus	00 – 08 – 24 – 10	Gemini
Saturn	04 – 00 – 28 – 36	Aries
Rahu	05 – 12 – 03 – 07	Aries
Ketu	11 – 12 – 03 – 07	Libra
Ascendant	04 – 20 – 39 – 12	Libra
M.C.	01 – 19 – 54 – 32	Gemini

The precession of the Equinoxes at the New year was 23° – 33' – 12"

Solar Return (5th Year)

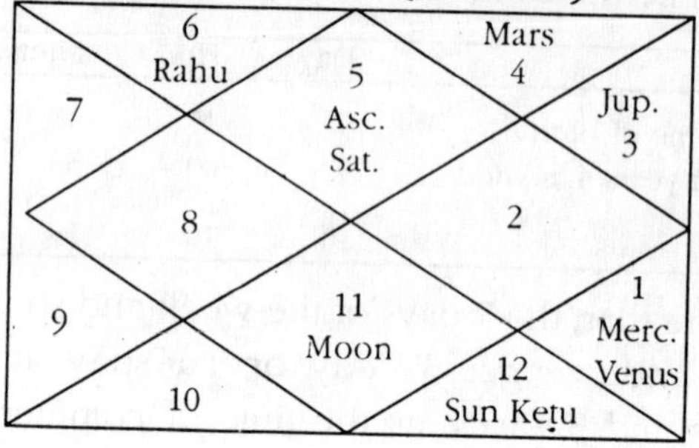

Navamsha Chart (5th Year)

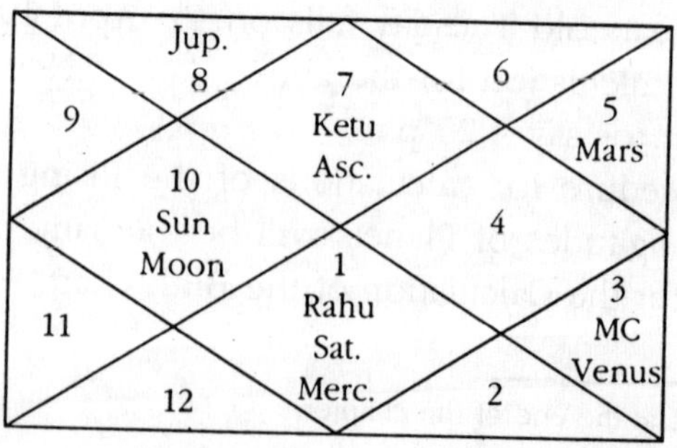

Balance of the Jupiter mahadasha at the time of the New year was 6 years 10 months and 1 day.

How to Place the Muntha in the New Year?

Muntha proceeds at the rate of one rashi per year in the birth chart and then the rashi (sign) in which Muntha falls in that year, the same sign it will occupy in the Solar Return chart irrespective of whatever house it is in. In the present case Leo is in the first house and so Muntha will be in Leo in the first year, in Virgo in the second year, in Libra in the third year, in Scorpio in the fourth year, and in the fifth year it will be in Sagittarius. This is the fifth year so we shall place Muntha in the Sign of Sagittarius in the Solar Return chart. Muntha goes to the fifth house again as the rising sign in the birth chart as well as in the Varsha chart is Leo and Sagittarius is in the fifth house in both cases.

How to Calculate the Mudda Dashas for the fifth Year?

For quick calculation of the Mudda Dashas for any year is the formula given below:

(Completed year + no. of the Moon's constellation at birth – 2) divided by 9. The remainder will show with which planet the Mudda dasha will start.

The dashas will be in the same cyclic order as in the birth chart but the duration of the Dashas will be different.

The Mudda dasha will start with Sun, Moon, Mars, Rahu, Jupiter, Saturn, Mercury, Ketu, and Venus according as the remainder is 1, 2, 3, 4, 5, 6, 7, 8 and 0 respectively.

In the present case the constellation of moon at birth was Purva Phalguni. This is the 11th Nakshatra, the completed years are 4, so with the above formula we have (11 + 4 – 2) divided by 9, or 13 divided by 9, gives us 4 as the remainder and so in the present case the Mudda dasha will begin with that of Rahu.

Total duration of the Vimshottari Dasha cycle for life is of 120 year and here we are concerned only with one year so the dashas of all planets will be proportionately reduced and they will consist of only the 1/120 parts of the full dasha.

Example Rahu dasha was 18 years and so the 1/120th part will be (18 multiplied by 12) divided by 120 = 1 month and 24 days. Similarly, the duration of Jupiter etc. will be reduced:

Table of Mudda Dasha for the fifth year

Planet	*Duration* *mo. days*	*Till (Date)* *year mo. date*
Rahu	1 - 24	1978 - 05 - 28
Jupiter	1 - 18	1978 - 07 - 16
Saturn	1 - 27	1978 - 09 - 13
Mercury	1 - 21	1978 - 11 - 04
Ketu	0 - 21	1978 - 11 - 25
Venus	2 - 00	1978 - 01 - 25
Sun	0 - 18	1979 - 02 - 23
Moon	1 - 00	1979 - 03 - 13
Mars	0 - 21	1979 - 04 - 04

These are the Mudda Dashas. The other type of dasha, i.e., the Hinansha and Patyamsha is already discussed earlier in the Introduction.

Joys of Planets

One more factor is impartant in the Annual charts and this is called the Joys of Planets. This is another way to measure the strength of planets.

There are five manners where a planet is in *Joy*. These five are:

1. Planets in exaltation.
2. Planets in their own signs.
3. Sun, Moon, Mars, Mercury, Jupiter, Venus, and Saturn are respectively in JOY when they are in the 9, 3, 6, 1, 11, 5, and 12th house in the Solar Return Charts.
4. Female planets (Moon, Venus, Mercury, Saturn) are in Joy in the 1, 2, 3, 7, 8, 9 houses from the Ascendant. Male planets (Sun, Mars, Jupiter) are in the 4, 5, 6, 10, 11, 12th houses from the Ascendants.

5. Female Planets are in Joy at Night and Male Planets are in joy during the Daytime. Sunrise to Sunset is the daytime and Sunset to Sunrise is the night time.

Five points are allotted for each type of Joy and the total number of points that a planet gets will indicate its strength.

Given below is the illustration of the Joys in the present Solar Return:

Manner of Joy	*1*	*2*	*3*	*4*	*5*	*Total*
Sun					5	5
Moon				5		5
Mars				5		5
Mercury				5		5
Jupiter			5	5	5	15
Venus				5		5
Saturn				5		5

Jupiter has 15 points so it is very strong. Other Planets are of average strength.

Western readers should note that sign notation is recorded in the Hindu Manner, wherein Aries = 0, Taurus = 1, and so on up to Pisces = 11. Hence the Ascendant in this chart is 20 degrees and 39 minutes and 12 seconds.

Another point which must be clarified is this: the Solar Return chart is always erected *for the latitude and longitude of the birthplace*. Some Western proponents of sidereal astrology advocate computing the Solar Return chart for the geographical location at which the native resides at the time of the Soalr Return, but Hindu astrologers traditionally use the place of birth in any event.

In addition to the nine planets, a "sensitive point" called *Muntha* is also included in the annual chart. The literal meaning of Muntha is "that which churns". At the exact time of birth, Muntha is regarded as having the same sign and degree as the natal Ascendant. At the beginning of the native's second year (1-2 years of age), Muntha is in the second sign from the Ascendant, having moved 30 degrees in the course of the year. Thus, Muntha makes one complete round of the twelve signs in twelve years, so that in the thirteenth year of life (12-13 years of age) it will once again occupy the natal Ascendant and begin another round.

Note that Muntha is in Sagittarius in the example chart because this is the Solar Return for the fifth year and, counted form the natal Leo Ascendant, Sagittarius is the fifth sign. Muntha's degrees and minutes in any sign at the time of the Solar Return will always correspond to the natal Ascendant or Lagna, i.e., our sample Ascendant is 13 degrees Leo, hence Muntha in our example Solar Return is 13 degrees Sagittarius. The significance of Muntha, its interpretation and judgement, will be explained at a later stage.

House Division

The system of house division followed in the Tajik is that of Shripati or Keshava. This is the same as the Western system known as Porphyry's, except for the fact that Hindu astrology defines a *cusp* as the *midpoint* of a house rather than its border or boundary, as in the West.

Tajik, in distinction to other branches of Hindu astrology, lays a great emphasis on house positions, house boundaries, and the placement of planets in houses. However, many factors—such as aspects and house rulerships—are determined according to the old Vedic rules in which one sign constitutes one house. Furthermore, many of the examples in this book are based upon the same principle.

Students who may wish to learn to compute the houses in the old manner are referred to Appendix—at the back of this book. Those who have access to a computer with a Vedic astrology program may easily select the Shripati system, then divide the degrees between house cusp in two to get the house *boundaries* and place the planets in their proper houses. This will allow the student to assess houses. This will allow the student to assess house positions in the classical way.

Subdivisions of Signs

After the chart has actually been cast and the houses determined, it is customary to derive twelve completely different charts from the Solar Return chart by subdividing the signs. These subdivisions or harmonic charts (vargas in Sanskrit) are also used in natal astrology, though the Tajik employs a somewhat different set of subdivisions.

The calculation of all these harmonic charts is, obviously, extemely time-consuming. Many eminent astrologers simply do not take the trouble to calculate all the vargas when analyzing a Solar Return chart. We are also of the opinion that there are other guidelines which yield similar information regarding the assessment of planetary strengths, and that the information derived from the vargas is not commensurate with the time and labor involved. Therefore, we shall not deal with the calculation of all the vargas in the body of the text, though for the sake of completness they are described.

The ninth harmonic or Navamsha, however, is fundamental to the Tajik as well as in natal astrology. It is derived as follows:

The 30 degrees of each sign are divided by 9, which equals 3 degrees 20' in each division or navamsha. The divisions, therefore, run from 0 to 3°.20, 3°.20' to 6°.40', to 10°.00' of each sign and so on. Beginning with Aries, the first navamsha is ruled by Aries, the second by Taurus, the third by Gemini and so on in sequence. Therefore, if a planet occupies 4° Aries 21' in the birth chart, it would be placed in Taurus in the Navamsha. The entire Navamsha system can be outlined in tabular form, to aid the reader in constructing this ninth harmonic or Navamsha for his birth chart or Solar Return.

We give below the Navamsha Table which will enable us to place the planets in their appropriate Navamsha.

Table III: Table of Navamshas

Degrees	*Fire Signs (Aries, Leo, Sag.)*	*Earth Signs (Taurus, Virgo, Cap.)*	*Air Signs (Gem., Libra Aquarius)*	*Water Signs (Cancer, Scor., Pisc.)*
3.20	Aries	Capricorn	Libra	Cancer
6.40	Taurus	Aquarius	Scorpio	Leo
10.00	Gemini	Pisces	Sagittarius	Virgo
13.20	Cancer	Aries	Capricorn	Libra
16.40	Leo	Taurus	Aquarius	Scorpio
20.00	Virgo	Gemini	Pisces	Sagittarius
23.20	Libra	Cancer	Aries	Capricorn
26.40	Scorpio	Leo	Taurus	Aquarius
30.00	Sagittarius	Virgo	Gemini	Pisces

Other Subdivisions

There are 12 subdivisions which are used for gauging the strength of planets. The names of 12 subdivisions are given as we discuss them.

1. **Rashi**, i.e., the sign a planet is in.
2. **Hora:** In one sign there are two 'Hora'. In the odd signs, i.e., 1, 3, 5, 7, 9, and 11 from 0 degree to 15 degrees is the hora of the Sun and from 16 degrees to 30 degrees is the hora of the Moon. In the even signs, i.e., 2, 4, 6, 8, 10, and 12 it is the other way round. From 0 degrees to 15 degree is the hora of Moon and from 16 degrees to 30 degrees that of Sun.

Signs	0° to 15°	16° to 30°
1, 3, 5, 7, 9, 11.	Sun	Moon
2, 4, 6, 8, 10, 12	Moon	Sun

3. **Dreshkana:** A sign is divided in three sections and each section consists of 10 degrees the first section of this Dreshkana or Drekkana always start with the same sign. The second section is the sign in the 5th from it and the third section is the sign which is the 9th sign.

	I	II	III
Sign	0 to 10 deg.	11 to 20 deg.	21 to 30 deg.
Aries	Aries	Leo	Sagittarius
Taurus	Taurus	Virgo	Capricorn
Gemini	Gemini	Libra	Aquarius
Cancer	Cancer	Scorpio	Pisces

and so on.

4. **Chaturthansha:** Four divisons of a sign, each consisting of 7 degrees and 30 minutes. The first portion is the same sign and the second, third, and the fourth sections are the signs which are in the 4th, 7th and 10th respectively from the sign itself.

	I	II	III	IV
Signs	0° to 7°30'	7° 30' to 15°	15° to 22° 30'	22°30' to 30°
Aries	Aries	Cancer	Libra	Capricorn
Taurus	Taurus	Leo	Scorpio	Aquarius

and so on.

5. **Panchamansha:** Five divisions of a sign each consisting of 6 degrees. In odd signs, i.e., in the 1, 3, 5, 7, 9, and 11 Mars,.Saturn, Jupiter, Mercury, and Venus respectively are the rulers. In the even signs, i.e., 2, 4, 6, 8, 10, and 12, Venus, Mercury, Jupiter, Saturn, and Mars are the rulers.

	I	II	III	IV	V
Signs	0 to 6	7 to 12	13 to 18	19 to 24	25 to 30
1, 3, 5, 7, 9, 11	Mars	Sat.	Jup	Merc.	Venus
2, 4, 6, 8, 10, 12.	Venus	Merc.	Jup.	Sat.	Mars

Here 1 stand for Aries. 2 for Taurus etc.

6. **Dwadashansha:** A sign is divided into 12 portions and each of this portion is of 2 degrees and 30 minutes. We start with the same signs in which the Dwadashansha is needed and the next divsions follow in order, i.e., from Aries to Taurus to Gemini to Cancer and so on.

D. - M	0	2-30	5	7-30	10	12-30	15	17-30	20	22-30	25	27-30
Sign	I	II	III	IV	V	VI	VII	VIII	IX	X	XI	XII
Aries	1	2	3	4	5	6	7	8	9	10	11	12
Taurus	2	3	4	5	6	7	8	9	10	11	12	1

and so on.

The numerical value of the signs is used here.

7. The other subdivisions will be calculated by coverting the longitudes into degrees. Place them in six places and then multiply them by 6, 7, 8, 9, 10, and 11 respectively. Divide each of the resultant product by 30. And we shall get in order the Shashtiansha, Saptamansha, Ashtamansha, navansha, Dashmansha, and Ekadashansha. The quotient so obtained viz., 1, 2, 3, 4, 5, etc. will give the signs starting with Aries, Taurus, Gemini, Cancer, Leo etc. respectively. *We shall discard the remainder as we do not need it*. The next step is to add one sign in it in order to get the present Sashtiamsha, Saptamamsha etc.

Example:

Let us work out the subdivsions of the Sun in a chart, The Longitude of Sun is 0 – 16° – 24' – 00".

Shashtiansha

Multiply the Degree and minutes by 6 and divide by 30 *Quotient* or (16 d – 24 m) × 6/30=(96 – 144)/30=(98 – 24)/30=3 signs add 1 sign

and we get 4 signs so Cancer is the Shashtiamsha.

Saptamansha

(16–24) × 7/30=(114–48)/30=3 signs

add 1 sign so we get 4 signs so Cancer is the saptamansha.

Ashtamansha

(16–24) × 8/30=(131–12)/30=4 signs

add 1 sign and we get 5 so Leo is the Ashtamansha.

Navansha

Multiply the longitudes of the Sun by 9 and divide by 30. Then add I sign in the quotient.

(16d 24m) × 9/30 = (147d – 36m) gives us 4 as quotient. Add 1 sign and we get 5 so Leo is the Navansha here.

Dashamansha

(16–24) × 10/30=(164–00)/30=5 signs
add 1 sign and we get 6 so Virgo is the Dashmansha.

Ekadashansha

(16–24) × 11/30=180–24\30=6 as the quotient
add 1 sign and we get 7 so Libra is the Ekadashansha.

Similarly, the subdivisions of the other planets should be calculated.

What is the purpose behind the calculation of all these subdivisions and how do they modify the effect of the planets?

The answer is that in order to measure the strength of a planet these subdivisions are useful. If a planet is in its exalted, own, friends, or in benefic subdivisions then its good effect is enhanced. However, if the subdivision lords are debilitated, in the signs of an enemy, or in that of a malefic, the effects of the planet will be bad.

If the number of benefic subdivisions of a planet are more than good results will ensue. However, if malefic, subdivisions out number the benefic than the resultant effect will be bad. The good and bad effects will be felt in their placement and more during the dahsasof planets.

If malefic are in the benefic subdivisions than even they would show good results and vice versa. If the subdivsions of a malefic are malefic than they would show drastic results.

Similarly, if the Lords of Ascendant and other houses are in exalted, own, friend's and enemy's subdivisions than the good or bad result concerning that house should be judged accordingly. These subdivision apply both to the Nativity as also to the Solar Return charts.

We give below a table of the sub divisions of Sun.

In the first column is the Rashi, Hora etc. in the second column the section it goes to; in the third column the sign; and in the 4th column the Ruler of the Sign. The next thing is to check if the subdivisions are benefic or malefic.

Subdivision of Sun

Name	*Section*	*Sign*	*Ruler*	
Rashi	I	Aries	Mars	M
Hora	II	Moon	Moon	B
Dreshkana	II	Leo	Sun	M
Chaturthansha	III	Libra	Venus	B
Pamchamansha	III	Jupiter	Jupiter	B
Dwadashansha	VII	Libra	Venus	B
Shashtansha	IV	Cancer	Moon	B
Saptamansha	IV	Cancer	Moon	B
Ashtamansha	V	Leo	Sun	M
Navansha	V	Leo	Sun	M
Dashmansha	VI	Virgo	Mercury	B
Ekadashansha	VII	Libra	Venus	B

From the table above examine the ruler, and the inner strength of Sun will be measured. Look into the subdivision (called Vargas) if the rulers of the Vargas are benefic, it is a plus point. The more the number of the benefic, the better would be the result of the planet. In the above table 'M' stands for malefic and 'B' for benefic. In the subdivisions the benefics out number the malefic by 8 is to 4. Therefore, Sun will show good effect.

Note: The day of birth is recorded as "5" not because the native was born on the 5th day of the month, which he was not. Rather, the day of birth is expressed in terms of the weekday. Sunday=1, Monday=2 etc. and so 5=Thursday, the day of the week upon which the native was born. Adding 5 days gives us a "weekday" of 10 in the example and since there are only 7 days in the week so we subtract 7 from 10 and then the remainder is 3, which signifies Tuesday. Hence, the Solar Return will occur on Tuesday, on or near the date of birth according to the Gregorian Calendar, at 16:19:39 hours, which equals 4:19:39 p.m. I.S.T. on Tuesday April 4, 1978. The Ascendant and Meridian Cusp are calculated by converting the Standard Time into the Local Mean Time according to the place of birth. The longitude of the planets are calculated according to the Standard Time. The ayanansha on 4th April 1978 was 23° – 33' – 12".

CHAPTER II

FIRST PRINCIPLES

Before dealing with the question of how to interpret the Solar Return chart, we will spotlight some of the principal differences between conventional Vedic Astrology and Tajik. The principles of Middle Eastern Astrology from which the Tajik takes its origin are similar in many ways to those of Western Astrology. Readers schooled in the Western tradition will readily recognize many such factors.

The Signs of the Zodiac

Hindu astrology recognizes numerous attributes which pertain to each sign of the zodiac. The utility of some of them will be immediately apparent, whereas others may seem to be curiosities from the medieval texts. A relativiely complete listing of such correspondences is given below (see Table IV). As regards the signs, there are no special differences between Tajik and natal astrology.

A brief word of explanation may, however, be required regarding the heading of "rising". In ancient India, signs were said to rise in an "even" or "odd" manner because in those latitudes Cancer through Sagittarius rise in a straight, i.e., even, fashion, whereas Capricorn through Gemini—the odd signs—rise diagonally. Because of this astronomical phenomenon, the even signs will rise for a somewhat longer period of time than the odd ones.

Planets

As with the signs of the zodiac, we include a table of correspondences for the seven planets (Table V). Note that each planet, like each sign of the zodiac, is assigned a time of day when it is "in strength". These correspondences are directly related to an element of Vedic astrology which will be familiar to students of that art, i.e., directional strength. For instance: Mercury and Jupiter get directional strength in the First house, which in the diurnal wheel of the houses, corresponds to early morning. Similarly, Mars and the Sun are strong in the Tenth house or at mid-day, and Venus and the Moon in the Fourth house or at mid-night. Saturn is strong at sundown or in the Seventh house.

Note that some of the indications of planetary gender are different than in natal astrology. In Tajik, the Sun, Mars and Jupiter are male, while the Moon, Mercury, Venus and Saturn are female. There are no androgynous planets in the Tajik system.

Table IV (Section 1)

We give below Table IV, which has four sections. However, before giving the table we would like to mention as to what these sections contain. In all the sections the first column indicates the sign whose attributes are mentioned. In the 1st section of Table IV, the second column contains modalities, i.e., Cardinal, fixed, dual, or moveable. In the 3rd column the elements viz., fire, earth, air, or water are mentioned. In the 4th column the gender is mentioned like male or female. The 5th column deals with the constitution, i.e., the Vata, Pitta, or Kapha—the tridosha according to the Ayurveda System, the imbalance of which is the root cause of all diseases. Column 6 mentions the colours of the signs. These colours are independent of the ruler-ship of the signs.

Sign	Modality	Element	Gender	Constitution	Colour
Aries	Movable (Cardinal)	Fire	Male	Pitta	Red
Taurus	Fixed	Earth	Female	Vata	White
Gemini	Dual (Mutable)	Air	Male	Vata	Green
Cancer	Movable	Water	Female	Kapha	Pink
Leo	Fixed	Fire	Male	Pitta	Yellow
Virgo	Dual	Earth	Female	Vata	Yellow
Libra	Movable	Air	Male	Vata	Multi-Coloured
Scorpio	Fixed	Water	Female	Kapha	White
Sagittarius	Dual	Fire	Male	Pitta	Golden
Capricorn	Movable	Earth	Female	Vata	Tawny
Aquarius	Fixed	Air	Male	All 3 (Tridosha)	Spotted
Pisces	Dual	Water	Female	Kapha	Yellowish

Table IV (Section 2)

Now we give below the second section of Table IV. In this section the second column mentions the species. There are 6 species, viz., Quadruped, Two-legged, Many legged, Human, Jalachar (those residing in water), and Reptiles. The third column mentions the pitch of the voice. These are 4 types—high, none (even), loud or broken. The third column indicates the abodes viz., the jurisdiction of the signs on different places. These are of utmost use in Horary Astrology in deciding where the crux of the problem lies. These are divided into 4 parts *viz.*, Mountains, Beautiful Places, Forests, and Water (like water resorts, Sea shores etc.) The fifth column indicates if the signs are strong at daytime or night-time. The last (i.e., the 6 column) indicates the caste of the sign. The caste system is the same as is prevalent in India viz., Brahmin, Kshatriya, Vaishya and Shudra.

Sign	Species	Voice	Abode	Strength	Caste
Aries	Quadruped	High	Mountains	Day	Kshatriya
Taurus	Quadruped	High	Beautiful Places	Night	Vaisya
Gemini	Two-legged	High	Forests	Day	Shudra
Cancer	Many-legs	None	Water	Night	Brahmin
Leo	Quadruped	Loud	Mountains	Day	Kshatriya

Sign	*Species*	*Voice*	*Abode*	*Strength*	*Caste*
Virgo	Human	Broken	Beautiful Places	Night	Vaisya
Libra	Human	None	Forests	Day	Shudra
Scorpio	Many-legs	None	Water	Night	Brahmin
Sagittarius	Human	Loud	Mountains	Day	Kshatriya
Capricorn	Quadruped & Jalachar	Broken	Beautiful Places	Night	Vaisya
Aquarius	Reptile	Broken	Forests	Day	Shudra
Pisces	Reptile	None	Water	Night	Brahmin

Table IV (Section 3)

In Table IV, Section 3, which we give below, the second column gives the Temperament of the signs. The temperament is further divided into two parts. In the first part,it shows if it is dry, cool, or hot. In the second part it shows if it is aggressive, rigid, humorous, protective, proud (not arrogant), passive, balanced, clever, restless, morbid, humanitarian and romantic. The next column indicates the directions upon which a sign rules viz., East, South, West, and North. The fifth column gives the hue of the signs viz., luster or without luster, smooth etc.

Sign	*Temperament*	*Nature*	*Direction*	*Hue*
Aries	Dry/Aggresive	Malefic	East	Luster
Taurus	Cool/Rigid	Benefic	South	Without Luster
Gemini	Hot/Humourous	Malefic	West	Smooth & Lustrous
Cancer	Cool/Protective	Benefic	North	Lustrous
Leo	Hot/Proud	Malefic	East	Without Luster
Virgo	Cool/Passive	Benefic	South	Without Luster
Libra	Hot/Balanced	Malefic	West	Smooth & Lustrous
Scorpio	Cool/Clever	Benefic	North	Lustrous
Sagittarius	Hot/Restless	Malefic	East	Without Luster
Capricorn	Cool/Morbid	Benefic	South	Without Luster
Aquarius	Hot/Humanitarian	Malefic	West	Smooth & Lustrous
Pisces	Cool/Romantic	Benefic	North	Lustrous

Table IV (Section 4)

In the Table IV, section 4, which we give below, the second column deals with the body type, i.e., strong and medium build, smooth, big or small frames. The third column shows the amount of interest in love-making. The fourth column indicates the number of children normally born; and the fifth column indicates the method of Rising, i.e., odd or even. Even signs are of longer duration where as odd signs are of short duration.

Sign	*Body Type*	*Involvement with Women*	*Number of Children*	*Rising*
Aries	Very Strong & of Medium Build	Infrequent	Few	Odd
Taurus	Medium Build	Average	Average	Odd
Gemini	Smooth	Average	Average	Odd
Cancer	Smooth	Frequent	Many	Even
Leo	Strong	Infrequent	Few	Even
Virgo	Big Frame	Moderate	Few	Even
Libra	Medium Build	Moderate	Few	Even
Scorpio	Smooth	Indulgent	Many	Even
Sagittarius	Strong	Infrequent	Few	Even
Capricorn	Small	Infrequent	Few	Odd
Aquarius	Small	Average	Average	Odd
Pisces	Small	Indulgent	Many	Odd

With the above four sections of Table IV, it would become easier to follow different signs as to their type, physical build, temperament etc. Generally, these are of great help in pinpointing to directions, the type of person etc. in the horary charts.

In addition to these standard planetary correspondences, there are several attributes relating to the Moon's Nodes, Rahu and Ketu. Rahu, for instance, is like Saturn in appearance, is associated with the lower castes and the southwestern direction, and rules over snakes and bones.Ketu resembles Mars,is a bit more benefic than Rahu,is multi-faceted, and is associated with black dogs. Rahu requires a special note as to terminology. In a chart say Rahu is at

7 degrees Sagittarius. Since Rahu's motion is always retrograde, the span from 0 to 7 degrees of Sagittarius remains to be traversed. This sector is called the mouth of Rahu, while 7 to 30 degrees of Sagittarius is called the back. The seventh or opposite sign in which Ketu is always posited (Gemini in the above example) is called the tail of Rahu. The Nodes are imaged as a gigantic serpent or dragon; hence, these expressions.

The Houses

The matters to be judged from each house are essentially the same as in natal astrology. A complete list is given here, however, in order to note some of the different meanings (italicized) specific to Tajik.

First House: self, head, body, personality, temperament, health.

Second House: eyes, face, upper throat, speech, wealth, family; *also friends.*

Third House: arms, lower throat, shoulders, brothers and sisters, valour; *also servants and failure or fall of the father.*

Fourth House: chest, heart, mother, real estate, vehicles, happiness; *also the father's wealth and money buried underground.*

Fifth House: stomach, education, intelligence, children; *efforts for the accumulation of wealth.*

Sixth House: navel region, sickness, enemies and competitors, debts, distress; *also cattle and dependence upon others (whether as a captive or otherwise).*

Seventh House: marriage, one's spouse, sexual relations, groin; *also trade and commerce, property destroyed, loss of memory or forgetfulness, ascertaining stolen property, quarrels, journeys.*

Eighth House: genitals and anus, death and/or longevity, wills and legacies; *also wealth accumulate long ago, the assets or money of the dead, battle, the destruction of an enemy's property, family and distress of mind.*

Ninth House: hips, thighs, religion and spirituality, prosperity, the guru; *also long journeys.*

Tenth House: knees, back, activity, career, fame, honor, worldly status; *also deeds of religious merit and any matters pertaining to the father.*

Eleventh House: calves of the leg, income or material gains; *also daughters, friends, cattle, money from the king, family.*

Twelfth House: expenses; teeth, loss, sexual pleasures, confinement; *also distress and being restrained by an enemy or restraining an enemy.*

Planets in Houses

The general effects of planets in houses are the same as in natal horoscopes, save for the fact that they must be interpreted within the framework of one solar year. Therefore, the solar or annual chart is primarily an aid or accessory to the basic indications of the annual chart, the planetary periods (dashas and antardashas), and transits. If, for instance, the Seventh house is afflicted in the birth chart, thus indicating possible loss of one's spouse, and if the Seventh house in the Solar Return chart is also afflicted, then one may be apprehensive about the spouse's health during that particular year.

In Tajik, as in natal astrology, planets in the angular houses (First, Fourth, Seventh, and Tenth) are considered strong; the Ascendant or First house, however, is by far the strongest. If a planet is auspiciously placed in a particular natal house and occupies the same house in the Solar Return chart, it bestows excellent results. Conversely, if a planet is inauspicious in a particular natal house and occupies the same house in the annual chart, the results are altogether unfortunate.

As regards the so-called evil houses of the birth chart—the Sixth, Eighth and Twelfth—Balabhadra states (on the authority of Satyacharya, who flourished some two thousand years ago) that if benefics occupy the Eighth house of the natal chart it is good for longevity, but that malefics may shorten one's life-span. If benefics occupy the Sixth house of the birth chart the native either has no enemies or else overcomes them. Benefics in the natal Twelfth house help curtail one's expenditures while malefics cause loss. Most of these judgements would also apply to the Solar Return chart, save for the fact that malefics in the Sixth house are considered well-placed under the rules of Tajik.

Aspects

One of the major points of difference between Jatak (i.e., natal astrology) and Tajik is the matter of aspects. In Jatak a planet aspects signs or houses which lie at a particular and stated distance from the planet making the aspect. Hence, it is possible that Mars may aspect Saturn while Saturn does not aspect Mars. But in Tajik, all aspects are mutual. Planets may aspect the cusps of houses or other planets situated at a particular distance away.

Aspects are either *friendly* or *inimical*. The friendly apsect is also called *helpful* and the planet making such an aspect is a *helper*. The inimical aspect may also be described as *hindering* and the planet in question as the *hinderer*. Whether friendly or inimical, an aspect may be of two kinds: *manifest* or *secret*. This is in regard to the *quality* of the aspect.

The table of Aspect Values (Table VI) shows the distance in degrees between a planet and another planet or house cusp, alongwith the usual value of that geometric relationship as an aspect. However, another medieval author named Waman has assigned the following, somewhat different, quantitative values to the aspects:

(a) Sextile (third or eleventh house aspect): 25%
(b) square (fourth or tenth house aspect): 50%
(c) trine (firth or ninth house aspect): 75%
(d) conjunction or opposition (0 or 180 degrees) 100%

Traditionally, aspects are effective within an orb of 12 degrees. The word "orb" will be familiar to students of Western astrology, but inasmuch as the concept is absent

1. See Chapter V, "the Sixteen Yogas" for this and other terms.

from classical Vedic astrology, we give the following definition for those who have been schooled only in the Vedic tradition:

The word "orb", which literally means a circle, globe, or sphere, is used in astrology to denote *the distance surrounding a planet to which its influence particularly extends.* In sanskrit, it is called 'Deeptansha'

Table V (Section 1)

We give below Table V, which deals with the planetary correspondences. But before that please note that it has been divided into four sections. The first column of all sections gives the name of planets and what else each of the section deals with, is mentioned before the table.

In the first section of Table V, the second column indicates if the planet is a natural malefic or benefic. The third column indicates the gender of planets viz., male, female. There are no eunuchs in the Tajik system. The 4th column indicates the caste viz., Brahmin, Kshatriya, Vaisya or Shudra; the fifth column gives the directions, East, north-east etc. The last column (6th) shows the Guna viz., Sat, Raja, or Tama.

Planet	Nature	Gender	Caste	Direction	Guna
Sun	Malefic	Male	Kshatriya	East	Sattwa
Moon	Benefic	Female	Vaisya	Northwest	Sattwa
Mars	Malefic	Male	Kshatriya	South	Tamas
Mercury	Benefic	Female	Shudra	North	Rajas
Jupiter	Benefic	Male	Brahmin	Northeast	Sattwa
Venus	Benefic	Female	Brahmin	Southeast	Rajas
Saturn	Malefic	Female	Shudra	West	Tamas

Table V (Section 2)

We give below Table V, section 2. The second column gives the appearance of planets. The third column shows when a planet is strong, i.e., during noon, mid-night, morning etc. The 4th column shows the Prakriti (humours) of planets viz., Vata, Pitta, Kapha, or mixed. The 5th column indicates the temperament viz., fickle, mild, easygoing etc.

Planet	*Appearance*	*Strength*	*Constitution*	*Temperament*
Sun	Square	Noon	Pitta	Fixed
Moon	Strong, Stout & fair complexioned	mid-night	Kapha	Fickle
Mars	Square and scarred	Noon	Pitta	Violent
Mercury	Circular and childlike	Early Morn.	All 3 (Tridosha)	Volatile
Jupiter	Two-legged and round	Morning	Kapha	Mild
Venus	Two-legged smooth and lustrous	Mid-night	Kapha & Vata	Easy-going
Saturn	Tall	Evening	Vata	Harsh, Cruel

Table V (Section 3)

Table V, section 3, which we give below, indicates in the second column, the metals which a planets rules. By wearing the metal of that planet which is showing bad effect, the negativity could be reduced. The 3rd column indicates the type of animal or bird over which a planet rules. By feeding the animals or bird which comes under a planet, the good effects can be enhanced. The 4th column shows the quality viz., changeable, violent, mild etc. of a planet. The 5th column indicates the abode of planets like water, rubbish, wetlands etc., and the 6th column gives the precious Gems, which come under a planet.

Planet	*Metal*	*Animals*	*Quality*	*Abode*	*Gems*
Sun	Copper	flour-legged	Fixed	With animals	Ruby
Moon	Silver	Water	Changeable	Wetlands	Pearls
Mars	Gold & Copper	Wild	Violent	Burnt ground	Coral
Mercury	Alloys	Birds	Fluctuating	Villages, high Places graveyards	Emeraled
Jupiter	Gold	"Living things"	Mild	Villages	Pukhraj/ Yellow Sapphire
Venus	Silver	Horses	Easy Going	Water, wetlands	Diamond
Saturn	Iron & Lead	Birds, Wild animals	Fixed	Wastelands, rubbish heaps	Blue Sapphire

Table V (Section 4)

We, in the end give the fourth section of Table V. In this table, given below, the 2nd column gives the age of planet like Saturn represents very old person, Mars rules young persons, etc. The 3rd column gives colour which a planet rules; the fourth column indicates the Tastes; The 5th column gives some of the other ruler ships of planets.

Planet	*Age*	*Colour*	*Taste*	*Other Rulerships*
Sun	Old	Reddish White	Bitter, Pungent	Grains, Roots, forest-dwellers
Moon	Very Young	White	Salty	Snakes
Mars	Young	Red	Bitter	Goldsmiths
Mercury	Very Young	Blue	All tastes	Birds (Parrots in particular)
Jupiter	Old	Yellow	Sweet	Business, places of worship, conjugal bliss
Venus	Medium Age	White	Sour	Marriage, Roots
Saturn	Very Old	Dark Blue	Astringent	Snakes

The matters dealt with in tables IV and table V are of great use not only in the Solar Return charts but in all branches of Astrology.

Suppose planet A lies at 15 degrees of Aries. His aspect on planet B at 15 degrees of Leo would be an exact trine. But if planet B lies at 7 degrees of Leo rather than 15, then the aspect is 8 degrees wide of being exact; still, we would say that A aspects B because B's location is ***within orb***. Simiarly, a planet may not lie precisely on the cusp of a given house, but if that cusp is within the planet's orb, then that planet will still be effective in producing effects pertaining to that house.

Table VI: Aspect Values

Distance Between Two Planets or Planet and House Cusp	*Aspect Value*
30°	0%
60°	66.6%
90°	25%
120°	75%
150°	0%
180°	100%
210°	0%
240°	75%
270°	25%
300°	16.5%
330°	0%
360°	100%

In summary, we may say that a planet:

- has no aspect upon the second, sixth, eighth or twelfth house from its own position.
- has a strong and friendly aspect called a trine upon the fifth and ninth houses form its own position.
- has a secretly firendly aspect called a sextile upon the third and eleventh houses from its own position (the sextile brings success).
- has a secretly inimical aspect called a square upon the fourth and tenth houses from its own position.
- has a manifestly inimical aspect called an opposition upon the seventh house from its own position.
- has a manifestly inimical aspect called a conjunction upon any planet occupying the same house as itself.

The trine and sextile are universally regarded as benefic influences which help to accomplish one's objectivies, while the square and opposition are just as universally regarded as destructive, malefic, and productive of quarrels. But there is a difference of opinion concerning the conjunction. The standard medieval author Nila Kantha regards the conjunction as essentially malefic. Waman states that any planet in its own house helps to accomplish affairs pertaining to that house, i.e., a planet which occupies the sign it rules will be auspicious even when conjunct other planets. The apparent difference between Nila Kantha and Waman is reconciled by Balabhadra in the 17th-century work *Hayan Ratna*. Balabhadra affirms that if two planets in conjunction are either exalted, in their own house or in a friendly house, the conjunction helps to accomplish the affairs of that house. But if, on the contrary, the planets are either debilitated or in an enemy house, the conjunction should be regarded as malefic. We may say that it is, in fact, quite reasonable to infer that a planet in exaltation, its own house or a friend's house would naturally do more good than harm.

Tajik Sara, another medieval work, states that:

- if a malefic aspects another malefic with an inimical aspect (i.e., square, opposition, or conjunction), then the effect should be regarded as fully malefic.
- if a benefic aspects another benefic by trine or sextile, the effect should be regarded as fully benefic.
- if a benefic casts a malefic aspect, then an effect which is only half malefic or half benefic is produced.

This is quite logical, because the square of Jupiter or Venus would not be considered nearly as harmful as that of Mars or Saturn. Conversely, a trine from Saturn or Mars would be considered less auspicious than one from Jupiter.

Before concluding this discussion of aspects, we would like to add three points.

1. The orb of 12 degrees is a general rule which applies to all planets, but for the purposes of the special combinations or yogas described later on, there are special orbs of influence:

Sun	-	15°
Moon	-	12°
Mars	-	8°
Mercury	-	7°
Jupiter	-	9°
Venus	-	7°
Saturn	-	9°

2. In the special yogas which are part of the Tajik system, a sharp distinction is made between aspects which are either *applying* or separating. These terms are common in Western astrology, and they mean precisely the same thing here. When a planet is approaching a particular degree of the zodiac where he will make a precise aspect (whether conjunction, sextile, square, trine or opposition) to another planet, he is *applying* to that aspect. When he is moving away from that exact degree, though still within orb, he is said to be *separating*. When we consider applying and separating aspects, we use those special orbs which are related to the yogas as listed above.
3. An aspect from a planet positioned in the *visible half of the zodiac* (from the Seventh house cusp to the First house cusp by way of the Tenth house, i.e., planets above the horizon) upon a planet positioned in the *invisible half of the zodiac* (from the First to the Seventh by way of the Fourth, i.e., below the horizon) is more powerful than an aspect from a planet in the invisible half upon a planet in the visible half.

Friends and Enemies

Tajik Sar gives us a listing of the natural friendships and enmities among planets which is different from the one followed in classical Vedic astrology. The same work also states that natural and temporal relationships should be combined to arrive at a composite set of relationships for any given chart. Most authors, however, do not follow this view either in theory or in practice. Typically only the *temporal relationships* between planets are taken into consideration, and these are determined according to the following rules:

- Planets in the third, fifth, ninth or eleventh houses from each other are friends.
- Planets in the second, sixth, eighth or twelfth houses from each other are neutrals.

- Planets in the same sign or in the fourth, seventh or tenth houses from each other are enemies

In essence, the system of planetary relationships follows the same principle as that of the aspects, e.g., just as the opposition aspect is considered inimical, so is the relationship between planets in opposite houses, and just as the trine is considered helpful, so are planets in the fifth or ninth houses from each other regarded as friends.

As we have seen, Tajik divides the houses according to the Shripati system described above rather than following the traditional Vedic practice of regarding each sign as equivalent to a house. Thus, the question naturally arises: When ascertaining planetary relationships, should we count from sign to sign, or from house to house? Current practice follows the opinion of Balabhadra, who, in his *Hayan Ratna,* advises assessing the temporal relationships according to the usual Vedic method, i.e., from sign to sign.

The planetary relationships from the example chart in Chapter I are given below (Table VII):

Table VII (Planetary Relationships)

Friends—Enemies—Neutrals Chart

Planets	*Friends*	*Enemies*	*Neutrals*
Sun	Mars	Jupiter	Moon, Merc. Venus, Sat.
Moon	Merc. Jup. Venus	Saturn	Sun, Mars
Mars	Sun	Merc., Venus	Moon, Jup. Sat.
Mercury	Moon, Jup. Sat.	Mars, Venus	Sun
Jupiter	Moon, Merc., Venus, Sat.,	Sun	Mars
Venus	Moon, Jup., Saturn	Mercury Mars	Sun
Saturn	Merc., Jup., Venus	Moon	Sun, Mars

CHAPTER III

THE LORD OF THE YEAR

The Lord of the Year (Sanskrit: Varshesh) is determined by an elaborate process of calculating the strength of the planets. There are five planets which become candidates for Lord of the Year. These are:

1. The lord of the Ascendant in the natal chart.
2. The lord of the Ascendant in the Solar Return chart.
3. The lord of the sign occupied by Muntha.
4. The lord of the sun-sign if the exact time of the Solar Return occurs during the day[1] of the lord of the moon-sign if it occurs at night.

Importance of the Lord of the Year

One of the important factors in the Solar Return chart is the lord of the year. Before we go into what is the lord of the year and how it is determined we would like to emphasize that it is no less important than the lord of Ascendant in the Natal chart. Just as Lagnesh or the Ascendant lord controls the intensity of effects in the life in the same manner the effect of the lord of the year should be judged. The strength of the Lord of the year in the chart will also increase or diminish the results of other planets. If the lord of the year is strong then the year will be good and prosperous. If the lord of the year is placed in houses other than the 'Trik', i.e., the 6th, 8th, and 12th houses, is rising, is strong in the

1. A day is defined in Hindu astrology as the period between sunrise and sunset, while night is the interval between sunset and dawn.

natal as well as in the Solar Return charts, then it will be able to show full good effect viz., good health, gains and promotion as well as extreme happiness. If it is strong only in the Annual charts then the good results will be more pronounced in the second half of the year (last six months).

If the year lord has full strength than the benefic results of all planets and dashas will be full otherwise these would be proportionately reduced. If the year lord is week than unhappiness, sorrow, danger from enemies, tax problems, tiring journeys and many other calamities will be felt.

Calculation of Muntha in a Horary Chart

We had said in the beginning that all the principles of Solar Return chart applies in toto to the Horary astrology. But the question here is how to decide as to which are the five planets entitled to become the lord of the horary chart. The answer is that in order to arrive at it, first we should decide as to where Muntha should be placed? Secondly, which planet should be taken in place of the lord of the Birth Ascendant? The method to decide these issues are as follows:

A. (i) Leave aside the sign and just take the degree, minutes, and seconds of the Ascendant in the horary chart,

(ii) Multiply this by 2 and divide by 5.

The quotient will be the sign, degree, minutes, and seconds of Muntha.

B. *The Lord of the year chart from the horary chart* is decided in the following manner:

(i) Prasna Lagnesh (Lord of the horary Ascendant) in lieu of the Lord of the Ascendant in the Solar Return chart.

(ii) The lord of the 4th house in the horary chart instead of the lord of the birth Ascendant.

(iii) The lord of the house which Muntha occupies. We had calculated the position of Muntha with the method explained above.

(iv) Trirashipati in the same usual manner as in the Solar Return charts.

(v) The dispositer of Moon or Sun according as the times of the question is in the night or daytime respectively. This also is the same as in Solar Return charts.

We would like to illustrate it with the following example: Let us cast a horary chart for Mr. David who asked certain questions while on a visit to New Delhi at 01.34 a.m. on 24th September 1938.

The horary chart was as follows:

Horary Chart

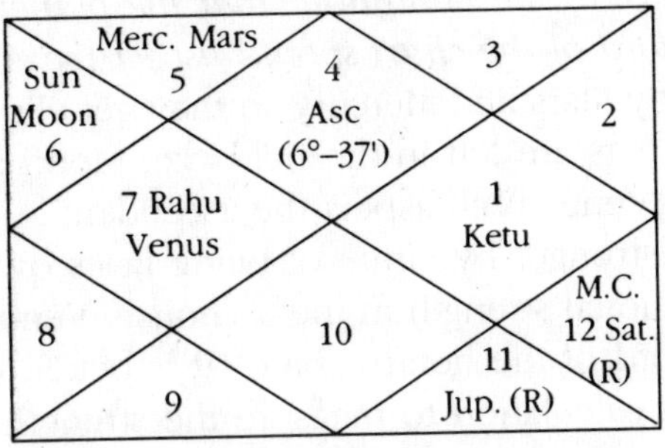

The horary Ascendant is 3 signs 6 degrees 37 minutes and 00 seconds. As per the rule above we put aside the sign and write the degree, minutes and seconds and then multiply it by 2.

Degree		*Minutes*		*Seconds*
06	–	37	–	00
			×	2
13	–	14	–	00

We divide this product by 5 and what we get will be the sign, degree, minutes, and seconds of *Muntha*. Please see below:

(13 – 14' – 00") ÷ 5 = 2 signs 20 degrees 12 minutes 00 seconds.

Muntha will therefore be placed in Gemini in the 12th house of the present horary chart. Munthapati here is Mercury.

The Lord of the ascendant in the horary chart is Moon (i) so it will be one of the planets entitled to become the lord of the horary chart. The 4th house here is ruled by Venus (ii) and so it will also be the planet to compete. The time of the question was during the night and as such the dispositer of Moon which is Mercury (iii) here is also entitled. The trirashipati is Mars (iv) and it is also an aspirant to be the lord of the chart. The Munthapti is Mercury (v) so it is again aspiring to control the horary chart.

We have therefore (i) Moon, (ii) Venus, (iii) Mercury, (iv) Mars, and (v) Mercury, the five aspirants to be the Lord of the Prasana. Here the *condition* that the planet entitled to become the lord of the chart should aspect the Ascendant* is not fulfilled by Mars and Mercury so they get eliminated and only two planets are left in the field viz., Moon and Venus.

Moon and Venus both aspect the ascendant but obviously Venus looks stronger by virtue of being in its own sign and has full directional strength in the 4th house. Venus therefore will be the lord of the horary chart. (It is better to have full mathematical calculation to measure the strength of planets before arriving at the final judgement as to who will be the lord of the chart).

We give below table of Trirashipati rulers, This table will enable us to see at a glance as to which planet will be the ruler. This rulership is dependent on two factors: (i) The rising sign and (ii) the birth time if it is during the day time or at nighttime. Here the *daytime* is from Sunrise to Sunset and the *nighttime* is from Sunset to Sunrise.

---

* Aspect on the Ascendant is essential in order to become the Lord of the Horary or Solar Return Charts.

Table VIII: Trirashipati Rulers

Sign	*Day Ruler*	*Night Ruler*
Aries	Sun	Jupiter
Taurus	Venus	Moon
Gemini	Saturn	Mercury
Cancer	Venus	Mars
Leo	Jupiter	Sun
Virgo	Moon	Venus
Libra	Mercury	Saturn
Scorpio	Mars	Venus
Sagittarius	Saturn	Saturn
Capricorn	Mars	Mars
Aquarius	Jupiter	Jupiter
Pisces	Moon	Moon

Thus, only a planet which qualifies under one of the five rules listed above may become the Lord of the year. *Of the planets thus eligible to become Lord of the Year, the one which is strongest and which also aspects the Ascendant is named Lord of the Year. If a planet does not aspect the Ascendant it cannot beocme Lord of the Year, even though it may technically be the strongest planet in every other way.*

The reader should remember that when we use the word "aspect" in this context, we are referring to the particular system of aspect employed in Tajik and which has been defined in the previous chapter. Rather than reiterate the entire discourse on aspects, let us simply note that *for all practical purposes a planet in the first, third, fourth, fifth, seventh, ninth, tenth or eleventh sign form the Ascendant is regarded as casting an aspect on the Ascendant whereas a planet in the second, sixth, eighth or twelfth position is not.*

The system does not discriminate between the *quality* of the aspect (i.e., friendly or inimical) or the *quantum* of the aspect (i.e., full, half, etc.) when determining the Lord of the year.

The above rule, though apparently simple, may sometimes be subject to extenuating circumstances. The circumstances and their resolutions are as follows:

1. If two planets are of equal strength and both aspect the Ascendant then the planet with the greater quantum of aspect becomes the Lord of the year.
2. If two planets are of equal strength *and* their quantum of aspect is likewise equal, or if all five planets are too weak to qualify, then the dispositor[1] of Muntha becomes the Lord of the Year.
3. If none of the five eligible planets aspects the Ascendant, then the strongest of the five becomes the Lord of the Year.
4. In the event that none of the five eligible planets aspects the Ascendant, a conflict may still arise if two of those planets are of equal strength. There are two schools of thought as to the resolution of this problem:
    a) The dispositer of the Sun becomes the Lord of the Year if the Solar Return occurs during the day, while the dispositor of the Moon becomes Lord of the Year if the Return occurs at night; or
    b) If the Moon applies to one of the five eligible planets within an orb of 12 degrees, then that planet will become Lord of the Year; if not, then the Lord of the Year is determined as under rule (a)

Three other points must be reiterated here to insure that they are fully understood:

1. Only a planet which becomes eligible under one of the five headings listed at the beginning of this chapter may be named Lord of the year. If a planet fails to qualify under one of these rules it cannot become Lord of the year, no matter how strong it may be or how powerfully it aspects the Ascendant.
2. Five is, in fact, the *maximum* number of planets which may be eligible. Often the number of eligible planets

---

1. The dispositor of a planet is the lord or ruler of the sign in which that planet is placed.

is less, due to the fact that the same planet may be eligible under more than one heading. For example: if the natal Ascendant is Pisces and if the Solar Return occurs during the day with an Ascendant of Leo, then Jupiter is both lord of the Ascendant and Lord of the Trirashipati.

3. When we use the term "strength" in reference to the planets eligible for lordship over the year, we refer to a *mathematically determined strength* computed according to the technique called Panchavargyabala (Sanskrit: "strength in five categories"). Predictions are made according to whether the Lord of the year is very strong, of middling strength, or weak in terms of Panchavargyabala. The substance of these predictions will be dealt with later in this chapter. First we must delineate the mathematical processes by which the quantum of strength is determined.

This brings us to Panchavargyabala which is discussed below:

Panchavargyabala — The Determination of Planetary Strength

The placement of Planet in a particular sign or to be more prescise in a particular degree will decide its five types of strenghth viz., Exaltation, Rashi, Hadda, Drekkana, and Navamsha.

There are five components of Panchavargyabala or Planetary strength. The strength of each planet eligible for lordship of the year is calculated according to each of these five components, then its total strength is determined by adding up its score for all five headings. The maximum number of points to be gained from each of the Five strengths is as follows:

Exaltation Strength	=	20 points
Rashi Strength	=	30 points

Hadda strength	=	15 points
Drekkana strength	=	10 points
Navamsha strength	=	5 points

It will be noted that the total number of possible points is 80. But this theoretical 80 is always divided by 4, so that the *actual* number of possible points is 20.

One may well ask: Why designate the number 80 and then take the trouble of dividing it by 4 ? The answer is that there is a facility of calculation attached to the number 20. Because this number once constituted a unit of area measurement for lands and fields, it was an easy and familiar integer for the people of India; hence its adaptation for use in the calculation of planetary strength.

Exaltation Strength

The calculation of a planet's Exaltation strength is very simple. There are 20 possible points attached to this component of the Panchavargyabala. If a planet occupies its highest point of exaltation it receives a full 20 points; if at its deepest point of debilitation (i.e., the point exactly opposite its exalation), it receives 0 points. Any position in between is calculated according to the rule of three.

Below is the table which shows the maximum exaltation and debitation degrees of a planets.

Table IX: Planetary Exaltations

Planet	*Exaltation*	*Debilitation*
Sun	Aries 10	Libra 10
Moon	Taurus 3	Scorpio 3
Mars	Capricorn 28	Cancer 28
Mercury	Virgo 15	Pisces 15
Jupiter	Cancer 5	Capricorn 5
Venus	Pisces 27	Virgo 27
Saturn	Libra 20	Aries 20

Rashi Strength

First of all we calculate if a planet is in its own sign, friends sign, neutral sign or in an enemy's sign and then we proceed further by the following method.

As regards strength by rashi or sign, a planet is assessed as follows:

- in its own sign = 30 points
- in a friends's sign = 22.5 points
- in a neutral sign = 15 points
- in an enemy's sign = 7.5 points

The assessment of friends and enemies follows the guidelines in the section "Friends and Enemies", Chapter II, p. 79.

Hadda Strength

The following table shows the degrees of the zodiac presided over by each planet in the Hadda system: However, before we give the table let us pointout that Hadda or Hadde is both a Persian and Arabic word and its literal meaning is 'Limit' or boundary. Each sign in the Zodiac is so divided that a particular planet is more powerful in between certain degrees and this in between is called its *Hadda*. Now please see Table X below which shows at a glance the 'Hadda' rulership.

Table X: Hadda Rulerships

Sign	*Hadda Divisions (By Degree and Planetary Ruler)*				
	Ist	*2nd*	*3rd*	*4th*	*5th*
Aries	0 to 6 Jupiter	6 to 12 Venus	12 to 20 Mercury	20 to 25 Mars	25 to 30 Saturn
Taurus	0 to 8 Venus	8 to 14 Mercury	14 to 22 Jupiter	22 to 27 Saturn	27 to 30 Mars
Gemini	0 to 6 Mercury	6 to 12 Venus	12 to 17 Jupiter	17 to 24 Mars	24 to 30 Saturn
Cancer	0 to 7 Mars	7 to 13 Venus	13 to 19 Mercury	19 to 26 Jupiter	26 to 30 Saturn
Leo	0 to 6 Jupiter	6 to 11 Venus	11 to 18 Saturn	18 to 24 Mercury	24 to 30 Mars

Sign	*Hadda Divisions (By Degree and Planetary Ruler)*				
	Ist	*2nd*	*3rd*	*4th*	*5th*
Virgo	0 to 7 Mercury	7 to 17 Venus	17 to 21 Jupiter	21 to 28 Mars	28 to 30 Saturn
Libra	0 to 6 Saturn	6 to 14 Mercury	14 to 21 Jupiter	21 to 28 Venus	28 to 30 Mars
Scorpio	0 to 7 Mars	7 to 11 Venus	11 to 19 Mercury	19 to 24 Mars	24 to 30 Saturn
Sagittarius	0 to 12 Jupiter	12 to 17 Venus	17 to 21 Mercury	21 to 26 Mars	26 to 30 Saturn
Capricorn	0 to 7 Mercury	7 to 14 Jupiter	14 to 22 Venus	22 to 26 Saturn	26 to 30 Mars
Aquarius	0 to 7 Venus	7 to 13 Mercury	13 to 20 Jupiter	20 to 25 Mars	25 to 30 Saturn
Pisces	0 to 12 Venus	12 to 16 Jupiter	16 to 19 Mercury	19 to 28 Mars	28 to 30 Saturn

With respect to Aquarius, two different readings are found in the old texts. According to *Hayan Ratna,* the first 7 degrees are allotted to Mercury and the next 6 to Venus, whereas the *Tajik Nil Kanthi* assigns the first 7 to Venus and the next 6 to Mercury. The latter division is followed here, inasmuch as it is by far the most commonly accepted in India.

The Hadda Strength is scored as follows. A planet:

- in its own hadda = 15 points
- in a friend's hadda = 11.25 points
- in a neutral hadda = 7.5 points
- in an enemy's hadda = 3.75 points

As with the signs or Rashi strength, friends and enemies are assessed according to the guidelines in Chapter II.

Drekkana Strength

The Drekkana or third harmonic chart as it is generally understood is explained in the appendix on Subdivisions. Although Drekkana Strength as employed in the Tajik system is likewise based upon a division of each zodiacal sign into three parts, it is worth noting that *the Drekkana subdivisions used in the calculation of Panchavargyabala are not the ones ordinarily used in the calculation of the third harmonic or Drekkana chart.*

The traditional Drekkana chart divides each sign into three parts, each ruled by a specific planet according to classical Vedic rules. But in the Tajik system, the division of each sign into three parts or decanates is governed by the so-called Chaldean system which entered the art of Tajik by way of the Middle East and which was also followed by some Western astrologers—for instance, Saint-Germain (see Table X, Decanates of the Tajik system).

Drekkana Strength is scored as follows. A planet gets the maximum point if it is in own Drekkana. Positionwise drekkanas are as follows:

- in its own Drekkana = 10 points
- in a friend's Drekkana = 7.5 points
- in a neutral Drekkana = 5 points
- in an enemy's Drekkana = 2.5 points

As with the Previous Strengths, the friends and enemies of the planets are assessed according to the guidelines in Chapter II.

Drekkana or Dreshkana in English means a decanate. A sign of 30 degrees is divided into three parts. Each of these part consists of 10 degrees. Each part is ruled by different planet. The degree of a planet will enable us to decide as to which decanate a planet should be placed. The next step is to know from the table as to which planet rules that decanate. For example let us say that Sun is in Virgo in 7 degree. Then we look for the column I of Table XI which says Virgo: In the 2nd column 0 degrees to 10 degrees, it shows that Sun is the ruler of this decanate.

The next step is to find out if Sun is in its (i) own drekkana (ii) in a friend's Drekkana (iii) in a neutral drekkana or (iv) in an enemy's drekkana. This way we will know the Drekkana strength of any Planet. We give Table of Drekkana according to the Tajik system:

Table XI: Decanates of the Tajik System

Sign	*Degrees and Rulers of the Decanates*		
	0 to 10	*10 to 20*	*20 to 30*
Aries	Mars	Sun	Jupiter
Taurus	Mercury	Moon	Saturn

Gemini	Jupiter	Mars	Sun
Cancer	Venus	Mercury	Moon
Leo	Saturn	Jupiter	Mars
Virgo	Sun	Venus	Mercury
Libra	Moon	Saturn	Jupiter
Scorpio	Mars	Sun	Venus
Sagittarius	Mercury	Moon	Saturn
Capricorn	Jupiter	Mars	Sun
Aquarius	Venus	Mercury	Moon
Pisces	Saturn	Jupiter	Mars

After the decanate is dealt with, we proceed to the Navamsha strength.

Navamsha Strength

Navamsha as we know is the most important division in Hindu astrology as well in the Tajik system. Earlier in Chapter I it has been discussed throughly and the Navamsha Table is also given on page no.... We should with the help of the table find out the Navamsha of all the planets and then see if the planets are in their own, friend's, neutral's or enemy's sign. In the Navamsha the maximum point a planet can have will be 5, if it is in its own Navamsha and then it is proportionately reduced by 1.25, i.e., 3.75 for being in a friend's, 2.5 for being in a neutral's, and 1.25 for being in an enemy's sign.

The calculation of the Navamsha, generally considered the most important of the vargas or harmonic charts, has been detailed in Chapter I. The rulerships are the same.

A planet:

- in its own Navamsha = 5 points
- in a friend's Navamsha = 3.75 points
- in a neutral Navamsha = 2.5 points
- in an enemy's Navamsha = 1.25 points

Friends and enemies are assessed as above.

Totalling the Planetary Strengths

Now we must total the number of points each eligible planet has attained under the Panchavargyabala, and then divide each total by 4 to obtain the final numerical strength of each planet. Here follow the total points for the planets from our example chart in Chapter I. Though only five planets, at most, can ever be eligible for the lordship over the year, we shall total each planet of the example chart, so that the student may check his or her work.

Table XII given below, gives the panchavargyabala of Sun, Moon, Mars, Mercury, Jupiter, Venus and Saturn. When the total of the two type of balas is divided by 4, the resulatnt quotient indicates the actual strength.

Table XII: Panchavargyabala

Planet	*Hadda*	*Navamsha*	*Rashi*	*Drek-kana*	*Exalta-tion*	*Total*	*Total/4*
Sun	Mars	Saturn	Jup.	Mars			
	Fr.	Neutral	Enemy	Fr.			
	11.25	2.50	7.50	7.50	17.863	46.61	11.65
Moon	Venus	Sat.	Sat.	Merc.			
	Fr.	Enemy	Enemy	Fr.			
	11.25	1.25	7.50	7.50	4.191	31.69	7.92
Mars	Mars	Sun	Moon	Venus			
	Own	Fr.	Neutral	Enemy			
	15.00	3.75	15.00	2.50	2.619	38.87	9.72
Mercury	Jup.	Mars	Mars	Mars			
	Fr.	Enemy	Enemy	Enemy			
	11.25	1.25	7.50	2.50	1.906	24.40	6.10
Jupiter	Merc.	Merc.	Merc.	Jup.			
	Fr.	Fr.	Fr.	Own			
	11.25	3.75	22.50	10.00	16.716	64.22	16.06
Venus	Venus	Merc.	Mars	Mars			
	Own	Fr.	Enemy	Enemy			
	15.00	3.75	7.50	2.50	18.733	47.48	11.87
Saturn	Jup.	Mars	Sun	Saturn			
	Fr.	Neutral	Neutral	Own			
	11.25	2.50	15.00	10.00	11.165	49.92	12.48

The abvoe is the table of the panchavargyabala. The last column 8 is the resultant strength which will enable us in deciding many factors related to the Solar Return chart or Horary Astrology.

Now that we have obtained our totals, we may determine the Lord of the Year. As we learned, there are five planets which may be eligible for lordship over the year:

1. The lord of the Ascendant in the Natal chart.
   In our example, Leo is rising. Therefore, the Sun rules the natal Ascendant.
2. The lord of the Ascendant in the Solar Return chart.
   In our example, Leo is rising again. Therefore, the Sun also rules the Solar Return Ascendant.
3. The lord of the sign occupied by Muntha.
   In our example, Muntha is in Sagittarius. Therefore, Jupiter rules the sign occupied by Muntha.
4. The lord of the sun-sign if the exact time of the Solar Return occurs during the day or the lord of the moon-sign if it occurs at night. As the solar Return is during the day so the lord of the Sun sign is Jupiter is a contender.
5. The lord of Trirashipati.
   In our example, the Ascendant is Leo. The Solar Return occurred during the day, and the daytime Trirashipati ruler of Leo is Jupiter.

As will be seen, an analysis of the five factors of eligibility shows us that, in this case, only two planets (rather than the maximum of five) are in fact eligible to become Lord of the Year—Jupiter and the sun.

However, we may also remember that a planet *must* aspect the Ascendant in order to qualify as Lord of the Year. Jupiter aspects the Ascendant (by sextile) whereas the Sun does not.

Therefore, Jupiter is the Lord of the Year.

As this example shows, it is sometimes possible to ascertain the Lord of the Year even without going through the full range of Panchavargyabala calculations. But these calculations serve another purpose in addition to simply helping us identify the Lord fo the Year.

The year under consideration for any Solar Return chart is divided into periods or cycles—in Sanskrit, the word is dashas. We will learn how to calculate these cycles in Chapter VIII. Whether or not a planet will yield good effects during the course of its dasha or cycle is dependent upon its strength in terms of Panchavargyabala. Hence, it is necessary for the student to master these calculations—even when the Lord of the year can be detemined without them. Here Jupiter get 16.06 strength and so it is very strong. Not only the period of Jupiter but the full year will be good.

Joys of Planets

There is another method, quicker and easier, which astrologers often use to judge whether a planet is well placed—or, in the traditional term, "joyously" placed.

1. A Planet is in strength if it occupies its own sign or
2. Its sign of exaltation
3. The following positions are also deemed strong:

    a) The sun in the Ninth house
    b) The moon in the Third house
    c) Mars in the Sixth house
    d) Mercury in the First house
    e) Jupiter in the Eleventh house
    f) Venus in the Fifth house
    g) Saturn in the Twelfth hosue

4. Male planets are strong during the day, female planets during the night (for male and female planets under the Tajik system, see Chapter II,).
5. Male Planets "rejoice" in the Fourth, Fifth, Sixth, Tenth, Eleventh and Twelfth houses (called "oriental"), while female planet do so in the First, Second, Third, Seventh, Eighth and Ninth ("occidental") house.

Each of the above criteria is allotted 5 points, and if a planet "rejoices" on at least two counts it is deemed well placed. According to *Tajik Muktavali,* a planet in a sign opposite its own sign is considered weak (Western astrologers use the term "detriment" to indicate such a position). However, this is a general consideration and no points are added or subtracted on this basis.

Interpreting the Lord of the Year

The Lord of the Year will show its best results if

- it lies in any house except the Sixth, Eighth or Twelfth
- it is rising
- it is strong in both the natal and Solar Return charts.

The Lord of the year is said to be

- endowed with full strength if it obtains more than ten total points in the Panchavargyabala
- of medium strength if it obtains between five and ten points
- devoid of strength if it obtains less than five points.

If the Lord of the Year is endowed with full strength, then it will yield its full benefic potential; if endowed with medium strength it will give mixed results; and if devoid of strength it will yield sorrow, unhappiness, mental apprehension from enemies and many obstacles or dangers.

Even though only these three basic categories are recoginized, it should nevertheless be taken for granted that the more points a planet has, the greater its strength, even within its own category.

Always remember that the effect of the Lord of the Year in the Solar Return chart will be realized according to its strength in the natal chart. For example: If the Fifth house of the birth chart, signifying children, is heavily afflicted, then it will not be possible for positve results concerning children to arise from the influence of the Solar Return.

The above set of rules is admirably summarized by the medieval author Nilakanth in his opening verses:

> If the Lord of the Year is posited in any house other than the Sixth, Eighth, or Twelfth; is not setting[1]; is very strong radically [i.e. in the birth chart] as well as in the annual chart, then there will be full good effects in respect to health, happiness, increase in prestige and position. If the Lord of the Year is of medium strength there will be only sorrow, distress, fear from enemies, and various impediments and losses during the year.

Effect of Planets when they are the Lord of the Year

The astrologer must always take into account the status, country of origin or cultural background, and the general circumstances of the times if he wishes to make an accurate Judgement. We now give below the effect of Sun, Moon, Mars etc. according as they are of full, medium or devoid of strength:

Sun

If the Sun is endowed with full strength as Lord of the Year, it brings acquisition of power, happiness from one's children, the respect and support of one's relatives, fame, gain of property and victory over one's enemies or competitors.

Endowed with medium strength, the Sun still brings the above effects, though to a lesser degree and side by side with physical weakness, differences of opinion with family members, loss of position, and trouble with the govenment.

Devoid of strength, the Sun's good effects fail to operate and the negative effects listed above will predominate and be very intense. It can also cause eye-sight problems.

1. The term "setting" refers to a planet which is setting *beliacally,* i.e., with the Sun. In terms of the birth chart diagram, this would be indicated by a planet which is conjunct the Sun in the Seventh house.

Moon

If the Moon is endowed with full strength as Lord of the Year, it brings wealth, relations with women or an especially close relationship with one's spouse, sons, friends and property. The native may also enjoy luxurious vehicles or clothes, a rise in his position (in accordance with his general circumstances) and friendships with those in power.

Endowed with medium strength, the Moon will produce the above results to a somewhat lesser degree, and if the Moon is separating from a malefic, then enmity with sons and friends, aimless and pointless wanderings, and physical illnesses involving kapha[1] will be the result.

If the Moon has little or no strength, then the native will suffer kapha disorders, fear from robbers and thieves, quarrels with relatives, and separation from one's spouse and/or children, along with a great deal of general anguish, both mental and physical.

Mars

If Mars is endowed with full strength as Lord of the Year, the native will be victorious, famous, may attain a high position in the army, the police force,or in a bank, and will gain wealth. His enemies or competitors will be vanquished. He will achive respect and will experience happiness on account of his sons.

Endowed with medium strength, Mars will produce some, but not all, of the results listed above. Loss of temper or qurrels with people in general and relatives in particular are also likely, and there is a possibility of pitta disorders, especially accidents, injuries, or diseases of the blood.

If Mars is devoid of strength then there will be danger from enemies or from fires, though if Jupiter aspects Mars

---

1. See 'aspects in Vedic Astrology'.

then these negative effects will not manifest. Dangers involving Mars tend to strike like a bolt out of the blue; precautions generally fail. Trouble with the government, stomach problems, or fevers are also likely. This is a particularly bad time for a woman to leave her husband; women who begin romantic liaisons at this time usually find themselves alone, sadder, and wiser afterwards.

Mercury

If Mercury is endowed with full strength as Lord of the Year, the native will excel in literary activity, public speaking or debate, and general comunication with others. He will be honored by those in power and attain a high position, perhaps administrative. This is a good time to deal with lawyers, inaugrate major business deals, or enter into long-term contracts.

Endowed with medium strength, Mercury still brings the same effects listed above, though in lesser measure. If Mercury applies to benefics there will be gains from business and/or commerce.

If Mercury is devoid of strength, there will be losses in business or in real estate, loss of memory or of friends, and legal problems. One may be cheated by one's maternal uncle. Carelessness on the part of the native will also create problems.

Jupiter

If Jupiter is endowed with full strength as Lord of the Year, there will be happiness, comforts, gain of wealth or over-all prosperity, travel to holy places, and general good fortune.

Endowed with medium strength, Jupiter brings the results detailed above, though in lesser measure. But if Jupiter is separating from another planet or planets, then there will be poverty and bad health.

If Jupiter is devoid of strength, the native will experience loss of money, disorders of the blood, chronic headaches, and the disapproval of one's elders. Gambling or speculation brings loss, and there may also be marital problems.

Venus

If Venus is endowed with full strength as Lord of the Year there will be good health, material comforts or luxuries, "favour from rich women" (i.e., productive or remunerative liaisons, whether in love or business, with women of substance), and a love of the fine arts. In some cases, the native may be drawn towards Divine love.

Endowed with medium strength, Venus produces the above effects to a lesser degree. But if Venus is conjoined with or aspected by malefics, then a certain amount of sorrow and loss will occur during the year.

If Venus is devoid of strength it will be a bad year, characterized by mental anguish, divorce, or loss of material comforts.

Saturn

If Saturn is endowed with full strength as Lord of the Year, the native will acquire property, particularly real estate. The classical texts mention gain of agricultural lands and cattle, a judgment which may still be applicable to those who live in rural areas. Saturn's influence may also bring an inheritance.

Endowed with medium strength, Saturn brings the same results in lesser measure. If the planet is associated with malefics, the results will be generally unfortunate.

Devoid of strength, Saturn will cause the native to waste a great deal of time in worthless pursuits, as well as experiencing the loss or destruction of his wealth.

Special Principles

Some of the more specific rules governing assessment of the Lord of the Year are given below.

The Lord of the Year shows its effects throughout the year. One must give consideration to its strength in the natal chart as well as in the Solar Return.

In general; it is said that a strong year lord produces its good effects, a medium year Lord its mixed effects and a weak year lord its misries throughout the entire year. But there are two schools of thought which make a more specific judgement in terms of time.

1. One school of thought stipulates that a Year Lord which is strong in both the birth chart and the Solar Return chart will manifest its good effects throughout the year, but a Year Lord which is strong only in terms of the Solar Return chart and weak in the natal chart will make for a troublesome first half of the year; the good results which may be indicated by transits or dasha cycles will be delayed. If the Year Lord is weak in the Solar Return chart rather than the natal chart then it is the second half of the year which will be troublesome.
2. The other school of thought affirms that one must perform the Panchavargyabala calculations on both the natal and Solar Return charts, add the totals, and divide the results by two in order to obtain the true strength of any given planet, in this case the Year Lord. The results for the year ahead should be predicted according to these calculations.

Any planet which applies to the Lord of the Year will most certainly show its effect during the year, according to its nature and strength. If a benefic makes application to the Year Lord, or if the Year Lord itself applies to benefic, the results will be good. But if the Lord of the Year is separating from a benefic, there will be only a little good fortune involved. And if the Lord of the Year is separating from a malefic, or if a malefic separates from the Year Lord, bad results will follow.

If the Lord of the Year (or any other planet) is in the same hadda as a planet to which it applies in both the natal and Solar Return charts, then that planet will produce its full effcts during the course of the year. Otherwise, it will give only mixed results.

If a planet which may generally be capable of good results is separating from the Lord of the Year or the lord of the Solar Return chart's Ascendant, that planet will give only inauspicious results. But if it applies to the Lord of the Year or the Solar Return Ascendant lord, then it will yield good results. If, on the other hand, it neither applies to nor separates from one of these planets, its effects will be felt according to its strength in the birth chart. For instance: if the ruler of the natal Fifth house aspects the Fifth and is strong enough to produce children for the native, there will nevertheless be no children forthcoming in a year where the lord of the Solar Return's Fifth house is separating from the Lord of the Year.

If Jupiter is the Lord of the Year and is natally placed in the hadda of a friend, and if the Moon applies to Jupiter with a friendly aspect in both the natal chart and the Solar Return, then the year will be an excellent one, full of good fortune.

The Tajik system recognizes three special combinations or yogas—namely Itthashal, Kamboola, and Israf—which must always be taken into account when assessing the Year Lord's strength (for the yogas, see Chapter V). If there is Itthashal between the Lord of the Year and benefic planets, then any negative results will be cancelled. But if the Lord of the Year does not apply to any benefic, then the wrost resutls may be expected.

If planet A in the birth chart is capable (by way of his position in a particular house or sign) of conferring good effects upon the houses he rules, and if this same planet A in the Solar Return chart separates from either.

a) the Lord of the Solar Return Ascendant or
b) the Lord of the Year

then during that year planet A will fail to confer the auspicious results promised in the birth chart.

Similarly, if planet A does not aspect either the Lord of the Year or the ruler of the Solar Return chart's Ascendant, then he may or may not manifest his natal qualities—whether for good or ill—during the course of the year. But if planet A does in fact aspect either of these two lords, then his effects, auspicious or otherwise, will most certainly be felt during the course of the year.

The student will wish to remember that the arduous calculations involved in Panchavargyabala are useful not only for determining the Lord of the Year, but for judging the strengths of the planets in general. This is important in regards to the dashas or periods of the planets (see Chapter VIII). A planet which is strong by way of Panchavargyabala, its period will be more favorable. In fact, assessing the trends and events for any given year is based primarily upon considering the strength of planets *and* of the year Lord in particular. The periods of the planets should be regarded as secondary factors compared to the strength of theYear Lord—i.e., if the Lord of the Year is strong, the Planetary periods will yield their full results, but if the Lord of the Year is weak the other planets will be less capable of exerting a favorable influence.

From the above rules we may glean, in essence, that the events of any given year must be predicted on the basis of the year Lord's strength in both the natal and Soalr Return charts, and by consideration of his aspects, especially whether these are applying or separating. It is particularly important to notice aspects between the Lord of the Year and the Moon (again in both the natal and Solar Return charts). In fact, the aspect of any planet to the Moon is of special importance, as well as the Moon's position by sign and house generally. The stronger the Moon, the better the results of the whole chart. Note also that planets must be considered not only in terms of their sign and house positions in both the natal and annual charts, but in terms of their hadda positions as well.

CHAPTER IV

MUNTHA AND SENSITIVE POINTS 'SAHAM'

In the Present chapter two important sections of the Solar Return chart are discussed. The first one is the 'Muntha' and its effect and the second one are the Sensitive points 'Saham'.

Muntha and the lord of Muntha are of prime importance and according to some of the old masters,if Muntha and its lord are well placed then the full year should be interpreted to be a good year.

There is one exception and that is if it is a 'Dwijanma Varsha' i.e., the Ascendant in both the natal and the solar chart, is the same then it will indicate sickness or any other problem according to the age and background of the person.

The sensitive points or 'Shaham' give a fair indication as to happiness and success, in the various department of life.

Equal importance should be given to the sensitive points in both the Natal as well as in the Solar charts.

SECTION 'A' : MUNTHA

Muntha is a special feature of the Solar Return. It is not a planet; rather, it is a symbolic placement.

What is the principle behind Muntha? According to tradition, the sign occupying the First house of the natal chart represents the first year of life, the sign, in the Second house the second year of life and so on. Thus, Muntha is placed in the sign which this progressed Ascendant would occupy in the natal chart during that year. Muntha progresses at a precise rate: the reader may refer back to the explanation in chapter I, p. 53.

Great emphasis is attached to Muntha. According to great masters the effect of muntha undergoes traumatic changes depending upon the following factors:

1. The association of Muntha with its dispositer, if it is a natural benefic like Jupiter, Venus, or Moon (which is in the 8th digit of bright half to the 8th digit in the dark half) will be full of happy events.
2. The dispositer of muntha is a malefic like Mars, Saturn, or Sun but Muntha receives a friendly aspect from it, then the full year will be good.
3. If muntha receives friendly aspects from natural benefics the year will be good.
4. If muntha receives inimical aspect from Malefics, the year will be bad. The above factors if they are mixed then the year will be a mixture of good and bad events. Keeping the above in view the following results of muntha, in different houses should be interpreted.

Muntha in the Houses

First House: Muntha in the First house of the Solar Return chart brings good health, happiness, "favours from the king" (i.e., the government), increase of valor, victory, success in one's endeavours, the annihilation of one's enemies (or, in a modern context, one's competitors), and general honour.

Second House: Optimism, an influx of money, an increase in reputation and the respect of others, the patronage of the king (i.e., government), success, good food and all kinds of happiness.

Third House: Big projects, an increase in physical prowess, early and successful culmination of one's endeavors, good friendships, happiness with respect to one's siblings, devotion to "gods and Brahmins" (i.e., positive spiritual concerns), and "the petronage of kings".

Fourth House: Physical illness and mental anguish, failure in one's endeavors or else a complete absence of endeavor, "fear from enemies", general dullness or lethargy, and some damage to one's reputation.

Fifth House: Wise counsel, religious devotion, the enhancement of one's valor and prestige, public recognition, happiness with respect to one's children, "royal favor", good income, good activities, and fame.

Sixth House: An increased number of enemies (or competitors), danger of robbery or burglary, loss of one's job or failure therein, physical distress, "royal displeasure", ill-conceived efforts, evil intentions, repentance.

Seventh House: Distress, illness, wrong action due to confused thinking, anxiety, ill repute, pessimism, loss of money and "irreligious conduct" (i.e., actions which are out of harmony with one's spiritual path).

Eighth House: "Foul diseases" (i.e., problems involving the eliminatory or reproductive system), distress due to thieves or other "wicked" people, fear from enemies, a general loss of one's health and wealth ("luster" is the classical term), "irreligious conduct", confinement, sorrow, long journeys (in ancient times a long journey was a dangerous and uncomfortable proposition).

Ninth House: Good luck, an increase in wealth and in "meritorious deeds" (i.e., behavior in accordance with one's spiritual path which builds up good karma), "auspicious cermonies" (i.e., spiritual preoccupations), success in one's enterprises, fame, "royal favor", and happiness with respect to one's spouse, children, and other contacts.

Tenth House: "Royal Patronage" (or the assistance and recognition of those in authority), an increase in one's status or respectability, the performance of meritorious deeds, success in one's enterprises, happiness, fame and wealth.

Eleventh House: Leisure time and pleasure, recognition from those in authority, the realization of one's hopes, an increases in one's income, happiness due to ones children, friends and associates.

Twelfth House: Loss of vitality, physical ailments, "bad company", quarrels with friends and relatives as well as with others, loss of money, possible trouble with the government, danger from thieves, failure in one's undertakings and general distress.

Interpreting Muntha

From the above, it will be seen that Muntha, in a general

way, is favourable in the First, Second, Third, Fifth, Ninth, Tenth and Eleventh houses, but unfavourable in the Fourth, Sixth, Seventh, Eighth and Twelfth. The following factors may modify these basic positions to a greater or lesser degree.

In order to assess Muntha properly, we must consider its ruler or lord. The lord or dispositor of Muntha is the ruler of the sign in which Muntha is located. The strength of Muntha's ruler should be examined in both the natal and the Solar Return charts. The stronger he is in both of these charts, the better his over-all influence. Muntha's lord may be considered afflicted and likely to yield negative results if it is:

1. in the Fourth, Sixth, Eighth or Twelfth,
2. Combust (i.e., conjunct the Sun within about 12 degrees),
3. retrograde,
4. conjoined with malefics and
5. conjoined with or aspected by the lord of the Eighth house.

Note that the house positions listed above apply equally to the natal chart or to the Solar Return. Similarly, the lord of Muntha should be deemed positively strong if it is:

1. exalted
2. in its own house or the house of a friend
3. in the First, Third, Seventh, Tenth or Eleventh
4. conjoined with or receiving friendly aspects from benefics.

Remember also that the Muntha lord will yield better results if he is himself a natural benefic rather than a malefic.

Aspects are important in judging Muntha, and here again we must study both the natal and annual charts. It is favorable if Muntha is conjunct with or aspected by its own lord or by benefic planets. Distress due to illness or enemies may result if Muntha conjoins or is aspected by malefics, especially through inimical aspects (the square or opposition). Other general principies are:

1. it is better to have a friendly aspect (trine or sextile) from a benefic than it is to have an inimical one (conjunction, square or opposition).
2. an inimical aspect from a malefic is inherently evil, but a friendly one is not.
3. it is better to receive an aspect from a powerful benefic rather than a r iddling or weak one.
4. aspects from a weakened malefic need not be considered evil if that malefic happens to be a friend of the Muntha lord.
5. an aspect within orb is more effective than a distant one (the conjunction is understood to be included among the aspects for our present purposes).

Any proper assessment of Muntha depends on a synthesis of four factors:

1. Muntha's condition in the birth chart
2. Muntha's condition in the Solar Return chart
3. the condition of Muntha's lord in the birth chart
4. the condition of Muntha's lord in the Solar Return chart.

If Muntha is strong and positive on all four counts, then all the affairs relating to its house position in both the birth chart and the annual chart will yield auspicious resluts. Similarly, when Muntha is in poor condition on all four counts then the affairs of its houses will manifest nothing but trouble during the year.

But what happens when Muntha is well placed in the birth chart but weakened in the Solar Return, or vice versa? In this case, the influence of the birth chart will be felt during the first half of the year, while the influence of the annual chart will be felt during the second half.

This principle is a general one in Tajik, and applies to all planets. It may be stated thus:

A planet which is auspicious in both charts yields positive results throughout the year, while a planet that is poorly placed in both charts yields negative results throughout the year. A planet which is positively placed in the birth chart but ill placed in the Solar Return will show good effects in the first half of the year and evil effects in the latter half, while a planet which is inauspicious in the birth chart and auspicious in the Solar Return chart will show poor results in the first half of the year and good results in the second half.

A few other interpretative points which the student may keep in mind are:

- If Muntha is conjoined with the Sun or in Leo and the Sun is strong, then the native will enjoy the favor and patronage of those in positions of power, but if the Sun is debilitated or afflicted then there will be no such results.
- If muntha is conjoined with the Moon, Mercury, Jupiter or Venus, or if it lies in signs ruled by these planets (Taurus, Gemini, Cancer, Virgo, Libra, Sagittarius or Pisces), then the situation is favorable and the affairs signified by the planet involved will flourish. But if Muntha is conjoined with Mars or Saturn, or if it lies in their signs (Aries, Scorpio, Capricorn, or Aquarius) the situation is unfavorable.
- Muntha in conjunction with malefics in the Fifth or Ninth encourages the native towards "sinful activities".
- It is auspicious if Muntha lies in the "mouth" of Rahu, especially when conjoined with or aspected by Venus or Jupiter (happiness, wealth and a good name are the results). But it is inauspicious when Muntha lies in the "back" or "tail" of Rahu.[1]

1. The terms "mouth", "back" and "tail" of Rahu are defined in Chapter II in the section entitled "Planets"

SECTION 'B' : WHAT ARE THE SENSITIVE POINTS?

The medieval texts identify as many as seventy-five sensitive points, also known as sahamas. Each relates to a specific matter, department or affair of life. Since each house of the horoscope signifies a number of affairs, it becomes difficult for the astrologer to ascertain whether *all* the affairs pertaining to a particualr house will prosper or suffer simply from studying the disposition of the applicable planets. The use of the sensitive points helps to restrict and define the field of inquiry.

On principle, all seventy-five of the sensitive points should be calculated, in the birth chart as well as the Solar Return chart, though most astrologers only calculate those points which refer to the question at issue. If a sensitive point is well-placed and strong in the birth chart by virtue of occupying a good house and being beneficially conjoined with or aspected by its dispositor, and if it meets these same conditions in the Solar Return chart, then it will show its effects in the strongest possible way. Some of these points obviously require a common-sense approach to the practical or cultural background of the subject. For instance, the points of Romantic Affairs or Birth of a Child could scarcely apply to the Solar Return of a four-year-old child, as also the days of Horses and Elephants are clearly long past.

The names of the sensitive points are given here primarily in English, for the sake of clarity. However, we have retained the term *punya,* meaning merit or good fortune, for the first and most important of all sensitive points because of its specificity and utility. When the Punya Saham is well-placed, the year will prove to be a good one; an afflicted Punya Saham will yield the opposite result. Just as Western astrologers calculate the Part of Fortune by deducting the longitude of the Sun from that of the Moon and adding the longitude of the Ascendant, so the Punya Saham is calculated. The other points are derived by the same principle of operation, though using different coordinates.

One more peculiarity applies to sensitive points in the Tajik system which is different from the way the Part of Fortune is approached in the West. In Tajik, a distinction is made between diurnal and nocturnal births (or Solar Return). Thus, the formula for calculation differs according to whether the birthtime occurs during the day or night.

Each sensitive point is derived from a combination of three figures, which we shall call A additive, B subtractive and C additive. In most cases, C is the longitude of Ascendant. The rules is: *If C does not fall between B and A, one sign is added to the result.*

Let us illustrate. Suppose, the Sun is at 8 degrees Leo, the Moon at 12° Libra and the Ascendant at 10° Sagittarius. We are going to find the Punya Saham. Since the Sun is above the horizon, this is clearly a daytime birth. The first part of our equation, therefore, will be Moon (6–12°) – Sun (4–8°)=4° Gemini.[1] Now we add the Ascendant (8–10°), which gives us 14 degrees Aquarius. But if we count from the Sun (whose longitude has been subtracted) to the Moon (from which substraction has been made), we will be counting Leo, Virgo, Libra. The Ascendant, being Sagittarius, does not fall in between B and A. Therefore, we add one sign or 30 degrees to reach the longitude of the Punya Saham, which is 14 degrees Pisces.

Let us try another example. The Sun is at 8 Leo, the Moon at 12 Taurus, and the Ascendant at 10 Satittarius. Again, we are concerned with a daytime birth. Since the longitude of the Moon is less than that of the Sun, we must add 12 signs to the Moon's longitude. Thus, (13–12°) – (4–8°)=(9–4°) or 4 degrees Capricorn. The next step consists of adding the Ascendant: (9–4°)+(8–10°)=(17–14°). Of course, there are only 12 signs, so 17–12=5. We now have 5–14 or 14 degrees

1. We use the traditional Hindu sign notation, in which Aries=0 rather than 1 and Taurus=1 rather than 2. In Western notation, Aries=1. See Chapter I, p.

Virgo. Again, let us count from the Sun (that which was subtracted) to the Moon: Leo, Virgo, Libra, Scorpio, Sagittarius, Capricorn, Aquarius, Pisces, Aries, Taurus. Since our Ascendant, Sagittarius, lies between the Sun and Moon, we need not add another sign, so the Punya Saham is 14 degrees Virgo.

Keshava, Ganesha, and Haribhatta—three eminent medieval authors—do not recommend adding one sign as in our first example. But standard practice in India follows the *Tajik Muktavali, Jeerna Tajik, Grahajnabharan, Tajik Nilakanthi,* and the *Hayan Ratna,* wherein one sign is added.

INTERPRETING THE SENSITIVE POINTS

When interpreting the sensitive points, the general rule is that a saham aspected by its dispositor and by benefics will prosper. The strength of the point's dispositor must also be considered—the stronger the planet which rules over the sensitive point, the better results it will yield. If the saham's dispositor aspects the Ascendant, this is also considered a favorable situation. A dispositor need not be in its own sign to be exceptionally strong—if it is in its own hadda, drekkana or navamsha as well as aspecting the Ascendant, it may be deemed quite strong.

If the lord of a saham is conjoined with or aspected by the lord of the Eighth, and if it applies to or receives application from malefics, evil results follow. The same is true if the dispositor appears in the Sixth, Eighth or Twelfth. However, we should note that the sensitive points of Disease, Quarrels, Death, Enemies and Poverty *should* be positioned in these evil houses with their lords weak in order to show favorable results. Traditionally, a saham's dispositor may also be considered weak if it fails to acquire many points through Panchavargyabala or through Planetary Joy.

The strength of a sensitive point should be considered in terms of the birth chart as well as the Solar Return, for a result may only be made manifest when it already exists as a potential in the brith chart. For instance, let us suppose that the Punya Saham occupies 7 degrees Aries in a Solar Return chart. If a debilitated Saturn occupies 7 degrees Aries in the birth chart, then the annual Punya Saham is afflicted by natal Saturn and cannot be expected to yield positive results. But if Jupiter occupies 7 Aries in the birth chart, then of course a Punya Saham at that degree would yield excellent results indeed.

We give below table XIV which gives the Sensitive Points called 'Saham' in Sanskrit.

In this table the name of the Sahams is given in the first column. In the second column, the method to obtain the Sahams if the time of birth is during the day. In the 3rd column the formula to get the Saham if the birth is during night. In the 4th column, we have mentioned the houses to which the matters related to the Saham will pertain to.

Please note that if (i) Saham, (ii) The house itself and (iii) the Significators, i.e., the 'Karka' are all strong then good results will be realized in respect of the Saham. If it is mixed that is below average then only average results will be felt.

Table XIV: Sensitive Points

Saham	*Day*	*Night*	*House*
Punya	Moon–Sun+Asc	Sun–Moon+Asc	9,1,4
Guru or Preceptor	Sun–Moon+Asc	Moon–Sun+Asc	9
Knowledge & Learning	Sun–Moon+Asc	Moon–Sun+Asc	3, 5
Fame & Reputation	Jupiter–Punya+Asc	Punya–Jupiter+Asc	8,10
Friends	Guru–Punya+Venus	Punya–Guru+Venus	11
Religious Ritual	Punya+Mars–Asc	Mars–Punya+Asc	9
Hope	Saturn–Venus+Asc	Venus–Saturn+Asc	9
Physical Strength[1]	Mars–Asc Lord+Asc	Asc Lord–Mars+Asc	1,3
Siblings	Jupiter–Saturn+Asc	Jupiter–Saturn+Asc	3,11
Respect	Jupiter–Moon+Asc	Jupiter–Sun+Asc	1
Political Authority	Saturn–Sun+Asc	Sun–Saturn+Asc	10
Father	Saturn–Sun+Asc	Sun–Saturn+Asc	10

1. The following formulas apply only if Mars is *not* the Ascendant lord. If Mars rules the Ascendant, then a different formula is used, applicable to both day and night, which is Jupiter–Mars+Asc.

Saham	*Day*	*Night*	*House*
Mother	Moon–Venus+Asc	Venus–Moon+Asc	4
Sons	Jupiter–Moon+Asc	Venus–Moon+Asc	5
Longevity	Saturn–Jupiter+Asc	Jupiter–Saturn+Asc	1,8
Luster	Moon–Venus+Asc	Venus–Moon+Asc	1,4
Action	Mars–Mercury+Asc	Mercury–Mars+Asc	10,1,6
Disease	Asc–Moon+Asc	Asc–Moon+Asc	6,1
Cupidity[1]	Moon–Asc Lord+Asc	Asc Lord–Moon+Asc	7,8
Quarrels	Jupiter–Mars+Asc	Mars–Jupiter+Asc	1,3
Forgiveness	Jupiter–Mars+Asc	Mars–Jupiter+Asc	1
Scriptural Study	Jupiter–Saturn+Mercury	Saturn–Jupiter+Mercury	5
Male Relatives	Mercury–Moon+Asc	Mercury–Moon+Asc	3,11
Defeat	Moon–Mercury+Asc	Mercury–Moon+Asc	6,12
Death	8th Hose Cusp –Moon+Saturn	8th House Cusp –Moon+Saturn	2,7,8
Foreign Lands	9th House Cusp –9th Lord+Asc	9th House Cusp –9th Lord+Asc	9,12,7
Wealth	2nd House Cusp –2nd Lord+Asc	2nd House Cusp –2nd Lord+Asc	2,11
Romantic Affairs	Venus–Sun+Asc	Venus–Sun+Asc	5
Working as an Employee	Moon–Saturn+Asc	Saturn–Moon+Asc	6
Mercantile Activity	Moon–Mercury+Asc	Moon–Mercury+Asc	3,2
Successful Endeavors	Saturn–Sun+Sun's Dispositor	Saturn–Moon+Moon's Dispositor	12,10
Marriage	Venus–Saturn+Asc	Saturn–Venus+Asc	7
Birth of a Child	Jupiter–Mercury+Asc	Mercury–Jupiter+Asc	5,11
Mental Anguish	Saturn–Moon+ +6th House Cusp	Saturn–Moon +6th House Cusp	3,12
Religious Devotion	Guru–Punya+Asc	Guru–Punya+Asc	9
Love	Venus–Mars+Asc	Venus–Mars+Asc	10
Armies	Jupiter–Punya+Asc	Punya–Jupiter+Asc	10
Body	Jupiter–Punya+Asc	Punya–Jupiter+Asc	1
Mental or Emotional Stupefaction	Mars–Saturn+Mercury	Saturn–Mars+Mercury	3
Commerce	Mars–Mercury+Asc	Mars–Mercury+Asc	2
Drowning	Saturn–Moon+Asc	Moon–Saturn+Asc	8
Enemies	Mars–Saturn+Asc	Saturn–Mars+Asc	6,12
Victory	Punya–Mars+Asc	Mars–Punya+Asc	6,10

1. If the Moon itself is the lord of the Ascendant, then the formula, whether for day or night births, is Sun – Moon + Asc.

Saham	Day	Night	House
Endeavours	Saturn–Jupiter+Asc	Jupiter–Saturn+Asc	3,1
Poverty	Punya–Mercury+Jupiter	Mercury–Punya+Jupiter	12,8
Spiritual Administration	10 Aries–Sun+Asc	3 Taurus–Moon+Asc	9,10
Travel by Water	3 signs 15–Saturn+Asc	Saturn–3 signs 15+Asc	8,9
Imprisonment	Punya–Saturn+Asc	Saturn–Punya+Asc	12
Daughters	Venus–Moon+Asc	Moon–Venus+Asc	5
Horses & Elephants	Punya–Sun +11th House Cusp	Sun–Punya +11th House Cusp	4

Timing of the Sensitive Points

What these Sensitive Points indicate by placements or by receiving aspects from other planets will come to be realized during:—

a. Transit of Planets in a friendly or inimical manner and forming an aspect to the degree of the Saham.
b. During the dashas of the ruler of the sign in which they fall, good results will be felt.
c. Negative results will ensue when the Dashas or Mudda Dashas or any other type of Dashas of a planet which rules the 6th, 8th, or 12th houses from the sign where the Saham is posited, are in the offing.

For example if the 'Punya Saham' is in Cancer 6 degrees, then the Mahadasha of Moon (because Moon is the ruler of Cancer), will bring in good fortunes and benefit from matters connected with property. It will be a good time for fame and wealth.

However, if the Dashas are that of Saturn, Mercury or to some extent Jupiter then some negative results will be felt. This is so becuase these planets rule the 8th, 12th, and 6th houses respectively from Cancer. The effect of Jupiter will be mixed as it also rules the 9th house. If a planet rules the first and 8th both houses as for Aries Ascendant, then the result will be good.

It will be a good indication if during 'Transit' a natural benefic forms a trine, sextile or conjunction with a Saham and not good if a malefic has an inimical aspect.

CHAPTER V

THE SIXTEEN YOGAS

Now we shall discuss the sixteen yogas, which, over and above the general principles of delineation, constitute one of the main planks upon which to base inferences concerning the Solar Return chart.[1] In the course of our discussion, we shall refer to terms in Persian or Arabic; these have been absorbed into the medieval Sanskrit texts. It is less important to memorize the terms themselves than it is to understand the principles and how they are applied. Western astrologers with an historical bent may note that some of these techniques bear a marked similarity to those discussed by William Lilly, Guido Bonatus, and Jerome Cardan, save for the fact that these Western writers limited their consideration of the data to horary practice.

As regards the yogas, the student must remember that particular orbs of influence are employed, as discussed in Chapter II and reiterated here:

Sun	15°
Moon	12°
Mars	8°
Mercury	7°
Jupiter	9°
Venus	7°
Saturn	9°

However, it is also worth mentioning that the *Tajik Tilak* advises a uniform orb of 12 degrees for all planets.

1. The sixteen yogas are applicable to horary techniques as well as to Solar Returns.

The Names of the Yogas

The Total number of Yogas are Sixteen. That is why these are called the *'Shodasha Yogas'*. See the touch of Sanskrit language in the yogas for which Persian words are used. 'Shodasha is Shashta plus Dasha. Shashta means Six and Dasha means ten and when added together Shodasha=16. In Persian the number when counted has many words which are also used in Sanskrit. This is so because the Persians were 'Aryans' like the Indians in the North of India.

Most of us understand the word Yoga viz., addition, i.e., combining together of two or more numbers or factors and this is what will be discussed in the present chapter. Here we shall be concerned with different Planetary combinations or placement. We shall discuss all the yogas and substantiate them by charts. We shall explain them under different heads but before we do that, we give the names of all the yogas.

1. Ikkabal, 2. Induvar, 3. Itthashal, 4. Israf, 5. Nakta, 6. Yamaya, 7. Manau, 8. Kambool, 9. Gairkambool, 10. Khallasar, 11. Radda, 12. Dufalikuttha, 13. Dutthothvir, 14. Tambira, 15. Kuttha, 16. Duraffa.

The above 16 yogas are the subject matter of this chapter. These are the main planks on which the results of the Solar Returns and Horary Astrology rests.

Ikkabal Yoga

The gist of this yoga is that no planet should be in a cadent house—all planets, including Rahu and Ketu, must be in angular and/or succedent houses.[1] The word Ikkabal in fact refers to such placement. When all planets are posited in

---

1. In traditional Vedic astrology, the outer planets—Uranus, Neptune,and Pluto—are not taken into consideration because they were not discovered until recent times. It is our opinion that they too should be considered.

this way, the year will be a good one for increase of wealth and a rise in status. This yoga also acts as an antidote for other unfavorable yogas in the Solar Return chart.

We give below an illustration of the Ikkabal Yoga. In the chart below all planets including Rahu and Ketu are in angles (1, 4, 7, 10) or in Succeedent houses (2, 5, 8, 11). This yoga will take place irrespective of whatever may be the rising sign.

The importance of this yoga increases as planets in angles and succeedent houses start to show their effects from the beginning of the year itself. Here, planets in the 2nd and 8th house will not aspect the Ascendant, and secondly 8th is also a Trik yet by virtue of other planets being in Angles and succeedent houses, the planets in the 2nd and 8th houses will also exert good influence.

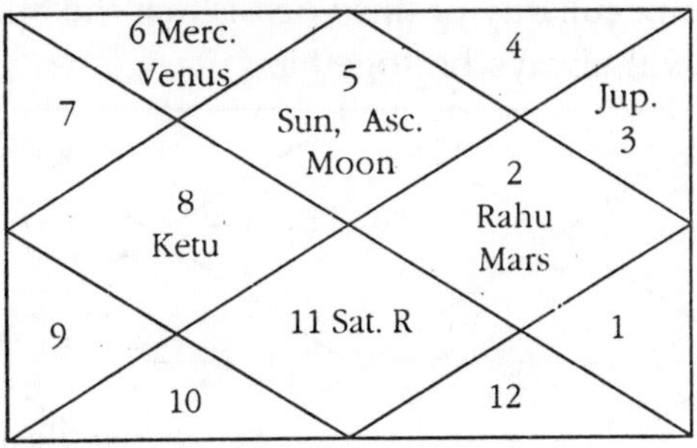

Fig. V: Ikkabal Yoga

If there be other good yogas viz., Itthashal etc. in the chart given above then the good results will be felt earlier.

This yoga should be applied in the birth charts as well in the Horary charts. In horary charts 'Ikkabal yoga' is an indication of accomplishment of the work at an early date. For example if there is a question as to when this girl will get married then the reply will be within a month, a year or weeks if the rising sign and the navansha of the Ascendant both are in dual, fixed or moveable sings. Similar answer should be judged for other questions.

Induvar Yoga

Planets in Cadent houses (3,6,9,12) do not show quick results. This yoga is not considered good—Planets in the 6th or 12th will also not aspect the Ascendant. In a horary chart it indicates delay in all matters for which the chart is cast. In the birth charts Planets in Apoklim (Cadent) show delayed results.

In the chart given below all planets are in 3rd, 6th, and 9th houses. These houses are Cadent houses. Planets can be 1, 2, 3, or 4 houses, i.e., not necessarily in all the four houses.

In this yoga, all planets are in cadent houses only, which is the meaning of the term Induvar. If all planets are cadent and none in angular or succeedent houses, the year will prove inauspicious; evil results follow. This yoga is evil whereever it is found, whether in nativities, Solar Returns, or horary figures. One peculiarity of this yoga is that the Sun, Mercury and Venus will always be together.

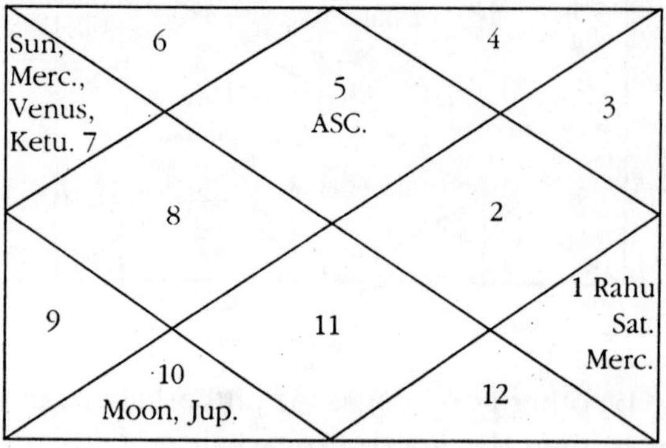

Fig. VI: Induvar Yoga

In the above chart Sun, Mercury, Venus and Ketu are together in the 3rd house, Saturn, Mars, and Rahu are in the 9th house; and Moon and Jupiter are in the 6th house. As all planets are in the 3rd, 9th and 6th houses so it creates Induvar yoga. The Solar Return in which this yoga occurs will be a listless year and may bring in discords, losses and separations. The same will be the result if this Induvar yoga is present in a birth chart. In the early part of life, the native will not be able to achieve much but in the later years of life better things can come.

Itthashal Yoga

'Itthashal Yoga' is one of the prime yogas of the Sixteen Yogas. When two planets meet (apply to) each other then this yoga take place. In the present day context it can be illustrated in the following manner: when we want to purchase an important item, then we go out to buy it. However, if

1. we do not reach the shop, or
2. when we reach the shop it is closed, or
3. the shopkeeper has left (not found in the shop), or
4. someone has already purchased the item that we want to buy, or
5. we get delayed due to some other work before we reach over there, or
6. when we have already purchased the item, we lose it or
7. it is forcibly taken away from us.

Similar are the problems that we shall come up with in Itthashal Yoga. Some of these are the matters that we shall be discussing in the coming yogas after Itthashal.

If there is a clear cut application between two planets then the work will be effectively done. One of the planets in this case has to be

A. The Lord of Solar Return Ascendant or
B. The Lord of the Year

and then it should apply to the other planet. The planet that they apply to will be the ruler of some house (or houses) and the work of that house indicated, will be accomplished.

Another important factor to be remembered is that both planets in application should aspect the Ascedant and the house whose work is to be accomplished.

We shall discuss below these points one by one.

This term refers essentially to application between two planets either through aspect or by way of conjunction. There are three conditions which combine to create this yoga:

1. *There must be some aspect between the planets involved, whether conjunction, sextile, square, trine or opposition.*

There is one exception to this rule. Let us suppose that two planets are in the second and twelfth from each other (i.e., in adjoining houses), that the faster planet is behind the slower (i.e., at an earlier degree of zodical longitude), that they are within orb and are heading towards conjunction. For example: Venus is at 28 degrees Leo and Jupiter at 3 degrees virgo since Venus is the faster-moving planet, it will soon catch up to Jupiter and form a conjunction. Hence Itthashal is deemed to be in effect. In terms of delineation, we should note that such a situation, one not yet completed, signifies an issue wherein the results of the yoga will take place in the future.

Below we give a chart where a faster moving planet Venus (28°) in the preceding sign (Leo) applies to Jupiter (3°) in the next sign (Virgo).

Ex. Chart 1

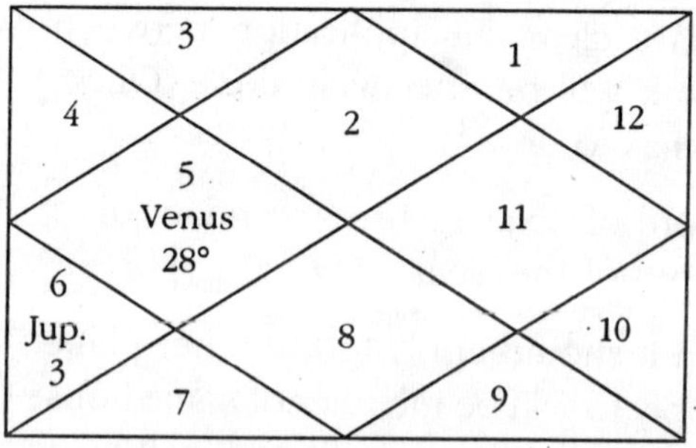

Fig. VII: Itthashal Yoga

Here, Venus and Jupiter are in orbs (Deeptansha). Venus is faster in motion and when it goes to Virgo, it will apply to

Jupiter. Venus and Jupiter are the lords of 1st and 11th houses respectively. So there will be gain of money and meeting with a friend or an older brother. These are the matter which falls under the purview of 11th house. The important thing here is that this application will take place in future as Venus has still to cross Leo and go over into Virgo which is the next sign. So this type of Itthashal indicates the accomplishment of the work in future.

The readers should note that it is Venus which is moving forward and applies to Jupiter—*Venus is the lord of the Ascendant and so it represent the native,* or the person whose chart is under discussion will make efforts, however, if it is the lord of the 11th house which moves forward and applies to the lord of the Ascendant then the gains and meetings will come on their own without efforts.

Let us look at another example. In the sample chart below, Venus and Mars are within orb of an opposition. Venus moves more quickly, and hence applies to Mars. This is also Itthashal.

Ex. Chart 2

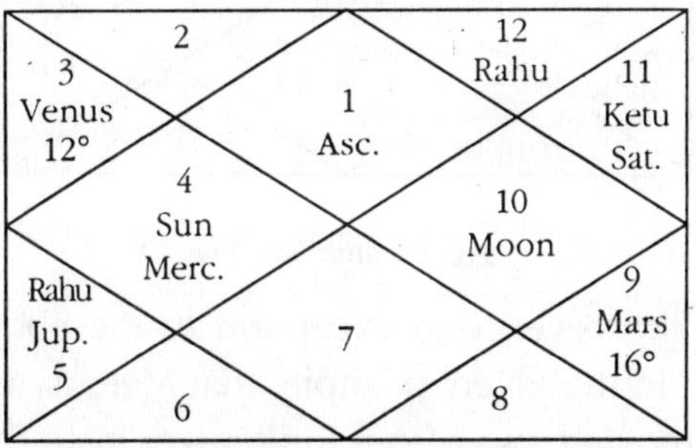

Fig. VIII: Itthashal Yoga

In the above chart, Venus is in the 3rd house in 12 degrees. Mars is in Sagittarius in 9th house in 16°, Venus here by virture of being faster in motion applies to Mars which is the slower moving planet of the two. This is an Itthashal Yoga. Venus rules the 7th house (marriage/partnership) and 2nd house.Mars rules the Ascendant (I house). Here the lord signifying the work moves forward to apply to the Ascendant lord — so proposal of marriage/partnership (which is judged from the 7th house) and wealth (2nd house) will come on their own.

2. *The aspect which creates Itthashal must be with in the accepted degree of orb.*
3. *The faster planet must be in an earlier degree than the slower planet, so that the exact aspect is still pending at some future time, whether hours or days.*

Les us suppose that Mercury is at 23 degrees of Aries and Jupiter at 26 degrees Sagittarius. Hence, Mercury, as the faster planet, will form an exact trine to Jupiter within the next few days.

Ex. Chart 3

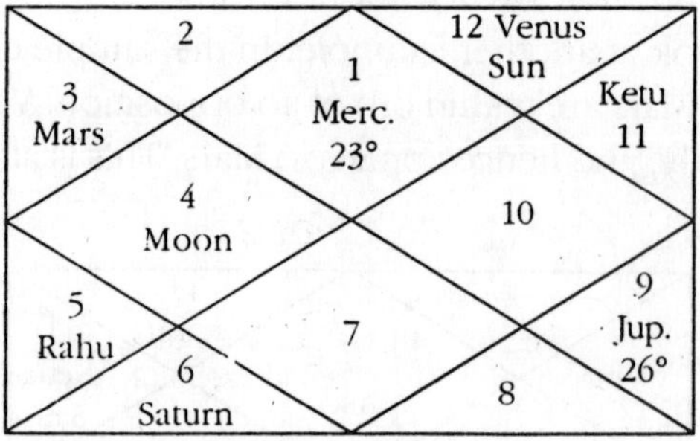

Fig. IX: Itthashal Yoga

There is, however, one exception to the above rule. Let us suppose, in the given example, that Mercury is retrograde and hence moving away from Jupiter—or even that Mercury, though direct at the time of the Solar Return, will turn retrograde before it reaches its exact trine with Jupiter. In this case, Mercury will never make its trine to Jupiter and hence there is no Itthashal.

One possible variation on this them is that Mercury may form its exact trine and *then* turn retrograde at (for instance) 28 degrees of Aries. In this event, the fruits of the trine will be made manifest during the year, but they will not be enduring; they will not last.

Some may argue that Mercury will eventually turn direct and catch up with Jupiter anyway, after its period of retrogression is finished. But by that time Jupiter may have moved forward into Capricorn. If one of the planets changes signs before the aspect can be formed, then there is no Itthashal.

Let us now illustrate yet another variation on Itthashal—how there can still be application even when the faster planet is more advanced in degrees than the slower one.

We shall assume that Jupiter is at 20 degrees of Sagittarius, and that Mercury is at 25 Aries, either retrograde or due to turn retrograde at the 26th or 27th degree. Ordinarily, Mercury will of course move much faster than Jupiter, but inasmuch as he is slowing down to a stationery and a retrograde transit, his longitude will descrease while that of Jupiter, in direct motion, will increase. Thus, there will, within a few days, be an exact trine. *The essence of Itthashal Yoga is that two planets should be within orb of a particular aspect at the time of the Solar Return and that the aspect will subsequently become exact.*

Note: Itthashal between benefics in any manner will always show good results and the accomplishment of events. Itthashal between malefic is also good but the intensity of the good effects is reduced if it is from inimical houses viz., 4th, 7th and 10th (Square and opposition).

Ex. Chart 4

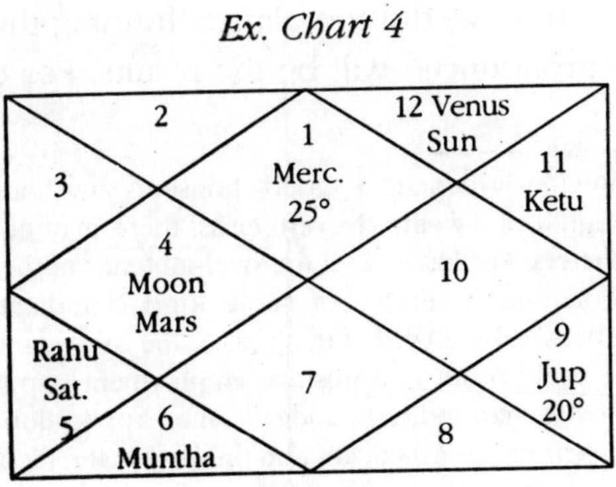

Fig. X: Itthashal Yoga

In the above chart Mercury is retrograde, i.e., moving backwards from 25 degrees to 24° and then to 23° and so on. At the same time Jupiter is moving forward so at one time Mercury and Jupiter will come in exact conjunction leading to the completion of the Itthashal yoga and the realization of the object.

This yoga is one of the most important foundations for judgment in any Solar Return (or horary figure), and throughout our text we shall understand the word "application" to mean Itthashal Yoga.

In the Solar Return chart, any application between:

a. the Lord of the Ascendant and that of a good house, or
b. the Lord of the Year and that of a good house

is considered a certain indicator that the affairs of that house will reach fulfilment during that year.[1]

other general principles relating to Itthashal Yoga are:

a. The more exact the orb, the more powerful the effect of the aspect; the wider the orb, the weaker the effect.
b. Application is more auspicious when it involves a friendly aspect (trine or sextile) than an inimical one (square, opposition or conjuction).
c. The more powerful the planets forming the yoga, the more pronounced will be the results. For example: If

1. We have previously defined a "good" house as any house except for the Sixth, Eighth or Twelfth. Nevertheless, there may occasionally be mitigating factors. For instance, if the over-all tenor of the Solar Return chart is good and if service of some kind is indicated, then an application between the Lord of the Year or the Ascendant and the lord of the Sixth could result in a positive employment opportunity. Similarly, if the natal chart indicates a legacy, then application between the Lord of the Year or the Ascendant and the lord of the Eighth may bring that potential legacy into manifestation.

Tarurus rises in the Solar Return chart, then an applying conjunction between Venus and Saturn in the Ninth would be a yoga between the lords of the First, Ninth and Tenth, with the lord of the Ninth and Tenth in its own very auspicious house. On the other hand, the same conjunction in the Twelfth house in Aries would be much less favorable.

Arguing from this same premise, we may also say that

- any application between two debilitated planets (e.g., Mercury in Pisces and Jupiter in Capricorn) cannot be regarded as favorable, and
- if the Lord of the Year and the Ascendant and the lord of the house to whom either of these planet applies should happen to be aspected by their respective dispositors or friends, the yoga is strengthened, and
- if planets aspect the Ascendant or the houses for which they are significators, the yoga is likewise strengthened.

Let us note that this passage introduces a somewhat different meaning to the word "significator". The Sanskrit word used by older writers is *karyesh*. The word *karya* in Sanskrit means "work", "business", "affair", etc., and the suffix *esh* means "lord". In other books we have used the word *karaka* to denote the planet which governs the affairs relevant to a particular house. If we were to use the term "the lord of the house in the Soalr Return chart regarding which the matters are to be judged", it would make for a very unwieldy text. Hence, the term significator.

Let us also note that when we speak of a particular yoga in terms of relationship between the lord of the annual Ascendant and the significator of a particular house, that yoga should also be examined with reference to the significator and the Lord of the Year.

Finally, we shall give a practical example of Itthashal Yoga. Suppose, that we are considering the Solar Return chart of a young man ready for marriage. If we find that the lords of the Ascendant and the Seventh house, both strong, apply to each other within very close orb, then we might predict that he will indeed be married during the year. An application between the lords of the First and the Fifth might denote the birth of a child or success in education or romance; between the lords of the First and Tenth, promotion or a new job.

Israf Yoga

This yoga, as well as several others which follow, are merely corollaries of Itthashal, but they have been given separate names for the sake of easier identification. Israf means "separation". When two planets have already reached an exact aspect *before* the time of the Solar Return or in a horary chart and are now moving away from that exact aspect due to the motion of the faster planet, they are said to be separating. There are two basic conditions:

- the planets must already have formed their exact aspect and be in the process of separating from each other at the time of the erection of the Solar Return, and
- they must be within conventional orb.

Look at the chart given below with Cancer rising. The two conditions are fulfilled, i.e.,

1. Moon was already in conjunction (aspect) with Saturn a few hours ago and since then it is moving farther and farther away due to faster motion.
2. Moon and Saturn are 6 degrees apart and so they are within orb.

Ex. Chart 1

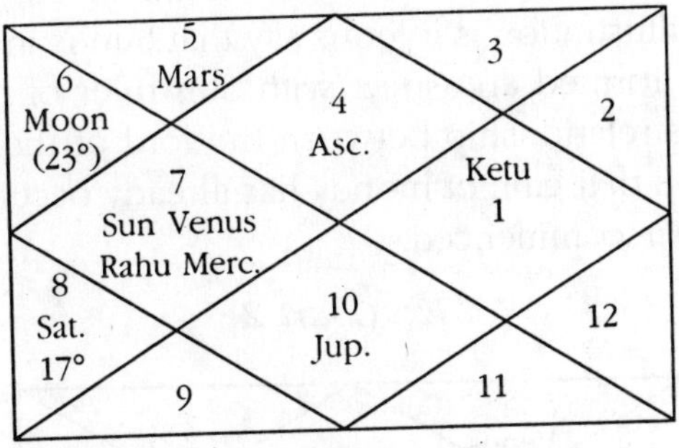

Fig. XI: Israf Yoga

Note that the Moon and Saturn are within orb in the above example. The Moon is the faster planet, and is already six degrees beyond its exact aspect with Saturn. Hence, there is Israf which, in the example given here, might well indicate separation from one's spouse or partner.

When this yoga occurs between the lord of the Soalr Return's Ascendant and the lord of any particular house in the annual chart, it indicates that the affairs pertaining to that significator will not be fulfilled. Thus, a separating aspect between the lords of the First and the Seventh would either be an indication of a possible separation from the marriage partner or, if the individual is not married, then there would certainly be no marriage during the course of the year.

But if the lords of the First and the Seventh are both strong, exalted, in their own signs and in angular houses, then marriage would be indicated despite the presence of Israf—*if* the sepration aspect is no longer within orb (see Figure XII below).

Sometimes, if the planets are within three degrees of orb, Israf may indicate an event which has occurred *before* the Solar Return or horrory chart is erected.

In the following chart Moon and Saturn are only 3 degrees away from each other. Their distance is increasing so it is an example of Israf yoga, however, as the orb is 3° as stated above it is an indication that marriage or partnership already took place before the Solar Return commenced.

Another illustration is if let us say that Sun is in 22° and as such Moon formed an aspect with Sun ruler of the Second House. This relationship between the lord of the I and II is an indication that gain of money has already occurred before the new year commenced.

Ex. Chart 2

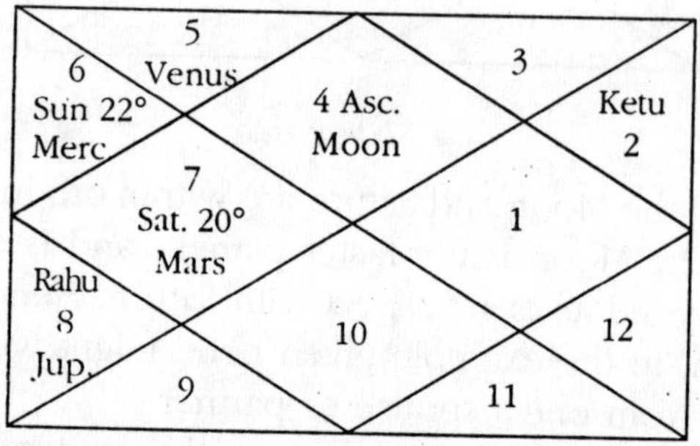

Fig. XII: Israf Yoga

The two yogas under consideration here (Itthashal and Israf) are most especially looked for between a given significator and the Lord of the Year or the Ascendant. But in general we may say that *any* applying aspect is good while any separating aspect is considered evil. Of course, it may be auspicious for a planet to be separating or moving away from the lord of an evil house. Also, it is not considered evil when a planet separates from a natural benefic—according to Hillaj, an old authority, even a separating aspect is good if it involves a benefic.

Nakta Yoga

If the lord of the Ascendant (Planet A) is *not* in aspect with a particular significator (Planet B), but another, faster planet (Planet C) aspects both A and B, thus "collecting light" from one and translating it to the other by forming an exact aspect within a few hours or days, then the results signified by the potential relationship between A and B will be accomplished through the help or agency of a third party. In other words, C acts as an intermediary. One qualifier here is that the faster of the two planets A and B must be behind the slower one in terms of degrees (i.e., must occupy an earlier degree of longitude).

To illustrate: Virgo is rising, and its lord, Mercury, is at 4° of Aquarius in the sixth house. Jupiter, lord of the seventh house, is in the seventh at Pisces 14°. Mercury and Jupiter are not in aspect with each other. But if the Moon, which moves faster than either Mercury or Jupiter, is at 8 degrees Taurus, it will square Mercury and sextile Jupiter, thus aspecting both planets. Therefore, the Moon "collects light" from Mercury (the planet at the earlier degree of longitude) and translates it to Jupiter, thus indicating the gain of a spouse (Mercury ruling the First and Jupiter the Seventh) through the intermediary of a third party.

In the following chart an illustration of Nakta yoga is given. Mercury and Jupiter do not aspect each other. However, Moon is in aspect to both Mercury and Jupiter and the degree of the Moon is more than that of Mercury and less than that of Jupiter—so Moon here takes the light from Mercury and transmits it to Jupiter. Therefore, matters connected with the 4th and 7th houses will come to pass through the help of a third party.

Example of the Nakta yoga is given below.

Ex. Chart 1

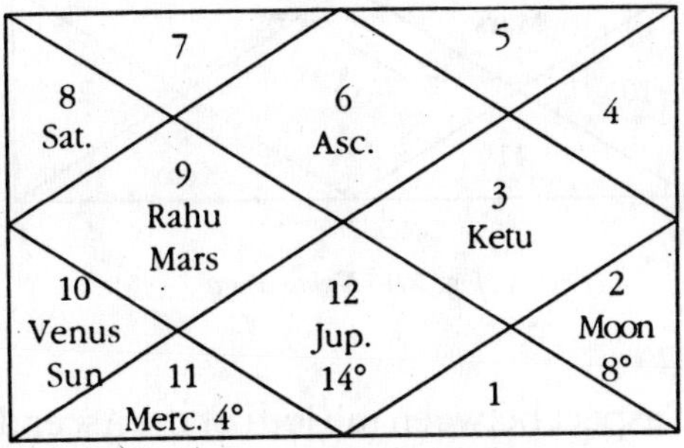

Fig. XIII: Nakta Yoga

Nakta Yoga is also present when

- two planets are in aspect by house but not within conventional orb, and
- a third planet aspects the first two within orb, thus collecting light from one and translating it to the other. (See Example#2, wherein Mercury and Jupiter are potentially in sextile though not in orb. The Moon aspects both Mercury and Jupiter within acceptable orb, thus acting as the intermediary.)

In the follow chart with Virgo rising Mercury is in 6° and is in sextile (aspect) with Jupiter in 20° in Cancer. They are not in orbs. However, Moon is in Scorpio in the 3rd house, in the 14° and is in aspect with Mercury (sextile) and Jupiter (Trine) so it takes light from Mercury and transmits to Jupiter, indicating again that the accomplishment of the works will be done through an intermediary.

The planet which transmits light or acts as the intermediary will signify the type of person involved—his age, position, social stature, etc.

Ex. Chart 2

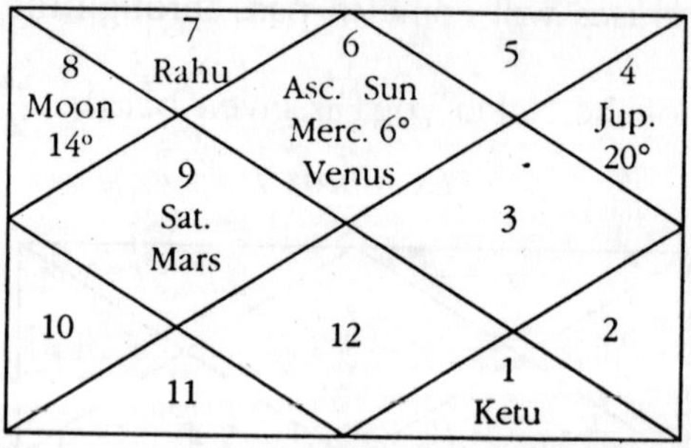

Fig. XIV: Nakta Yoga

Yamaya Yoga

If there is no aspect between the lord of the Ascendant (Planet A) and a particular significator (Planet B), and another planet

(Planet C), slower in motion than either A or B, is at a degree of longitude in between that of A and B, there is Yamaya yoga. Planet C receives light from one planet and passes it on to the other, another indicator that results will be achieved through the intermediary of another person. An old master furnishes the following example:

Libra is rising, and its lord, Venus, lies at 16 degrees Aries in the Seventh house. The inquiry regards "gain of kingdom" (or, in modern terms, a rise in status); thus the matter is referred to the Tenth house. The Moon, ruler of the Tenth, is at 6 degrees Taurus in the Eighth house. If Jupiter, which is slower than either Venus or the Moon, occupies the Tenth house at 10 degrees Cancer, it will aspect the Moon by sextile and Venus by square. Fruther more its position at 10 degrees lies in between that of the Moon at 6 and Venus at 16. Thus, it forms a connecting link to collect light from the Moon and pass it on to Venus. According to the medieval texts, one gains one's kingdom "through a minister". Why a minister? Since Jupiter is exalted, benefic, and placed in an angular house, we may assume that the intermediary is "strong" i.e., well placed and inclined to do good. The Moon, too is exalted, and even though it occupies the Eighth, it should be remebered that the Eighth is a succedent house, hence better than a cadent one. Note also that the Moon aspects its own house, the Tenth, with a friendly sextile (which also affects Jupiter). In modern terms, when the inquiry would most likely involve a rise in satuts due to promotion within some corporate structure, this would indicate that a vice-president or CEO (our contemporary equivalent of King's minister) is well disposed towards the querent and inclined to be helpful.

The following chart, the details of which are mentioned above illustrates the principles of Yamaya Yoga. This horary chart was erected when the late Maharaja of Alwar (a princely state in Rajasthan) passed away and as he did not had an heir, the question of succession was wide open. The question was asked by the Uncle of the late Maharaja for his son, "If he would become the ruler". The son Sewai Tej

Singh succeeded with the help of the Minister of Justice and the Resident.

Ex. Chart 1

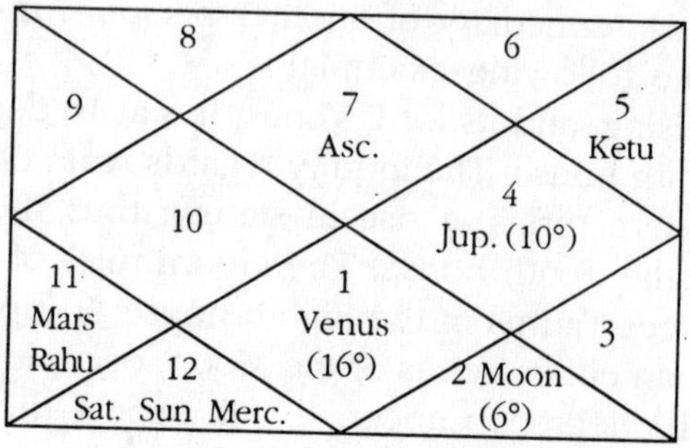

Fig. XV: Yamaya Yoga 'A'

The abvoe chart is a practical example of Yamaya Yoga. The same principles are used in the Solar Return chart. See the chart given below which illustrates the principle.

In the following Solar Return chart, the question was related to the child birth of a girl who was married for five years.

Here, the rising sign is Taurus, Venus is the lord of the Ascendant, Mercury is the lord of the 5th house children.

Yamaya Yoga 'B'

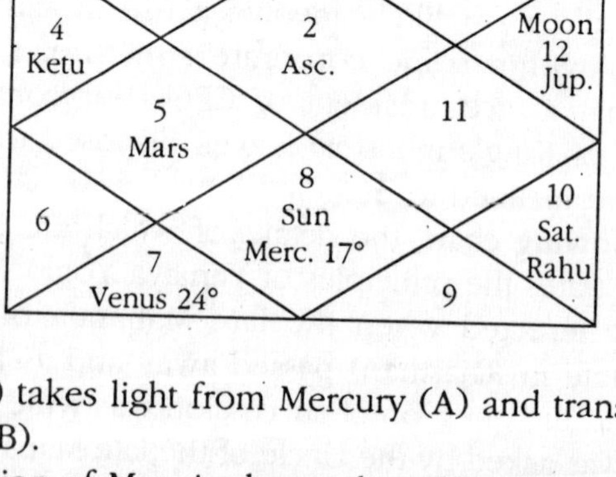

Mars (C) takes light from Mercury (A) and transmits light to Venus (B).

The motion of Mars is slower than that of either Mercury

or Venus. Its Longitude is also in between that of Mercury and Venus. So it acts as a mediator indicating children and acquisition of wealth because Mercury in the birth chart is the ruler of the 5th and 2nd houses (children and wealth).

Manau Yoga

This yoga is based upon the principle of "frustration"—a technical terms used in Western horary astrology of the 17th century. In the *Anima Astrologiae* (1676), frustration is defined as:

> ...a term solely applicable to horary questions. It is when one planet is applying to (within orbs) or forms an aspect with another planet; but before the aspect is complete, another swifter or nearer planet forms an aspect with the latter, which is supposed to destroy or frustrate that which was promised by the first aspect.

> The term frustration has also been defined as follows:

> The cutting off or preventing anything shown by one aspect by means of another. Thus, if Venus, lady of the ascendant, were hastening to the trine of Mars, lord of the seventh, in a question of marriage, it might denote that the match would take place; but if Mercury were to form an opposition of Mars before Venus reached her trine of that planet, it would be a frustration; and would show that the hopes of the qurent would be cut off, and if Mercury were lord of the twelfth, it might denote that it would be done by a private enemy or due to interference by religious people as Mercury also rules the ninth house (see chart example below).

In the follow chart Libra rises. Venus is the Lord of the Ascendant in 17 degrees and faster in motion and is moving towards Mars in Leo in the 23 degrees. However, Mercury in 19 degrees is more in advance (nearer) to Venus and is in a inimical position (opposition) with Mars, it will also apply to Mars much before, Venus does. Therefore, there is prevention of the application between Venus and Mars on account of Mercury. The result is frustration. This is called Manau Yoga.

Ex. Chart: 2

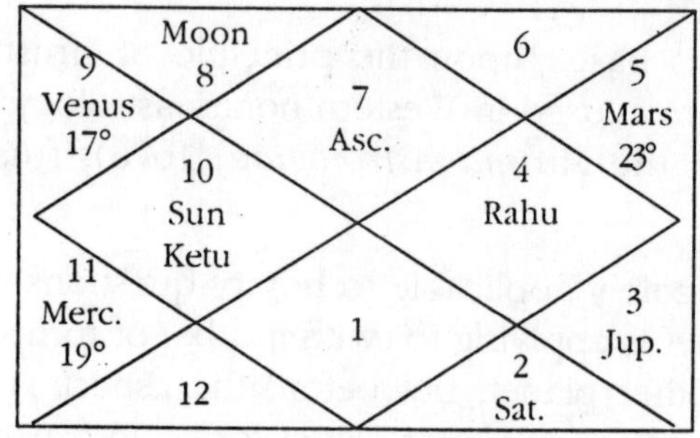

Fig. XVI: Manau Yoga

We have given an acutal chart to illustrate the above yoga. Miss Prema Wadia was going to get married to Ajay Babu, but before the marriage could take place, she was forced in to marrying a middle aged business rival of Ajay. These type of things do happen in actual life, i.e., why the proverb "there are many a slips between the cup and the lips." The planet obstructing should be a natural malefic. Hence, the formula for Manau Yoga should be enunciated as follows:

If there is application between the lord of the Ascendant (Planet A) and any significator (Planet B), and if either Sun, Mars or Saturn is also in inimical aspect (either applying or separating but within orb) with the faster of the two planets (A or B), then the positive results of application between A and B will be destroyed.

From this we may see that there are three essential ingredients of this yoga:

a. All the standard conditions of application between A and B must be fulfilled
b. Sun, Mars or Saturn should be in inimical aspect (conjunction, square or opposition) to A or B, and

c. Sun, Mars or Saturn must also be within acceptable orb of the aspect (whether applying or separating) to A to B.

In the chart given below with Virgo rising the above three conditions viz., a.b.c. are fulfilled. It illustrates that

i. When any other planet forms an application to a planet which is one of the planets we are banking on to complete an Itthashal to indicate an accomplishment,

ii. If one of the planets has just completed an Itthashal and is still within orbs then as it has already transmitted its energy and as such is not left with much force,

In both the cases, frustration will result. This yoga indicates a finer point that what milk a cow will yield when it has already been milked just before.

In the illustration given below, note that Mercury at 12 degrees virgo applies to Jupiter at 16 degrees Pisces. But Saturn at 13 degrees Sagittarius steals Mercury's energy away so that its work is frustrated. Or if Mercury separates from

Ex. Chart 3

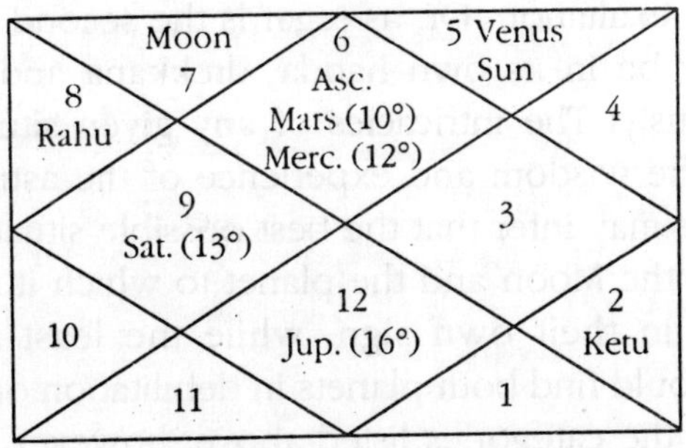

Fig. XVII: Manau Yoga

Mars at 10 degrees Virgo, it is weakened and cannot give Jupiter the benefit of its full strength, hence its work is frustrated.

Kamboola Yoga

This yoga is an embroidery on the principle of Itthashal or application—but the embroidery increases in value according to whether the thread is of cotton, silk, silver or gold.

When the Ascendant lord and a given significator apply within orb and the Moon also applies wihhin orb to either of the other two planets, it is called Kamboola. It greatly fortifies the Itthashal Yoga, enhancing its efficacy and beneficience.

To judge the extent of this beneficience, we must asses both the Moon and the planet to which it applies with respect to the following categories:

a. in exaltation or its own sign
b. in its own hadda, drekkana or navamsha though not in its own or its exaltation sign
c. in any other location, though not debilitated or in an enemy's sign
d. debilitated or in an enemy's sign.

It will be understood, of course, that the above categories are not static—a certain amount of mixture is bound to occur. For instance, the Moon may be in its own drekkana as well as being in exaltation. Or, as regards the second category, a planet may be in its own hadda, drekkana and navamsha simultaneously! The intricacies of any given situation must be left to the wisdom and experience of the astrologer.

Thus, we may infer that the best possible situation occurs when both the Moon and the planet to which it applies are exalted or in their own sign, while the least favourable situation would find both planets in debilitation or an enemy sign. Using the categories listed above, however, we would have 4 × 4 = 16 possibilities or permutations. Beyond this, there are actually *three* planets involved in the yoga, i.e., the Moon, the Ascendant lord, and the significator in question. Some of these may be strong while others are weak. In order to make some headway in all of this, it is sometimes useful to employ the techniques of Panchavargyabala to the planets in question, add up their total strength, and divide the sum by three. The quotient will give one an idea of precisely how strong the Kamboola Yoga is.

In the chart given below, the three planets Moon, Mercury, and Jupiter are in application. The two of them are in their own signs but Moon and Jupiter does not have much directional strength. Mercury however has full directional strength and so, although an average Kambool yoga, it will show good results. It is a 'stately mansion' in 'grand style' of the English language.

Ex. Chart. 1

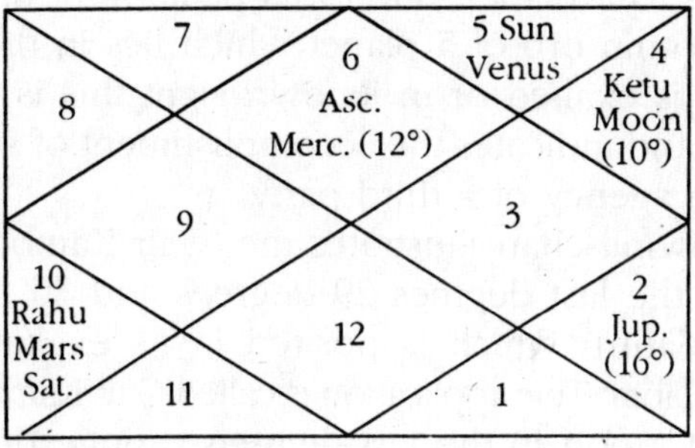

Fig. XVIII: Kambool Yoga

In the above chart indication of accomplishment regarding marriage and gain of property is clearly shown. It also shows extra support. However, when marriage is pointed out the age of the person, his status etc. should be considered.

In the example given above, Mercury applies to Jupiter within orb, and the Moon applies to Mercury. This is Kamboola Yoga. If we seek to ascertain its relative strength, we reach a Panchavargyabala value of 7.56 for the Moon, 11.79 for Mercury, and 4.58 for Jupiter etc. The total is 23.93. When this sum is divided by three, the quotient is 7.976. Any number above 10 indicates an excellent Kamboola Yoga, so this one should be deemed only average, and its results mixed.

Gair Kamboola

In order to understand this yoga, we must first acquaint our readers with the technical term "void of course". Jerome Cardan (b. 1501) defines void of course as a situation when a planet "forms no aspect before it leaves the sign it is in". In the classical Tajik texts a Sanskrit term, *shoonya marggat* (literally "on an empty track") is used, though here it refers to a planet which is neither exalted, in its own sign, in debilitation, *or* forming any aspect to any other planet before it leaves the sign it is in. We shall use the traditional Tajik definition here.

When the Ascendant lord and the significator apply within orb, *and* the Moon is void of course, but after change of sign applies to a planet, due to its position at the very end of a sign, within orb of a planet which lies in the next sign *and* which is exalted or in its own sign, this is called Gair Kamboola, and indicates the accomplishment of some matter through the agency of a third party.

The following chart illustrates the 'Gair Kamboola Yoga'. Moon is in the last degrees 29 degrees and 30' in Virgo. It applies to Saturn which is posited in its exaltation in the next sign of Libra. This application is called Gair Kamboola Yoga. However, if Moon in the last degrees applies to Jupiter in Capricorn where Jupiter is debilitated than it would indicate frustration. This is so because Jupiter is debilitated and does not have the status to achieve success.

Ex. Chart 1

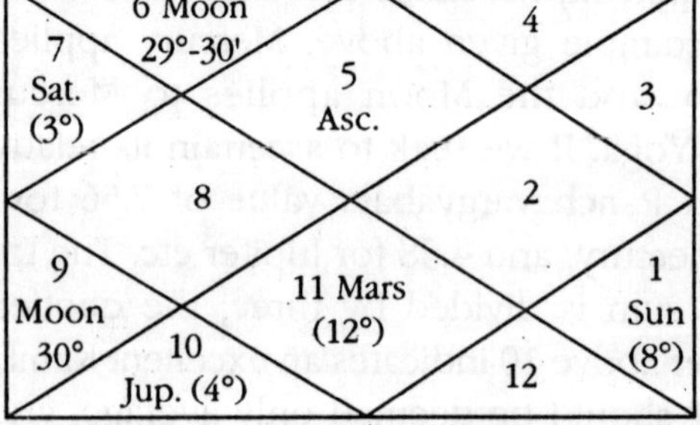

Fig. XIX: Gair Kamboola Yoga

Illustration: Leo is the Ascendant and its lord, the Sun, is in the Ninth house at 8 degrees Aries. The client's question is: "shall I enjoy comforts in my home?" To answer this question we must, of course, look to the Fourth house. Mars is the ruler of the Fourth, and lies at 12 degrees Aquarius in the Seventh house. The Moon is in the final or 30th degree of Virgo, within orb of an exalted Saturn at 3 degrees Libra; hence, there is Gair Kamboola Yoga. But should the Moon be applying to a similar conjunction with a planet which is *not* either exalted or in its own sign, there would be no yoga and no accomplishment.

Khallasar Yoga

When the Moon is void of course and without any of the features noted above under Gair Kamboola, then the situation is called Khallasar Yoga and menas "no accomplishment". According to one school, there must also be no application between the lord of the Ascendant and the given significator in order for accomplishment of a goal to fail absolutely. We concur with this view. However, it is only fair to mention that the *Jeerna Tajik* claims that Gair Kamboola acts as a bar to accomplishement even when Itthashal or Kamboola Yoga are also present.

We have stated the opinion of the oldmaster about 'Khallasar Yoga'. 'Khallas' menas finished, demolished etc. But in actual result in our experience out 30 chances that we were able to check this yoga 18 resulted in the accomplishment of the work through an agency. So the chances of success are almost fifty-fifty. The only reasoning could be that if more benefics are involved than the chance of success in the realization increases.

Radda Yoga

This is a Persian word meaning "cancellation". When any planet which applies to an aspect with another planet is either

a. combust
b. debilitated

c. in an enemy's sign
d. retrograde, or
e. in the same degree as a malefic and hence overpowered by it,

then that planet is so weak that it has very little light to rasnmit to the other planet, and hence the good effects of its application are canceled out.

In general, there must be more than one of the five negative factors noted above be present in order for the effects of application to be completely eradicated. Another dictum is that if the weakned planet lies in an angular house while the planet to which it applies lies in a cadent house then there will be a certain amount of accomplishment at the beginning of the matter, though it will end in failure. If the situation is reversed (i.e., an afflicated planet in a cadent house applies to another planet in an angular house), then there will be trouble at the beginning of the venture but success at the end.

In the chart below Mars is debilitated. It however applies to Saturn in the 3rd house. Therefore, the good effect is cancelled. This is called 'Radda Yoga'. Radda means rejection, cancellation etc. One of the above condition viz., (b) is fulfilled. It is also in an enemy's house (c).

Therefore, the chance of success on account of the application between Mars and Saturn does not exists.

Ex. Chart 1

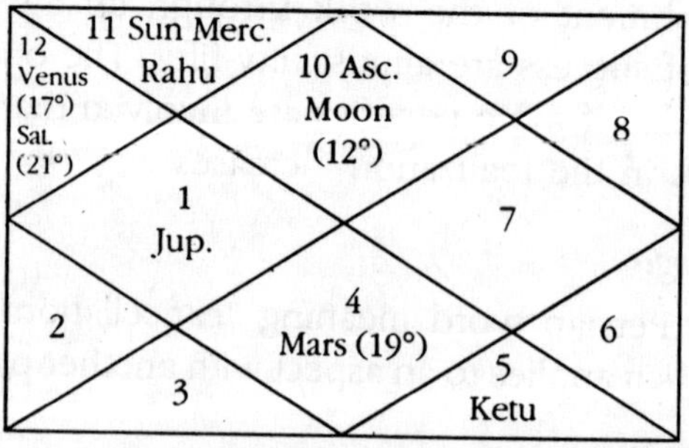

Fig. XX: Radda Yoga

Here the afflicted planet is in an angular house so in the beginning it may appear to be leading to success but ultimately the end will be nothing. If the situation is reversed that Mercury is debilitated in 3rd house and it applies to Moon in the first house (Angular position) than in the end success will come but only after a big effort.

Please note that the first condition that (a) if a planet is combust then an allowance should be made if (i) Sun is the ruler of the Ascendant (ii) The year lord or the lord of the Ascendant in a horary chart and (iii) the combust planet is within 7 minutes of Sun. In these cases the combustion effect will not be negative.

Dufalikuttha Yoga

This yoga is a variation on Itthashal, and signifies a situation in which the swifter planet is *not* exalted or in its own sign, but the slower planet *is* in such a condition. It leads to accomplishment. In the example given here, the yoga is comprised of Mercury applying to an exalted Jupiter.

In the Chart given below Mercury is faster in motion than Jupiter and it is neither exalted or in own sign. Jupiter is slower and it is also exalted so this Itthashal will lead to success.

Ex. Chart 1

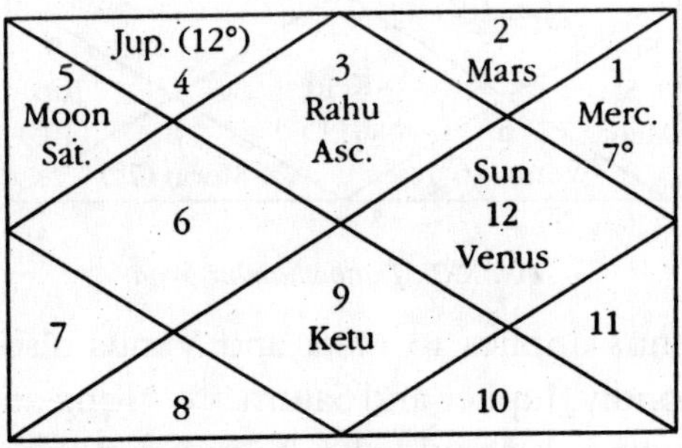

Fig. XXI: Dufalikuttha Yoga

Mercury in the above chart in the 11th house (7°) applies to exalted Jupiter (12°) indication of smooth sailing in the accomplishment of work.

Dutthothambir Yoga

This yoga is comprised of the following factors:

a. The Ascendant lord and the significator in question are both weak (i.e., combust, debilitated, etc.), but in application, while
b. One of them applies to a third planet which is strong by virtue of being in its own sign, etc., or two other planets are strong (though not necessarily in their own signs) and one of them applies to the Acendant lord or significator.

This yoga results in the accomplishment of a goal through the assistance of a third party.

In the chart below, Mars and Moon are both debilitated and in application. This is condition number (a) Mars applies to a third planet, i.e., exalted Saturn so condition (b) is fulfilled. This should be taken as an indication of accomplishment.

Ex. Chart 2

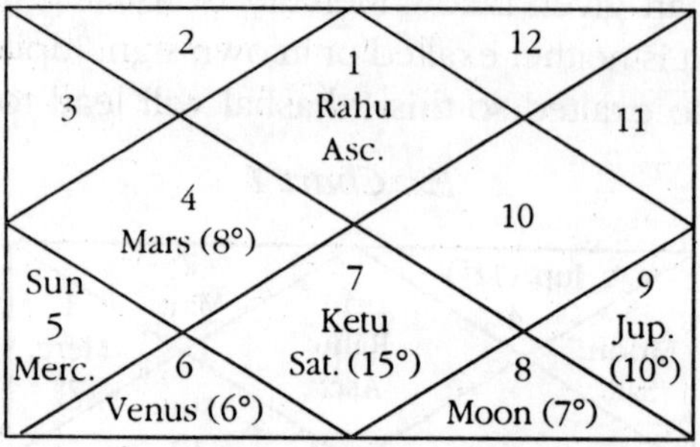

Fix. XXII: Dutthothambir Yoga

Here, Venus applies to Mars and Venus also applies to Jupiter. Secondly, Jupiter and Saturn are strong and Mars also applies to Saturn. It should also be noted in the above chart that Sun and Saturn are strong and Sun also applies to Moon which fulfills (b) (ii). The condition (a) also exists so there would be accomplishment.

Tambira Yoga

The following conditions comprises this yoga:

a. The lord of the Ascendant and the significator in question are not in aspect to one another
b. Either the significator or the Ascendant lord is strong *and* positioned at the very end of a sign within orb of conjunction with a planet in the next sign, this third planet being relatively strong.

This yoga indicates success, though somewhat belated.

Please note that in the chart given below Mercury and Moon are not in aspect but Moon (with in orb) applies to Jupiter in the first house so money will be realized though after some delay.

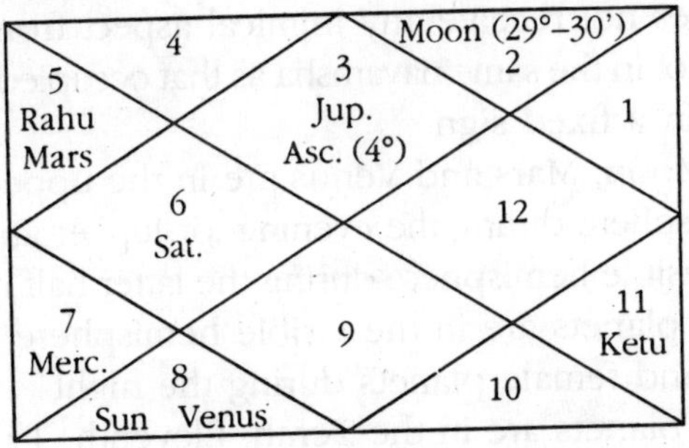

Fig. XXIII: Tambira Yoga

In the above example, the Ascendant is Gemini. Its ruler, Mercury, is in Libra in the Fifth. Let us assume that the inquiry regards the Second house. Therefore, the significator in question is the Moon, ruler of the second, which lies at 29°-30' Taurus in the Twelfth. Jupiter lies at 4 degrees Gemini, within orb of conjoining the Moon. Hence, there will be accomplishment. Note that the efficacy of the yoga (i.e., the extent of the accomplishment) will be dependent upon the planet to which application is being made, in this case Jupiter.

Kuttha Yoga

If all planets (especially the Ascendant lord and the

significator in question) are strong, then there is Kuttha Yoga, indicating a good year and general success. A planet may be said to be in strength when:

- it is posited in the Ascendant or in an angular or succedent house
- it aspects the Ascendant
- it is in its own house or exaltation
- it is in its own hadda
- it is in its own drekkana
- it is in its own navamsha
- it is moving at average speed (the less the better)
- it rises heliacally (as opposed to setting)
- it is direct rather than retrograde
- it is not conjoined with a malefic
- it does not receive any inimical aspect from a malefic
- it is not in the same navamsha as that occupied by the Sun
- it is in a fixed sign
- the Moon, Mars and Venus are in the upper or visible hemisphere during the evening, or Jupiter and Saturn in the visible hemisphere during the latter half of the night
- male planets are in the visible hemisphere during the day and female planets during the night
- male planets are in the Tenth, Eleventh, Twelfth, First or Second houses and female planets in the Fourth, Fifth, Sixth, Seventh, Eighth or Ninth
- male planets are in odd signs or female planets in even signs
- male planets are in odd navamshas and female planets in even navamshas

A planet should also be assessed for strength according to the Panchavargyabala.

Duraffa Yoga

This yoga is formed when all planets, including the lord of the Ascendant and the significator in question, are weak.

Naturally, the results are extremely inauspicious. A planet may be said to be weak when:

- it is posited in the Sixth, Eighth or Twelfth house
- it is retrograde
- it is in an enemy's sign
- it is debilitated
- it is about to turn retrograde
- it is in conjunction with a malefic
- it applies to a planet which is either malefic, retrograde, debilitated or in an enemy's sign
- it is inimically aspected by a malefic
- it is applying to or about to apply to a planet in the Sixth, Eighth or Twelfth
- it is located in Rahu's mouth or tail (see Chapter II)

In addition, there are several other special factors which contribute to the weakness of the Moon:

- when the Moon is in the twelfth house from the Sun
- when it occupies the latter half of Libra or the first half of Scorpio
- when it is void of course, i.e., not in aspect with any other planet, especially its dispositor
- when it is neither in its own sign, in exaltation, or in its own hadda, drekkana or navamsha
- when it is from 26 degrees 40' to 30 degrees of any sign
- from the tenth day of the dark fortnight to the second day of the bright fortnight
- when it is in inimical aspect with Saturn during the dark fortnight or Mars during the bright fortnight. This difficulty may be somewhat mitigated if:

    a. it is aspected by Saturn located in an odd sign or
    b. it is aspected by Mars located in an even sign at night during the dark fortnight.

CHAPTER VI

TRIPATAKI CHAKRA

The Tripataki Chakra is an important constituent of the Solar Return chart. This combines together the (i) the birth chart (ii) The Solar Return chart and (iii) the age factor according to which the planets are moved up to four places from their placements in the birth chart. There is an exception for the Moon that where all the remaining planets move to 4 places, it can move up to 9 places from its radical position in the nativity. The position at birth is counted as 1, the second sign from it as 2, the third sign from it as 3, and so on.

The purpose of the Tripataki Chakra is to see if Moon in particular or any other planet, has 'Vedh'. *Vedh* is a sanskrit word and it means piercing and as such obstructing or modifying the effects.

Vedh is also taken in account when we consider the transit of planets in the birth chart. However, in Transits, the transiting planet *obstructs or nullifies the good and bad both effects when in Vedh**. But it is different in the solar return charts. Here, the progressed planets will give good or bad effects according to its nature when in Vedh. *It will not eliminate or nullify any effect whatsoever.*

The Tripataki Chakra gives a full view of the Vedh of Moon or for that matter of all the planets at a glance. The Sanskrit word Tri-Pataki-Chakra means Three-Flags-Diagram, i.e., a diagram with three flags. As the figure will show when it is constructed with the method given below.

---

* See Astrology and You by the Authors.

Construction

To construct this figure, we should follow the following procedure:

Draw three horizontal parallel lines at an equal distance from each other, then draw three vertical parallel lines at an equal distance from each other so that they cut the horizontal lines. Flag the three ends of the vertical lines as in the figure XXIV) below. Select twelve points on both side of the six lines and join them in the following manner so that they pass through the intersections of the six lines (see figure XXIV) The method of joining is as follows:

Join 1 to 4 and 10; join 2 to 3 and 9; join 3 to 8; join 4 to 7; join 5 to 6 and 12; join 6 to 11; join 7 to 10; join 8 to 9; and join 11 to 12. Now our Tripati Chakra or Tripataki Chakram is ready.

(Basic Structure)

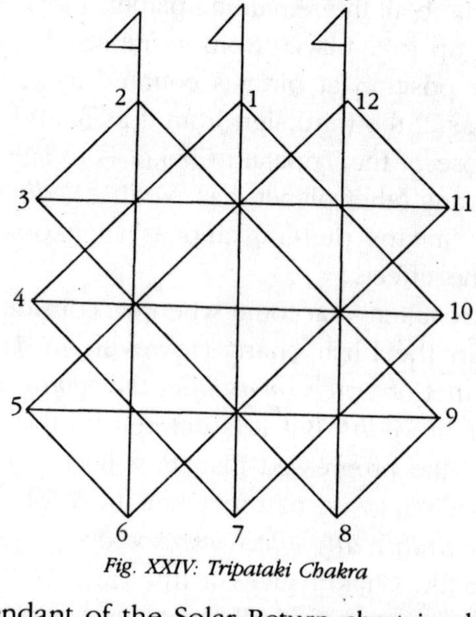

Fig. XXIV: Tripataki Chakra

The Ascendant of the Solar Return chart is placed at the top centre and the other signs follow sequentially in a counter-clockwise direction. Numbers rather than the conventional astrological symbols are used to designate the signs. Earlier in the book we familiarized the readers with the Hindu sign notation wherein for purposes of the arithmetical calculations,

0=Aries. 1=Taurus, 2=Gemini etc. But in this instance we will follow the conventional neumeration as it is practiced in the West, where 1 = Aries, 2 = Taurus and so on.

Returning to our example chart from Chapter I, we note that the Solar Return Ascendant is Leo, as is the natal Ascendant. Please note that Leo will occupy the position at the apex of the Tripataki Chakra by virtue of its being the Ascendant in the Solar Return chart and not beacuse it is the rising in the Natal or Birth chart.

Placement of Planets

After erecting the basic scheme of numbers, we compute the position of planets as follows:

Begin with the number of the years elapsed which in this case is Four (4). Now add one (1) to the elapsed years so we get 4+1=5. The root number is five (5). We now divide this root number by nine (9), forget about the quotient. We now divide this root number by nine (9), forget about the quotient. We are only concerned with the remainder and as it is not divisible so the balance or remainder is 5 itself. Therefore Moon will be placed in the fifth sign from the sign it occupied in the Natal or birth chart. When counting we start from the sign occupied which in this case was Leo as 1, 2 for Virgo, 3 for Libra, 4 for Scorpio, and 5 for Sagittarius. So the Moon in the Tripataki Chakra is placed in Sagittarius or where we have written 9 (indicating the number of the sign).

But what happens if the our root number is exactly divisible by 9? For instance 36 is exactly divisible and the remainder is zero. In this instance, we regard 9 itself as the remainder.

We have already placed the Solar Ascendant Leo (5) in the center at the top position (the center at the top in the Basic Structure is mentioned as 1, so 5 replaces 1. The other signs as mentioned earlier follow anti clockwise, and in order.

In order to place the other planets we divide the same root number 5 by four. 5 when divided by four leaves a balance of 1. So the other Planets will remain in the same signs which they occupied at birth. In this case we will now place Sun in Pisces, Mars in Taurus, Mercury in Aquarius, Jupiter in Aquarius, Venus in Aquarius, Saturn in Gemini, Rahu in Scorpio, and Ketu in Taurus.

The positions of Rahu and Ketu are determined by counting backwards, because they are in retrograde motion. Obviously this has no bearing in the present context, where the reminder is 1, indicating that Rahu will be in the same natal sign of Scorpio. But if the remainder were 2 then it will move backwards or clockwise from Scorpio which will be counted as 1, and Libra as 2, and so on. In the same way Ketu will also move backwards as they are always moving in the retrograde manner.

What happens if a planet is retrograde at birth? According to one school of thoughts, Planets in retrograde motion at birth should also be moved clockwise when computing for the Tripataki Chakra.

For ready reference the Natal Chart is given below. It is followed by the Tripataki Chakra for the Solar Return for the fifth year.

If for example the root number is 6 which when divided by 4 leaves a balance of 2, the planets will move up to the next signs. viz., like Sun from Pisces to Aries etc. If the number is exactly divisible by 4 and there is no remainder then we take 4 as the remainder and move the planets to four places.

Natal Chart

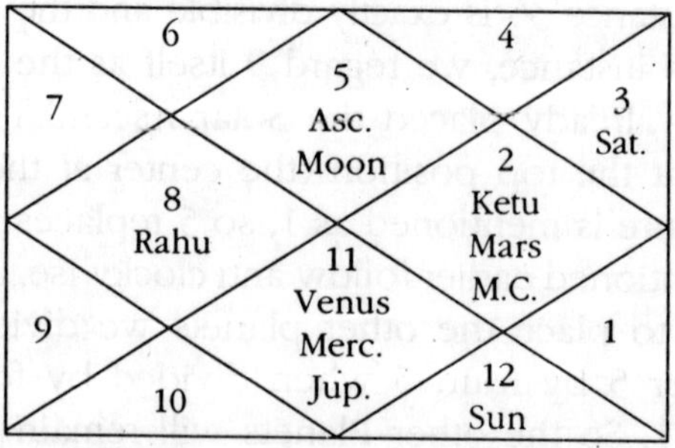

The above horoscope has been calculated for 4th April 1974, at New Delhi for 15.43 in the afternoon.

It shows Ascendant is Leo and Moon is also placed in Leo; Rahu in Scorpio in 4th; Mercury, Jupiter, Venus in Aquarius in the 7th house; Sun in Pisces in the 8th; Mars, Ketu and M.C. in Taurus in 10th house and Saturn in Gemini in the 11th house.

(Complete Diagram)

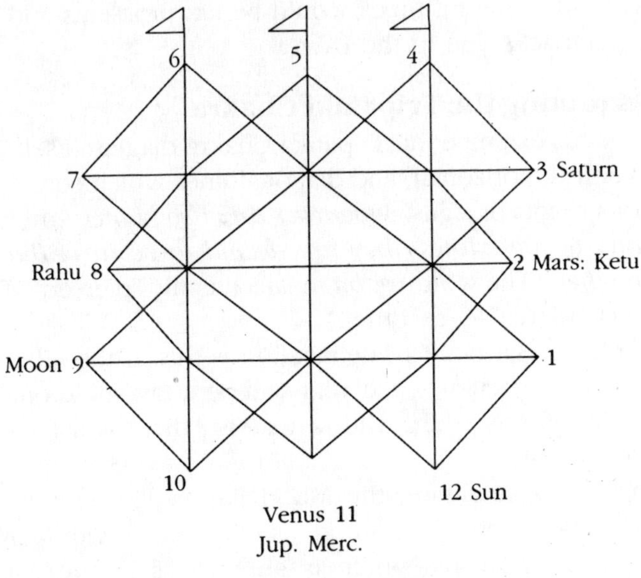

Fig. XXV: Tripataki Chakra

We have put more emphasis on the Vedh of Moon as in Hindu Astrology. Moon is considered the most important not only because it reprsents the emotions of a person but also because all good and bad is felt by the 'Mana' and Maṇa is Moon. If a person is happy even though lacking in luxuries than his Moon is strong and smaller negative things in Chart will not cause him distress. Good and bad is a comparative matter. It should be noted that in the annual chart full importance should also be given to the *Lord of the Year* called 'Varshesh' particularly in reading the effects of Tripataki Chakra.

Note: Please note that if the birth Chart and the Solar Return chart has the same rising signs as in the present case (Leo) then it is called 'Dvijanma' Varsha, i.e., twice born year and it is in general not considered good. If other factors are not strong enough in the year chart then sickness and punishment from the kings (which in the present times would be tax problems and legal setbacks due to the Law.

Interpreting the Tripataki Chakra

Now let us examine the Tripatika Chakra diagram itself. Note the vertical, horizontal, and diagonal lines which connect the various points or signs. *Whenever any two planets are linked by any of these lines, they are deemd to be in vedha with each other.* (The word *vedha* means literally "pierced". These planets "pierce" each other.)

The essential point of delineation is this: If the Moon has vedha with a benefic , the year will be a favorable one. But if the Moon has vedha with a malefic, there will be worry and/or illness.

In the above figure, the Moon has vedha with Jupiter, which is very good. The Moon also has vedha with Mercury, Venus, and Saturn—which is auspicious in the case of Mercury and Venus, though unfavorable as regards Saturn.

If the *Moon has vedha with:*

The Sun	:	there will be loss of prestige and danger from the government, or difficulties on account of one's father.
Mars	:	physical pain and danger.
Mercury	:	increase of knowledge.
Jupiter	:	happiness, wealth, good food and good fortune on account of one's children.

Venus	:	pleasant times and all kinds of enjoyment.
Saturn	:	disease
Rahu	:	danger
Ketu	:	disease

Type of Person—Obstructing

Note that we have been concerned here only with the Moon, because the Moon represents the native. But what happens when two other planets have vedha with each other—such as, in our example, Jupiter and the Sun? In this instance, judge the effects according to the *kind of person* indicated by the planet. For instance, Jupiter would indicate one's guru or one's children, while the Sun would indicate one's father. A full list of the kinds of individuals signified by the various planets is given here:

Sun	:	government officials, political leaders, or one's father.
Moon	:	one's mother.
Mars	:	enemies, soldiers, siblings and other relatives.
Mercury	:	friends, one's maternal uncle, writers, astrologers, merchants.
Jupiter	:	teachers, gurus, one's children or (in a woman's chart the husband.
Venus	:	one's spouse, singers, dancers, actors
Saturn	:	servants (or employees), thieves, old people.
Rahu	:	one's paternal grandfather, foreigners, outcastes (in India), widows.
Ketu	:	maternal grandfather, witches and sorcerers.

CHAPTER VII

THE TIMING OF EVENTS

Several different methods are employed to assess the timing of events. First we shall take up two systems of dashas (periods) and antardashas (subperiods). These priods are based on but *not* identical to the periods and subperiods of the natal chart. In natal astrology, a single period may last for as long as twenty years; in Tajik, the entire round of planetary periods takes place within the confines of a single year and adds up to 360 solar days.

What do we mean by a solar day? A solar day is the time taken by the Sun to travel 1 degree of zodiacal longitude. As soon as the Sun has traveled 360 degrees and traversed the entire chart, another year commences and a new Solar Return chart is cast. All influences and indications for the previous year, whether good, bad or indifferent, now come to an end. In the following paragraphs, a "day" should be interpreted as a solar day. A year constitutes 360 solar days rather than the usual 365 or 366 calendar days.

The medieval texts outline several different dasha systems,though we shall confine ourselves to the two which are most popularly used in India today. These are 1) the Mudda Dasha and 2) the Hinansha Patyansha.

The order of cycles or periods is the same here as in the Vimshottari Dasha system customarily used in natal astrology But as we have noted, our total allotment of time is 360 solar days—as opposed to the 120 years which constitutes a complete Vimshottari Dasha cycle in natal astrology. The duration

Table XV: Mudda Dasha Planetary Periods

Planet	*Number of Days*
Sun	18
Moon	30
Mars	21
Rahu	54
Jupiter	48
Saturn	57
Mercury	51
Ketu	21
Venus	60
Total	360

of each planetary period in the Mudda Dasha is as given above. Remember, days are given in terms of *Solar* days. For any given year, however, the student may take days to mean degrees of longitude in the ephemeris. If, for instance, Mudda Dasha begins with the Sun period, and if the Sun is at 10 degree in Gemini in the Solar Return chart, then the Moon period will begin on the day that the Sun reaches 28 degree in Gemini, as per the ephemeris.

But from which planet's dasha should we begin? For this we must consult the birth chart. In natal astrology, the periodic cycle of the dasha begins with the planet which rules the nakshatra or lunar mansion in which the natal Moon is positioned.

Many readers are familiar with the Term Nakshatras. This is a Sanskrit word which in the English Language means 'Constellation'. But those who do not understand it well, a Nakshatra is a mansion which constitutes one by twenty-seventh part of a Zodiac. When the 360 degrees are divided by 27, we get one constellation which is equal to 13 degrees and 20 minutes. These 13°— 20 is further divided into four parts and each of these consists of 3 degrees and 20 minutes. Therefore, in Hindu Astrology each Nakshatra has 4 quarters and so 27 Nakshatras all together has 108 quarters. The system of division was such in India that all measurements, clock timings, money measurements, weights etc. was according to the breath that we inhale and exhale. The 108 is an auspicious number so much so that the names of Ascetics, Spiritual Masters, and Rulers are prefiexed with this number before their names. The string of beads that is used has 108 beads in the 'JAPA' (continuous repetitions of Mantras). We conclude this matter here for fear of enlarging on an issue which is not the subject matter of this book.

The names of the Nakshatras are given in the second column of Table XVI, which is given below. In the first column the number of the nakshatras is given; The third column gives the spread out in the degrees and minutes of the nakshatras; The fourth column gives the planet which is the ruler of the Nakshatras; The fifth column gives the duration of the Mudda dashas in months and days.

Table XVI: Table of Nakshatras

S.No.	*Name*	*Zodical Longitude*	*Ruler*	*Duration*
1.	Ashwini	0.00 to 13.20 Aries	Ketu	0 - 21
2.	Bharani	13.20 to 26.40 Aries	Venus	2 - 0
3.	Krittika	26.40 Aries to 10 Taurus	Sun	0 - 18
4.	Rohini	10.00 to 23.20 Taurus	Moon	1 - 0
5.	Mrigashira	23.20 Taurus to 6.40 Gemini	Mars	0 - 21
6.	Ardra	6.40 to 20.00 Gemini	Rahu	1 - 24
7.	Punarvasu	20.00 Gemini to 3.20 Cancer	Jupiter	1 - 18
8.	Pushya	3.20 to 16.40 Cancer	Saturn	1 - 27
9.	Ashlesha	16.40 to 30.00 Cancer	Mercury	1 - 21
10.	Magha	0.00 to 13.20 Leo	Ketu	0 - 21
11.	Purva Phalguni	13.20 to 26.40 Leo	Venus	2 - 0
12.	Uttara Phalguni	26.40 Leo to 10.00 Virgo	Sun	0 - 18
13.	Hasta	10.00 to 23.30 Virgo	Moon	1 - 0
14.	Chitra	23.20 Virgo to 6.40 Libra	Mars	0 -21
15.	Swati	6.40 to 20.00 Libra	Rahu	1 - 24
16.	Vishakha	20.00 Libra to 3.20 Scorpio	Jupiter	1 - 18
17.	Anuradha	3.20 to 16.40 Scorpio	Saturn	1 - 27
18.	Jyeshta	16.40 to 30.00 Scorpio	Mercury	1 - 21
19.	Mula	0.00 to 13.20 Sagittarius	Ketu	0 - 21
20.	Purvashadha	13.20 to 26.40 Sagittarius	Venus	2 - 0
21.	Uttarashadha	26.40 Sagittarius to 10.00 Capricorn	Sun	0 - 18
22.	Shravana	10.00 to 23.20 Capricorn	Moon	1 - 0
23.	Danishtha	23.20 Capricorn to 6.40 Aquarius	Mars	0 - 21
24.	Shatabhisha	6.40 to 20.00 Aquarius	Rahu	1 - 24
25.	Purvabhadra	20.00 Aquarius to 3.20 Pisces	Jupiter	1 - 18
26.	Uttarabhadra	3.20 to 16.40 Pisces	Saturn	1 - 27
27.	Revati	16.40 to 30.00 Pisces	Mercury	1 - 21

In our sample horoscope (from Introduction), the natal Moon at 11° – 25'–10" Gemini falls in Ardra Nakshatra, ruled by Rahu. Obviously, the birth chart itself must serve as the Solar Return chart for the first year of life; therefore, the Mudda Dasha for the native's first year of life will begin with the Rahu period. After this, the years and dashas follow in succession: Jupiter begins the second year, Saturn the third, Mercury the fourth year and so on. After all nine planets have taken their turn at beginning the yearly cycle, the tenth year begins with Rahu again.

The whole cycle for the first year (or the tenth), will unfold according to the patern in the table given below:

Table XVII: Sample Mudda Dasha

Planet	*Solar Days or Degrees*	=	*months and Days*	
Rahu	54	=	1 Month, 24 days	then
Jupiter	48	=	1 Month, 18 days	then
Saturn	57	=	1 Month, 27 days	then
Mercury	51	=	1 Month, 21 days	then
Ketu	21	=	21 days	then
Venus	60	=	2 Month, 0 days	then
Sun	18	=	18 days	then
Moon	30	=	1 month, 0 days	then
Mars	21	=	21 days	then
Total	360	=	12 months, 0 days	

The actual calendar dates can, of course, be determined by checking the ephemeris and noting the solar degrees. But as a rule of thumb it makes little material difference whether we use the ephemeris or simply estimate accoriding to the calendar days.

There are several easy ways to calculate the initial dasha period for any given year of the native's life. Let us say that we wish to determine the beginning period for the 56th year of a native whose natal Moon was in the mansion Revati, ruled by mercury. If we divide 56 by 9, we get a quotient of

6 and a reminder or balance of 2. We are not concerned with the quotient. Instead, we begin with Mercury and count forward 2 dashas: Mercury = 1, Ketu = 2. The initial dasha for the native's 56th year (i.e., 55 years completed will be Ketu.

There is another method, based on the table given below. Add the number of *years completed* to the *number of the birth star* (nakshatra), then subtract 2 and divide by 9. The *remainder* or *balance* will be the number of the dasha with which the year commences.

Table XVIII: Planetary Numbers

Number	1	2	3	4	5	6	7	8	9
Planet	Sun	Moon	Mars	Rahu	Jup.	Sat.	Merc.	Ketu	Venus

The table of nakshatras tells us that Revati is the 27th mansion. So: Years completed (55)+Nakshatra Number (27)=82–2=80. Then we divide 80 by 9. This gives us a quotient of 8 as well as a remainder of 8. We are concerned with the remainder, which established that the initial dasha is that of Ketu.

Another easy reference table can be constructed to give us the same information. The left-hand column indicates the *number* of the birth nakshatra, as found in our table of nakshatras. The series of numbers above represents the applicable year of the native's life. Find the year involved, and read down the column until you reach the list of planetary periods. Then locate the appropriate birth nakshatra to the left, by number. For instance, let us say that we are examining the same birth chart we have used as an example immediately above. So we will look for 56, the year of life, which will be found in the second column of numbers. Reading down from there, we look to the left and find 27, the number of Revati, the lunar mansion of birth. We will find Ketu listed in the appropriate number column, indicating that Ketu is the initial cycle for the native's 56th year.

Table XIX: Nakshatras and Years of Life

Nakshatra	*Year of Life*								
	1-46 10-55 19-64 28-73 37-82	2-47 11-56 20-65 29-74 38-83	3-48 12-57 21-66 30-75 39-84	4-49 13-58 22-67 31-76 40-85	5-50 14-59 23-68 32-77 41-86	6-51 15-60 24-69 33-78 42-87	7-52 16-61 25-70 34-79 43-88	8-53 17-62 26-71 35-80 44-89	9-54 18-63 27-72 36-81 45-90
1-10-19	Ketu	Venus	Sun	Moon	Mars	Rahu	Jup.	Sat.	Merc.
2-11-20	Venus	Sun	Moon	Mars	Rahu	jup.	Sat.	Merc.	Ketu
3-12-21	Sun	Moon	Mars	Rahu	Jup.	Sat.	Merc.	Ketu	Venus
4-13-22	Moon	Mars	Rahu	Jup.	Sat.	Merc.	Ketu	Venus	Sun
5-14-23	Mars	Rahu	Jup.	Sat.	Merc.	Ketu	Venus	Sun	Moon
6-15-24	Rahu	Jup.	Sat.	Merc.	Ketu	Venus	Sun	Moon	Mars
7-16-25	Jup.	Sat.	Merc.	Ketu	Venus	Sun	Moon	Mars	Rahu
8-17-26	Sat.	Merc.	Ketu	Venus	Sun	Moon	Mars	Rahu	Jup.
9-18-27	Merc.	Ketu	Venus	Sun	Moon	Mars	Rahu	Jup.	Sat.

Those who are familiar with the Vimshottari Dasha as it is practiced in natal astrology will know that each planet has a subperiod or antardasha within the context of the major periods or dashas, and that the first antardasha within a planetary period is always the same as the major period or dasha itself. In the context of the Tajik, these antardashas can be worked out by the rule of three. For example, let us assume that we wish to determine the first antardasha in the period of Venus, which will of course be that of Venus itself. The dasha of Venus is 60 days, so its proportional antardasha will be comprised of 10 days.

The medieval astrologers worked out their planetary periods down to the hour, but this is not really worth the effort. It is, however, relevant to note (at least in terms of academic interest) that the medieval authorities would not ordinarily have begun our example period above with the *full* 48 solar days of Jupiter's dasha. In natal astrology, the dashas may last many years. If the natal Moon is, for example, half way through the nakshatra it occupied at the time of birth, then the native is regarded as being halfway through the dasha involved. In our example chart from Introduction, the Moon is at 11 degrees of Gemini. This is just over a quarter over Ardra nakshatra, So that the native would be born just a little over a quarter of Rahu Mahadasha with about 12 of the 18 years still to run. So in terms of the Solar Return, we would recognize the same proportions; instead of running for a full 54 days, Rahu would begin its cycle with a run of about 36 days, and the other 18 days would be tagged on at the end of the year. All the other dashas on subsequent years would similarly begin a little more than a quarter through their run.

Although there is a great deal of logic in this method, it is no longer practiced in India today. Each initial dasha is given its full quota of days at the beginning of each year, as we have outlined in the main body of this section.

Hinansha Patyansha

In this method, the total year of 360 solar days is divided up among the Ascendant and the seven planets (the effect of Rahu and Ketu, and Moon's Nodes, is said to manifest during the dasha of Saturn). We begin by writing out only the longitudes of the Ascendant and the planets in ascending order and regardless of sign they are in. In the next column, we begin by writing out the degrees and minutes occupied by the first planet. After that, the next planet receives the *difference* in degrees between its own position and that of the initial planet. The next planet in line is listed in terms of the difference in degrees between itself and the previous planet and so on and so forth. We have worked out examples of this earlier for the learned readers in the introduction of the book itself.

Guidelines for Timing

- The general principle that a planet shows its effects during its dasha and/or antardashas holds good for the annual chart as well. Remember that a planet *expresses* its effects in terms of its house lordships, its sign and house position, and the planet with which it is conjoined or by which it is aspected. Muntha's effect is felt primarily during the dasha or antardasha of its dispositor, as well as during the periods of planets with which it is conjoined or by which it is aspected.

- The technique for timing the effects of the sahamas or sensitive points is as follows: Count the number of degrees from the longitude of the saham's dispositor up to the sensitive point itself. The number of degrees so obtained represents the number of solar days after which the effect of the sensitive point will be felt.
- Think of the twelve houses as representing the twelve *solar* months of the year —the First house is equivalent to the first month, the Second house to the second month, and so on. If a given house as well as its lord is strong, well tenanted and well aspected, the month will be a good one and vice versa.
- When considering the sixteen yogas, note how far the planets are from forming the exact aspect which defines the yoga. (Remember that the maximum orb for any aspect is 12 degrees.) Multiply the number of degrees of orb by 15. The product equals the number of days after which the effect of the yoga will be felt. The closer the orb, the earlier the result and so on.

Another method for determining the timing of the various yogas is as follows: Let us assume a timeline in which cardinal signs are equivalent to days, fixed signs to months, and mutable signs to weeks. Then note the degrees of orb involved in the aspect. If the planets involved are in different kinds of signs, then the resulting *average* is used as the determinant of time. Let us say a planet in Cancer aspects another in Pisces with an orb of 6 degrees. Thus, the effects will be felt in 3 weeks (mutable Pisces) and 3 days (cardinal Cancer.)

- The Ascendant can be progressed at the rate of 1 degree per solar day. When the progressed Ascendant degree forms exact friendly aspects — especially with benefics —the results will be good. Inimical aspects with malefics are, of course, unfavorable. The Sun, Moon, and Midheaven can be progressed according to the same principle. However, all indications based on these techniques should be regarded as secondary to the general tenor of the annual chart.
- Examine transits to the positions of the planets in the annual chart.

The medieval texts recommend the use of monthly and even daily charts. In our example chart, for instance, the Sun is 25° pisces 42' 16". Monthly charts would be erected for the time at which the Sun reaches 25° Aries 42' 16", 25° Taurus 42' 16", and so on.

Similarly, daily charts can be erected for the precise moment that the Sun reaches 42' 16" of any degree of the zodiac. However, these daily charts are subordinate to the effects of the monthly chart, which are in turn subordinate to the annual chart. We urge our readers to confine their explorations to the annual chart alone.

Nevertheless, the lunar return chart technique deserves a few words of mention. Such charts are cast for the time when the Moon occupies the same position as in the birth chart — an event which occurs once a month. For instance, if the natal Moon was at 6 Virgo 54, then the monthly lunar chart would be cast for the time at which the Moon returns to 6 Virgo 54 every month.

The lunar chart is interpreted in precisely the same manner as a Solar Return chart. The only differnce is that instead of months, weeks and days the results are judged in terms of days, ghatis and palas[1] according to whether the planets are in fixed, mutable or cardinal signs respectively. The lunar chart is judged in relationship to both the natal and annual charts and is subsidiary to them.

The lunar chart is a very significant factor in horary astrology.

SOME SPECIAL FEATURE

A. Moon's Special Effects:

Moon has been ascribed with special importance in the Solar Return charts as well as in the Horary charts. We give below some effects over and above of what has already been mentioned.

1. A weak Moon, (waning Moon in very few digits), if placed in the first or eight houses and is also conjoined with or aspected by Malefics then disease, danger from enemies, fears and mental anguish will take place.
2. If Moon and Mars are together in the 6th or 8th house then injury from weapons afflicted by an enemy; if other malefics are in the Ascendant then disease in the body and mind, should be judged; if other malefic/malefics are simultaneously in the 4th house then danger of falling down from a vehicle, horse etc. will take place.
3. If the commencement of the Solar Return is during the day time then the result of the year will depend upon the "Awastha" of the Moon.

The following are the 12 'Awastha' (State, condition or Situation) of the Moon.

1. Parvas; 2. Nasha; 3. Marana; 4. Jaya; 5. Hasya; 6. Rati 7. Kidrit; 8. Supta; 9. Bukta; 10. Jwara; 11. Kampa; 12. Isthira.

The above names are Sanskrit names and they themselves

---

1 One Ghati=24 minutes, 60 palas=1 ghati, and 24 hours=60 ghatis.

depict the effects but for those who do not understand them we give the results.

The following will be the results of the Moon in different situations.

1st Situation:	It cause foreign travels or living away from home.
2nd Situation:	Destruction; Loss of wealth
3rd Situation:	Death or suffering to that extent
4th Situation:	Victory, Success
5th Situation:	Happiness and luxuries
6th Situation:	Happiness from wife and other women
7th Situation:	Indulgence in sports
8th Situation:	Deep fatigue or sleep
9th Situation:	Fears
10th Situation:	Fever, heat stroke, blood pressure etc.
11th Situation:	Losses or Parkinsons's disease
12th Situation:	Happiness and contentment.

Calculation of the Avasthas

Leave aside the sign of the Moon, multiply only the degrees, minutes, and seconds of Moon 2, and then divide by five. The quotient will indicate the Avasthas which has elapsed. Add I to the quotient to know the present Avastha of the Moon.

Example

Moon is in Gemini 11 degree and 17 minutes and 00 seconds. Leave aside the sign which would be 2 for Gemini, then we have (11deg. – 17 m.) × 2/5 = (22d – 34m)/5=4.

This 4 is the quotient and it points that the 4 Avasthas of the Moon has elapsed and the next one, i.e., 4+1=5 is running, the 5th Avastha is that of 'Hasya'–so Happiness and luxuries should be interpreted.

B. Benefics

If benefics are in the 7th house then victory, success in legal disputes if any, favour from superiors; in the second house benefic confer contenment and wealth; in the 9th house they bestow spiritual advancement, wealth, favour from rulers, awards and fame: in the 11th house gains of elephants, horses and vehicles.

C. Results according to the Ascendant when Sun enters into Aries

The Ascendant at the time of the Sun's entry into the first sign of the Zodiac, i.e., Aries (Sidereal Zodiac), will give an indication in the Birth chart as to how the year should pass.

Whichever house of the nativity the ascendant falls in, if that house is conjoined with or aspected by benefic at birth then good results will be felt for the matters connected with that house. However, if malefics occupy or aspects the house then there would be losses related to the matters of the house.

The following results will occur according as the Ascendant, at the time of the Sun's entry in Aries, falls in different houses.

1. Good health and popularity. Lustur on the face.
2. Wealth, happiness, and increase in family.
3. Good for brothers/sisters, short trips.
4. Happiness from mother, gain of property.
5. Birth of a son (grandson) / success in education
6. Danger from enemies, new job.
7. Gain of wife, marriage etc.
8. Inheritance, fame and if bad then danger from sickness, tiring journeys.
9. Gain of wealth, foreign trips, spiritual development.
10. Gain of place and wealth. Rise in status. Good for father .
11. Vehicles, houses, gains, new friends.
12. Losses, expenses, danger from secret enemies.

All these matters should be blended together before conclusion is drawn.

D. New Moon, Full Moon, Eclipses

1. If a new Moon or full Moon occurs with in two degree orb of a planet in the nativity then that planet gets excited and good results will be felt and new opening will also occur. New Moon on the radical Jupiter indicates, gains, birth of a son, a new office etc. on Venus it leads to a love affair, birth of a child, happiness and expenses in luxuries things. Similar interpretation should be done for other planets.
2. However, if an eclipse (Solar or Lunar) occurs on the Longitude of a planet then the effects are long lasting. They start 6 months prior to the eclipse and can last up to one year. In one instance there was a full Solar eclipse on the Sun (Radical) in a male nativity. He met with an accident shortly after and did not survive. At the same time, this eclipse in a woman's chart occurred on her radical Sun as well. She developed an eye problem where a blood vessel burst in the eye and it took a few months to heal. Eclipse on a sensitive point can be good or bad, depending upon the strength of the planet in the nativity.

CHAPTER VIII

GUIDELINES TO INTERPRETATIONS

General Guidelines

In the present chapter, we have dealt with the guidelines which will be of much use in the interpretation of the Solar Return Charts. We should also note that all the factors that are dealt with are linked together. We cannot ignore any of them and only then the proper results will come.

General

The five most important factors in the Solar Return chart are:

1. The lord of the natal Ascendant.
2. The lord of the Solar Return's Ascendant.
3. The Lord of the year.
4. Muntha.
5. The dispositor of Muntha.

In taking into account the various planetary combinations and drawing inferences therefrom, we must always assess:

1. The general configuration of planets.
2. Their strength or weakness.
3. Their placement in signs and houses.
4. Their lordship.
5. Whether they are naturally benefic or malefic.
6. The aspects they receive from other planets.
7. Whether these aspects are friendly or inimical and whether they are from benefics or malefics.

8. The general potentialities of any given matter as shown in the birth chart, and how far a particular planet is capable of either promoting or damaging a particular house, either in the natal or annual chart.

The five factors which contribute to the strength of a planet are:

1. Location in its own or a friend's sign, hadda, drekkana or navamsha
2. Occupation of a favorable house
3. Aspects from friendly benefics
4. Direct motion
5. Heliacal rising

The five factors which contribute to the weakness or affliction of a planet are:

1. Location in an enemy's sign, hadda, drekkana or navamsha
2. Occupation of an evil house
3. Aspects from inimical malefics
4. Retrograde motion
5. Combustion

If the planets (and Muntha) noted above as of special importance to the Solar Return chart are all strong, then the year will prove exceptional in regard to health, wealth, status and general happiness. If they are weak and afflicted, the opposite will be the case. If some are strong and others weak (which is the usual situation) , they must be judged and synthesized in due proportion.

The Natal and Annual Charts

In India, it is customary to have the Solar Return chart erected each year. Sometimes it is worked out in detail; sometimes it is considered only as a framework. But even in the most cursory reading, the birth chart is always placed on the same page just below the Solar Return chart. Why? Because the lordship of the houses and placement of the planets in the birth chart should always be taken into account when interpreting the Solar Return. It is instructive to remember that millions of people throughout the world will have their Solar Return on exactly the same day, and many thousands of these will even have the same Ascendant in that Solar Return. And yet their lives are very different. Why? Of course factors of age and cultural background play a role, but the astrological answer is that their lives are different because their natal charts are different.

Another way to look at the natal-annual inter-relationship is to remember that even though Solar Return charts for any given individual will vary from year to year, a rich man continues to be rich for decades at a time, or even throughout his life, despite the fluctuations of the annual chart. Persons may hold important offices for a long stretch of time or keep their good health until the day they die. Others lead lives of continual sickness and poverty. The nature of planetary motion militates against any individual having favorable (or unfavorable) Solar Returns throughout an entire lifetime. Yet one's fortunes may remain *relatively* constant. When the natal chart is strong, an unfavorable Solar Return will cause only a little evil, and when the birth chart indicates a life of trouble and distress, the most favorable Solar Return is capable only of alleviating one's problems to a limited degree.

This general outlook must be applied to the details of the charts. A man whose natal Third house is strong, tenanted and aspected by benefic planets, with the lords of the First and Third well placed and mutually fiendly will not have serious quarrels with his siblings even when the Solar Return indicates that he will. A person whose birth chart denies him the possibility of offspring is unlikely to be blessed with a son even when planetary configurations in the annual chart support such a judgment. A person whose natal Seventh, its lord and Venus are all weak and afflicted may never enjoy a healthy marriage no matter how many favorable marriage aspects appear in a given annual chart —though such favorable aspects may provide a relatively peaceful year of respite in the midst of an essentially stormy relationship.

Despite these close relations between the natal and annual charts, we have observed that many astrologers completely ignore the birth chart or else do not give it the importance it deserves—even though the medieval texts provide detailed expositions as to the method of comparing the natal and annual charts. In this chapter and in the ones which follow, we shall therefore provide some guidelines which have a bearing on the relationship between the two charts, so that the student will not lose sight of the birth chart's all-important role.

Some readers may well argue that if everything is so dependent upon the birth chart, then of what value is the Solar Return? A Solar Return has its basis in the natal chart, like the foundation of a multi-storied building. Though each floor may be different to some degree, the basic pattern of the building must be founded upon a solid set of dimensions. The birth chart represents this set of foundations, while the Solar Return orchestrates the variety inherent in each separate storey or floor. The annual chart throws a remarkable light upon trends or events within the context of a particular year. Like transits, Solar Returns are helpful tools which allow us to drill a peep hole and provide ourselves with an additional glimpse into the future. The Solar Return has the virtue of narrowing the field of inquiry to a particular year, thus, virtue of narrowing the field of inquiry to a particular year, thus establishing boundaries within which predictions may be fine-tuned.

Some of the important guidelines we must take into account when comparing the natal and annual charts are as follows:

1. Whenever inferences are drawn on the basis of planetary configurations in the Solar Return, we must judge the strength of the planets involved in both

charts, natal and annual. A planet which is strong in both charts will bestow its optimum good effects, while a planet weak in both respects will yield extremely poor results.

A planet which is strong in the Solar Return but weak in the natal chart will be incapable of yielding all the good results implied by its position in the annual chart. Similarly, a planet which turns out to be afflicted in the Solar Return will not do all the damage of which it seems capable if that same planet is favorably disposed in the birth chart.

2. This principle may also be applied to questions of *timing*.

If a planet is strong in the birth chart but weak in the Solar Return, then the first half of the year will yield favorable results while the latter half will prove unfavorable. But if a planet is weak in the natal chart and strong in the Solar Return, the reverse is true, i.e., the first half of the year will be unfortunate and the second half more favorable. Of course, it follows that a planet strong in both charts will yield favorable results throughout the year, while one that is weak in both cases will produce the opposite effect.

3. If a planet occupies *the same house* in both the natal and annual charts, then its influence will be absolutely certain to manifest —for good, if the planet is favorably disposed, or for ill if unfavorable.
4. If a planet is favorably placed in the birth chart but ill disposed in the Solar Return, then one may expect that the affairs pertaining to the planet's natal house will suffer during the course of the Solar Return year. Similarly, if the natal sign occupied by a planet is strong in the Solar Return, then during that year the planet in question will yield all the benefits (in terms of that sign or house) of which the birth chart renders it capable.

Planets in Houses

We give below the effects of a planet when `posited in different houses in the Solar Return charts. These also apply to the Horary Horoscopes viz., Horoscopes cast for the time of the question or where there is no availability of a birth chart. We would like to make it clear that at places the influence of planets may differ to some extent from the effects which planets exert in the Natal Charts.

The second point to be noted is that the good effects will proortionately undergo changes depending upon the panchavargyabala of planets. The next thing that should be kept in view is that the strength of the Lord of the Year as well as its placements in a particular house, is of great significance.

If Sun is the ruler of the Ascendant in the Solar Return chart or if it is the Lord of the year then even *combust* planets will show their full effects: If applying to Sun then good results and if separating from Sun then frustration of the matter indicated by the other planet.

We have already indicated earlier that if a planet is in the same house in the Natal and Annual charts then it will show good results.

The effects of the various planets in each hosue of the Solar Return chart can be generalized as follows:

First House

The Sun, Mars or Saturn in this house cause fever, illness, and loss of wealth, though Saturn may show excellent results in Libra, Capricorn or Aquarius. The Moon will tend towards ill health and financial loss if conjoined with a malefic, though it will promote good health and happiness if it is conjoined with a benefic. Mercury, Jupiter and Venus bring all-around good results and confer wealth—Mercury is especially favorable here. Rahu gives one cause to fear from enemies or competitors and may cause illness either to one's self or one's spouse. Ketu gives rise to quarrels, illness, and general unhappiness.

Second House

The Moon, Mercury, Jupiter and Venus lead to the acquisition of wealth; they also confer happiness and elevation in rank. The Sun, Saturn and the Nodes cause loss of money, though the Sun may have the opposite effect and bring wealth to the native if it conjoins a benefic. Saturn causes loss through frustration in work and troubles with the government, while Rahu, in addition to bringing one into conflict with the government, also damages one's health and reputation and tends towards general loss of money. Ketu causes quarrels and confusion of mind and curtails both happiness and wealth. Mars may be good for money here — though the money is both easlly earned and easily spent. However, Mars in this house is unfavorable for health.

Third House

The malefics (Sun, Mars, Saturn, and the Nodes) are well placed in the Third house; if strong they may confer financial gain, especially in terms of real estate or other fixed assets. The Nodes are especially good in promoting an increase in valor and the ability to overcome one's enemies. The benefics induce various comforts and pleasures, and the Moon in particular causes some event of great elation.

Fourth House

If the Moon is strong, waxing, and/or conjoined with a benefic it will confer happiness, but if it conjoins a malefic it indicates both anguish and illness. The other benefics (Mercury, Jupiter and Venus) give rise to comforts and auspicious events of various kinds, while the malefics lead to loss of health and wealth and induce a feeling of apprehension. Rahu causes a great deal of travel; Ketu may actually be favorable in some respects but is a bad sign for the mother's health.

Fifth House

The effects generated by the malefics show their worst qualities in respect to one's children; they may also cause confusion of mind, quarrels and thefts. The benefics give joy in regard to one's children, wealth and general happiness. Venus is especially good here, and usually produces an outstandingly joyous event.

Sixth House

The malefics are favorable here and lead to a gain of money and happiness. Mars is most prized here, for he causes great joy and insures the annihilation of one's enemies or competitors. The benefics do not do well in this house; they cause apprehension, loss of money, and quarrels. If conjunct a malefic, the Moon can cause illness.

Seventh House

The Moon conjunct and/or aspected by a malefic causes sickness. Malefics impair the health of one's spouse and provoke marital quarrels as well as causing dissension with servants (employees in a modern context). Rahu tends toward illnesses of the genitals or reproductive system, while Ketu adds loss of prestige to the other features of the malefics here. The benefics give rise to financial gain, comfort, reputation, amity with one's relatives, respect from the government and success in legal disputes.

Eighth House

The Moon conjoined with a malefic causes illness and anguish of mind, or, in the classical texts, even death. The malefics generate very inauspicious events in general. Even benefics may cause illness here (according to the dosha or humor indicated by that planet), as well as loss of money. On the other hand, a benefic which enjoys an Itthashal relationship with another benefic will confer very auspicious results. The Nodes should be deemed very unfavorable here, though there is one school of astrologers which regards Ketu as favorably placed in this house.

Ninth House

The Sun in this house is a prized position, for it enhances power and prestige, but the other malefics cause one's siblings to quarrel with the native or suffer illness, as well as provoking legal troubles. The benefics confer all kinds of auspicious results in this house —increase of wealth, acts of religious merit, etc. According to one school of thought, all planets are favorable here, be they benefic or malefic.

Tenth House

All planets are good here, regardless of their essential nature. The Sun and Mars increase one's drive and ambition; the native will attain success due to his personal efforts. The benefics are especially good for increasing one's income. Even Saturn is good here, though it may cause "loss of cattle" (i.e., some of the native's assets may decline)

Eleventh House

All planets are generally favorable here. In birth charts as well as in Solar Returns, the malefics are regarded as conferring excellent results in the Eleventh. However, we believe that a malefic should be strong in order to show its best results, otherwise its weakness may bring on illness or other trouble to one's children and give the native problems in planning his projects with clarity. Strong benefics bring in a great deal of money; even weak benefics are helpful in this regard, though the amount is proportionately less.

Twelfth House

Malefics cause quarrels, penalties imposed by the government (such as a tax audit), and loss of money whether in business or through theft. Saturn, however, is regarded as favorably placed in this house and conducive to happiness.

The benefics lead to expenses, though for good reason, i.e., acquisition of property, comforts, and social or religious celebrations. However, another view —with which we concur — regards all planets as conducive to illness, quarrels and financial loss when placed in the Twelfth house.

It is said that a house will prosper whenever it is tenanted or aspected by its lord or by benefics. It follows that the evil effects pertaining to a given house must preponderate if that house is tenanted or aspected by,malefics, and that mixed influences foster mixed results. But what happens when the lord of a house is itself a malefic? The sages disagree on this issue. Some insist that the lord of a house *always* benefits that house, even when the ruler is a malefic. Others believe that a malefic is troublesome in any house, even when it rules that house.

It is also said that the aspect of Saturn or Mars upon a house is always inauspicious, even if these planets are aspecting their own houses. For the most part we agree with this judgment, though with the proviso that *the malefics benefit non-living or inorganic matters, whereas they are harmful towards living things.*

To illustrate some of the variables inherent in this issue of malefics and benefics, let us examine the chart of the avatar Rama, hero of the epic *Ramayana*. This horoscope, passed down from antiquity, is one of the most celebrated "example charts" in Vedic astrology.

Example Chart: Shri Ram

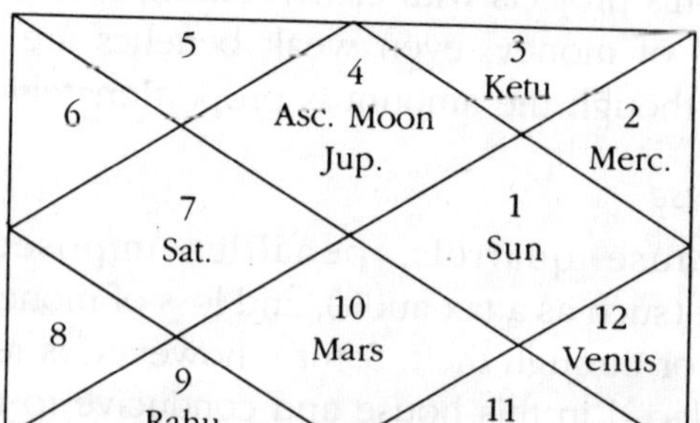

Note the Malefic Mars in the 7th house of marriage is exalted but it has created a Kuja dosha or mangalik dosha and has destroyed the house. Rama's wife was beautiful and virtuous endowed with all the qualities most desirable in women, but all His trouble was focussed on Her. Mars and Saturn are exalted and they aspect the Exalted Sun in the 10th house, yet his father was the one who sent him to the Forests for 14 years.

The readers should note that the Saturn is exalted in the 4th house, Sun is exalted Jupiter is exalted but none of these were able to change his destiny. It did not show good results. The mother (step mother) became the cuase of his exile and Mars in the 7th house made Sita the cause of all his Problems. Due to an exalted Mars, Moon and Venus he got married to the most beautiful women who was second to none and endowed with all the positive symptoms of physiognomy, still Mars made him fight to win her in marriage and fight again to get her back and still no happiness from her. Mars in his chart endowed Sita with an adamant nature and she insisted on going with Ram to the forest and then used sarcastic remarks to send Lakshaman (younger brother of Rama) in search for Him, making the field all clear for Ravana to kidnap her. The question arises if exalted planets are they good? From our experience we have seen that Saturn if exalted do not show very good happiness in the way we as layman understand Happiness. In the horoscopes of saintly persons it drives them toward an Asetic life and Sannyas.

The Lord of the Year

There are many professional astrologer who, in the context of a busy practice, feel that they do not have time to calculate the entire Panchavargyabala. Consequently, they neglect to determine the Lord of the Year. In many ways, this oversight is understandable: successful astrologers cater to a large clientele, and the labor involved in working out such detailed systems is not commensurate with the fees which an average client is able to pay. The problem is that without the Lord of the year any predictions based on the Solar Return chart are liekly to be lopsided or only partially applicable. A few very general indications concerning the interpretation of this all-important factor have been given in the chapter devoted to identifying the Year Lord. A few more guidelines may be introduced or reiterated here.

1. The Lord of the Year is so important that, for practical purposes,we may interpret the annual dashas as if the year Lord were the main ruler for any given period and the other planets simply sub rulers.
2. We should remember (from Chapter III) that the Lord of the year must aspect the Ascendant, and that special rules apply when none of the eligible planets make such an aspect. In this event, we must deem the whole quality of the Soalr Return chart to be weakened becuase the year Lord itself is so lacking in strength. Be particularly alert to some of the combinations in the following chapters which place the Year Lord in the Sixth, Eighth or Twelfth. The Lord of the Year *cannot* aspect the Ascendant from any of these inauspicious houses, which tells us that the Solar Return chart is already weakened accordingly.
3. Any combination involving the Lord of the Year increases its capacity for benefic results if the Year Lord itself is extremely strong. On the other hand, a weak Lord of the Year weakens any of the combinations involving that planet.
4. Judge the strength of the Lord of the Year by a variety of factors (especially those listed at the beginning of this chapter re: strengths and weaknesses of planets), not just by the Panchavargyabala alone.
5. Among the factors which aid our assessment of the year Lord, one of the most important is the condition of that planet in the birth chart. Never judge the Lord of the Year by its annual position alone. However,

we must not confuse oursevles by judging the Year Lord's natal position according to the rules of Jataka or natal astrology then turning round to judge his position in the annual chart by way of the rather different rules which apply in Tajik! Make your assessment entirely in terms of the Tajik system.

CHAPTER IX

HEALTH AND ILLNESS

The combinations for health and illness frequently mention death; this was the practice of the old masters. We have attempted to be as faithful as possible to the spirit of the classical writers, and have left these aphorisms unvarnished and unedited. However, death occurs only under a whole chain of sinister influences acting upon the birth chart. When such influences exist, we must then examine the Solar Return to determine whether the annual influences confirm or contradict the possibility of actual death.

General Considerations

Whenever the astrologer seeks to determine the nature of an illness, he or she must first note the planet which is *causing* the disease and *its* nature. In the Tajik system, each planet is associated with one of the principal doshas or constitutions of Ayurvedic medicine:

Table: The Doshas of the Planets

Sun	Pitta
Moon	Kapha
Mars	Pitta
Mercury	Tridosha (All 3)
Jupiter	Tridosha (All 3)
Venus	Kapha
Saturn	Vata
Rahu	Vata
Ketu	Pitta

Next, note the part of the body which will be afflicted by

the disease or planet. The part of the body may be ascertained by noting the sign or navamsha (whichever is stronger) occupied by the afflicting planet (see Table IV-Chapter II) .

In determining the quantum of health and happiness the native is likely to experience during a given year, the astrologer must consider the following five planets:

a. the lord of the natal Ascendant,
b. the lord of the Solar Return's Ascendant,
c. the Lord of the Year,
d. the Trirashipati lord and
e. the dispositor of Muntha.

If any of these planets proves to be extremely weak in terms of Panchavargyabala, it will give evil effects according to its own nature, as follows:

Sun: diseases of the skin and eyes, indolence and pessimism, trouble with or because of one's parents, base behavior or humiliating jobs.

Moon: eye trouble, loss of job, professional failure, defeat, humiliation, poverty, domestic quarrels, ill health and mental anguish.

Mars: fickleness and cowardice.

Mercury: confused thinking, unwise decisions, errors in judgment, defeat.

Jupiter: impious or evil actions leading to loss of spiritual merit (poorvapunya).

Venus: quarrels with one's spouse or with women, loss of comforts and pleasures.

Saturn: trouble with servants (or, in a modern context, one's employees) or with "low" characters, illnesses arising from an imbalance of vata (i.e., gout, rheumatism, pain in the joints or muscles).

Faorable Combinations

The following combinations are traditionally said to cancel

out bad effects, thus promising a happy and prosperous year for the native. Yet it should be remembered that even these raja yogas (kingly combinations) may also be canceled. If the Lord of the year, the dispositor of Muntha, the lord of the annual Ascendant and the other planets eligible for lordship of the year are conjoined with or aspected by malefics, combust or debilitated while the chart's benefics are all devoid of strength, then the fine effects of these combinations may suffer.

In general, we may say that if the lord of the natal Ascendant, the lord of the Solar Return Ascendant, the Lord of the Year, the lord of Muntha and the lords of both the natal and annual Eighth houses are:

a. endowed with strong Panchavargyabala and
b. placed elsewhere than in the Sixth, Eighth or Twelfth

then the year will be happy and prosperous and the native may expect excellent results. But if the above planets do occupy the Sixth, Eighth and Twelfth houses, and/or they are devoid of strength or fail to receive aspects from benefics, then the year will be miserable, characterized by unhappiness and sorrow.

- If the annual Ascendant lord is strong, posited in an angle or a trine, and conjoined with or aspected by benefics, this in and of itself will overcome almost any evil effects generated by any other unfavorable planetary configurations; it will preserve one's health and bestow wealth and happiness. (Similarly a weak Ascendant lord brings hardship and trouble.)
- If the lords of the natal and annual Ascendant are both placed in angles or trines while the dispositor of Muntha is strong, then the year will bring "gains in gold, clothes and happiness".
- If a potentially harmful planet has Itthashal with a benefic, its evil yogas are canceled or at least greatly mitigated.

- If the Fourth house is occupied by its own lord or if benefics occupy or aspect the house, it brings fame, contentment and prosperity.
- If the lords of the Second and Ninth are both in the Ascendant, endowed with strength and free of malefic aspect, then the native will acquire status and prosperity. This combination "destroys the bad effects of other planets and gives an everlasting fame".
- If malefics occupy the Third, Sixth and Eleventh while benefics occupy the angles and trines, then all negative effects are destroyed and the native will have "happiness, ornaments, jewels, clothes and good health"! The same is true if the Sun and/or Mars (two malefics) occupy the Third, Sixth, Tenth or Eleventh house from Muntha in the Solar Return.
- If either Jupiter, Venus or Saturn occupies its sign of exaltation and has Itthashal with a benefic, it gives benefits from "people of different religion" (in India, at least, this ususally indicates people from the Arab countries) .
- If the Sun, Jupiter and Venus mutually apply to each other then there will be gain of status, wealth and happiness.
- If there is Israf between Mercury and Venus while Jupiter occupies the Third house, then the native will gain "kingdom, fame, gold, pearls and coral". during the year.

Since Jupiter is the "greater benefic" and the most favorable planet, a number of very auspicious combinations are based upon the position of Jupiter alone.

- When the annual Jupiter occupies an angle or trine, is aspected by benefics and free from the aspect of any malefic, it will nullify the evil effects of any other combination which afflicts the Ascendant, the Moon, or Muntha; it will bring gain of money and comforts.

- If Jupiter is lord of the natal Ascendant and occupies the First, Second, Third or Fourth of the annual chart, then the "year will usher in happiness".
- If Jupiter and the lord of the Seventh are both in the Ascendant and both aspected by friends and benefics while remaining free of malefic aspect, then their dashas will cancel out all negative effects and bring the native happiness as well as "favour from the king".

Unfavorable Combinations

The following combinations create problems or difficulties:

- If the lord of the Solar Return's Ascendant, the lord of the Eighth house and Muntha are together in the Sixth, Eighth or Twelfth, then there will be disorder of one of three doshas (vata, pitta or kapha), depending on the ruler of the sign involved.
- If the lords of both the natal and annual Ascendants are conjoined with malefics in either the Fourth, Sixth, Eighth or Twelfth there will be illness. If either or both of these planets should also happen to be combust and/or lacking any aspects from benefics, there may even be death.
- If the lord of the natal Ascendant, the Lord of the year and Muntha are all conjunct in the Fourth, Sixth, Eighth or Twelfth it is inauspicious for the native's health, especially if the combination is also conjoined with, squared or opposed by malefics.
- If the dispositor of Muntha as well as the lords of both the natal and annual First house are all conjunct in the Fourth, Sixth, Eighth or Twelfth, then there is a possibility of death; this becomes a virtual certainty if the combination is aspected by malefics.
- If the dispositor of Muntha and the Lord of the Year are in enemy signs, combust or setting, then disease and danger will be the result.
- If the lord of Trirashipati is debilitated and inimically

aspected by a malefic, one's endeavors or undertakings will end in frustration.

- If the lord of the natal I house is devoid of strength in the Solar Return while the lord of the Eighth is setting and aspected by the Sun, then the native will suffer from death-like pains, leukoderma or leprosy, eczema and general danger.
- If Venus is debilitated (in Virgo) while Jupiter occupies an enemy's sign in the Navamsha, then there will be no happiness during the course of the year. If there is also an exchange between the lords of the First and the Eighth, there may even be danger of death.
- If the lords of the Second and Ninth are weak (devoid of strength) and malefics occupy the First house, then all the native's wealth will be destroyed "even if he is protected by Indra, the King of the Gods."
- If a malefic which occupies the natal Eighth should fall in the annual First house, then the native will experience disease and mental distress during the year. If the Moon and the lord of the annual Ascendant are also very weak, there is even a possibility of death.
- Distress and disease results when Muntha is conjunct two malefics, or even if it is conjunct with or aspected by Saturn alone. If Muntha is in the annual Eighth, and if the annual Eighth is the Fourth, Sixth, Seventh, Eighth or Twelfth sign from the natal Moon, and if this Eighth house is also occupied or aspected by malefics, death is possible.
- If the birth is diurnal, and if both the natal and annual Ascendants are in a hadda, drekkana or other subdivision ruled by the Sun or Mars, there will be health problems resulting from an imbalance of pitta. But if the Ascendant of the annual chart is also aspected by benefics, the trouble will fade by the end of the year and there will be happiness.
- If weak benefics occupy the Sixth and Eighth while

the malefics are strong, there will be mental distress, general ill health, quarrels, losses, and "dire consequences".

- If the Sun and Moon are combust in the Fourth, Sixth, Eighth or Twelfth there will be diseases arising from an imbalance of the three doshas *unless* Jupiter aspects the combination.
- If the Lord of the year (or the lord of the Eighth) is in the Sixth, Eighth or Twelfth while the lord of the Tenth is weak both natally and annually, the year will be an unfortunate one.
- If both the Ascendant lord and the dispositor of Muntha are combust and aspected by Saturn there will be destruction, death, trouble, and sickness of body and mind.
- If the Lord of the Year or the dispositor of Muntha is combust the Sun in an enemy's sign, there will be trouble and illness.
- If Muntha is in the Fourth or Seventh and inimically aspected by Saturn, the native will suffer from a disease causing intense pain. If Muntha is aspected by the Sun and Mars as well, then the disease will be more severe.
- If the Point (Saham) of Death or its ruler is rising and weak (i.e., in the first five degrees of the sign) there will be illness, extreme anguish of mind, and one's life will become "listless like death".
- If the Punya Saham is afflicted by malefics while the Eighth house lord and either the Year Lord or Muntha's lord fall in the Sixth, Eighth or Twelfth, there is a possibility of death.
- If the Moon and the Punya Saham are conjunct in the First house under the following conditions, death may result:

  a. Malefics are in the Seventh house.
  b. Malefics are in the Second and Twelfth, hemming

in the Moon and Punya Saham (see below for "Hemming In".)

c. The lords of both the natal and annual Ascendants are in the Eighth house.

Hemming In

An unfavourable situation is said to result when a planet, a sensitive point, or (especially) the Ascendant is "hemmed in" by malefics. This means that a malefic planet occupies both the sign preceding the planet or point in question as well as the sign immediately following it.

The ancient texts affirm that if a planet occupies the annual Twelfth house in direct motion while another planet occupies the Second in retrograde motion, there will be illness. Similarly, a direct planet in the twelfth and a retrograde planet in the second *from:*

a. the lord of the Natal Ascendant
b. the lord of the Annual Ascendant
c. the lord of the Year

will cause some sort of confinement, whether through imprisonment or hospitalization. The present authors would prefer to modify this classic dictum and to say that this rule should be applied only when the two planets involved are malefics.

Another especially difficult situation arises when the lords of Muntha and the annual Ascendant are both hemmed in by malefics. Health problems are the likely result.

Another combination based on the hemming in of the Ascendant is: Mars in the Twelfth with the Sun in the Second brings on arguments or "bad speech".

Planetary Combinations

Sun

If the Sun is a candidate for Lord of the year and occupies an angular house, then trouble with those in authority may occur, or the native may experience ill health if the Sun and Venus are separating in the natal chart.

Moon

In broad general terms, it is said that death may occur if the Moon is in the Sixth, Eighth, or Twelfth. If the Moon is aspected only by malefics and occupies the Fourth, Sixth, Seventh, Eighth or Twelfth, then dangers and calamities will almost certainly arise. If such a Moon is aspected by Mars, then there will be danger from fire or weapons. If aspected by Saturn or the Nodes, there will be fear of enemies and disorders of vata. If aspected by the Sun, poverty will result. Even such a Moon, however, may yield good results if it is aspected by Jupiter.

Mars creates numerous difficulties for the Moon. For instance, if the annual chart's Moon occupies the natal sign of Mars and is also a candidate for Lord of the year, there will be "hidden fear" pertaining to the government or ill health. The Moon and Mars conjunct in the Sixth, Eighth or Twelfth signifies a serious illness.

Some good, however, may come from Moon-Mars combinations. If the native's birth occurred at night during a waxing Moon, and if the Moon and Mars apply to each other in the annual chart, good health will result. But if the Moon applies to Saturn, one's health is somewhat endangered. The reverse is true if the birth occurs by day during a waning Moon.

If the Moon occupies a Saturnian sign (Capricorn or Aquarius) in both the natal and annual charts and is also hemmed in by malefics, there will be controversy with others.

If the Moon is debilitated (in Scorpio) while benefics are combust with a weak Sun, then the native may suffer separation from his family, illness, distress, and sorrow.

Mars

If Mars is in combustion with the Sun in the annual chart and in a sign occupied by either Jupiter or Venus in the natal chart, then there will be an imbalance of pitta; Mars with the Moon under the same conditions brings on hemorrhoids or (in times past) leprosy; Mars with Mercury, diseases arising out of excess cold.

Mercury

If Mercury is closely combust the Sun (within about two degrees) , then one may be imprisoned during foreign travels or even die in a foreign country. If Mercury is in conjunction with both the Sun and Ketu (the South Node of the Moon) , and if the combination applies to Mars, there will be health problems throughout the year. The same is true if Mercury and Ketu are in conjunction with a planet which is natally strong and which aspires to lordship of the year in the annual chart.

If Mercury is one of the five candidates for Lord of the year and appears in the natal sign of Mars, there will be ill health. If Mars itself should afflict Mercury in the above case, then the problem will involve disorders or impurities of the blood.

It is also said that when Mercury is debilitated (in pisces), devoid of strength, or in the Sixth, Eighth or Twelfth house while applying to Mars with an inimical aspect, death may occur. But if Mercury is also in a hadda of Mars, it is the native's wealth rather than his life which is destroyed, and if Mercury in this condition is aspected by benefics, some good may actually occur.

Jupiter

If Jupiter conjoins with malefics in the Eighth house and Mars is in the Ascendant there will be "drowsiness caused by fainting" (i.e., narcolepsy) .If the Moon is also involved by way of conjunction with Mars or Jupiter, there may be the loss of a limb.

Venus

If Venus is weak in Leo in the Sixth, Eighth or Twelfth house, and if the Point of Disease is in the Sixth house conjunct with malefics, there will be some serious ailment.

Venus in a biped sign (Gemini, Virgo, Libra, or the first half of Sagittarius and Aquarius) aspected by a malefic brings diseases arising from an imbalance of kapha.

Saturn

If Saturn is weak both natally and annually and occupies the Moon's natal sign while the Sun is Lord of the year, there will be failure in all one's enterprises. The same is true if Saturn is simply retrograde or combust. If the Tenth and its lord as well as the Point of Action and its lord are conjoined with or aspected by Saturn, all one's efforts will be in vain.

If Saturn is in the Tenth and eligible for lordship of the year there will be "fear of hurt by iron".

Natal-annual Combinations

- If the Lord of the Ascendant in the natal chart is a malefic, and if it receives an inimical aspect from the Lord of the year, sickness is indicated. If it is also conjunct with malefics in the annual chart, such health problems may be very serious indeed.
- If the lord of the natal Ascendant is weak in the Solar Return chart while the lord of the Solar Return's Eighth house is in the Ascendant and aspected by the Sun there will be calamities and illnesses, especially skin problems such as dermatitis, etc.
- If the sign which rises in the Solar Return chart happens to be the eighth sign from either the natal Ascendant or natal Moon, and if that sign is tenanted or aspected by malefics, there will be illness and trouble. If the affliction is very severe, there may even be death.
- If the sign tenanted by Muntha happens to be the Fourth, Sixth, Seventh, Eighth or Twelfth sign from the

natal Ascendant, and if that sign constitutes the annual Eighth house and is occupied or aspected by malefics, there will be a serious illness—the more serious the affliction, the more serious the illness.

- If a malefic occupies an angle or kendra in the birth chart, and the sign occupied by that malefic —or the malefic itself — appears in the Ascendant of the annual chart, health problems are indicated.
- If the Punya Saham's dispositor occupies the eighth house from the Punya Saham itself while the lord of the natal Eighth house is in conjunction with Punya Saham (as well as suffering the affliction of malefics), death is indicated.
- If the annual Punya Saham occupies the sign of the natal Eighth house and is conjunct its own dispositor, death may occur.

Solar Combinations

- If the Sun in the Solar Return chart occupies the same sign as the natal Moon, and if Saturn is afflicted in both the natal and annual charts, then there will be total failure and frustration in all work. (Note that this is only possible when the Sun and Moon are conjunct in the birth chart.)
- If the Solar Return occurs during the daytime and the ascending degrees of both the natal and annual charts fall in the sign, drekkana, hadda or navamsha of the Sun or Mars, there will be illness (probably fever) during the course of the year. But if the Solar Return's Ascendant is aspected by benefics there will be happiness towards the end of the year.
- If the Sun in the Solar Return occupies the natal sign of Venus, and if that sign falls in the annual sixth house while the Point of Disease is conjunct a malefic, then there will be venereal diseases or diseases of the reproductive system. (Since the Sun is always in same

sign in the Solar Return as that which it occupied in the natal chart, this combination can only occur when the Sun and Venus are conjunct in the birth chart.)

- If the Sun, as one of the candidates for Lord of the Year, separates from natal Venus and occupies an angle in the Solar Return, there will be a "slow and wasting disease".

Other Planets

- If the natal Moon is waxing and the annual Moon is in Itthashal with Mars during a Solar Return which occurs at night, any illnesses contracted by the native will abate. But if the situation is reversed —i.e., the natal Moon is waning and the Solar Return is diurnal —the aspect of Moon and Mars will cause illness. The Moon in Itthashal with Saturn may induce illness under any circumstances.
- If the annual Moon as a candidate for Lord of the year occupies the sign of natal Mars there will be illness and possible trouble with the government.
- If Mars' natal sign become the annual Ascendant, and if that sign receives the inimical aspect of Mars in the annual chart, there may be diseases resulting from an imbalance of pitta or danger from fire, and if a weak Mercury happens to be Lord of the year, then the year in general will not be a good one. If the sign in question is aspected by benefics, the intensity of the problem is reduced.
- If Mercury, as a candidate for Lord of the year, is natally in Aries or Scorpio, there will be illness during the year. And is such a Mercury is in inimical aspect to Mars in the Solar Return, there will be illness resulting from impurities of the blood. Or again, if such a Mercury happens to be combust and afflicted by malefics, the native may suffer imprisonment or death in a foreign country or far away from birth place.

- If the lord of the natal Ascendant is conjunct with both Ketu and Mercury in the annual chart there will be a protracted illness.
- Note the natal sign positions of Venus and Jupiter. If Mars is combust the Sun and occupying one of these signs in the annual chart, the native may suffer from boils, pox, fever, or diseases of the neck and/or throat. If such a Mars is also conjunct with both the Moon and Mercury there may be glandular swelling in the neck, fistula, or (in some countries) leprosy.
- Note Saturn's natal sign. If this sign rises in the Solar Return, there may be diseases involving emaciation or biliousness. But if the annual Ascendant is aspected by Saturn itself, the problem will be less intense. On the other hand, if the Ascendant is occupied by a malefic there may even be death.

Combinations with the Lord of the Year

- If the Lord of the year and the lord of the natal Ascendant are weak and posited in the Sixth, Eighth or Twelfth (whether jointly or separately), then the resulting ill effects must be judged according to the sign or signs involved. For example: Venus in the Sixth in a dwipada or two-legged sign (Gemini, Virgo, Libra, Sagittarius) brings loss of servants, but in a four-legged sign (Aries, Taurus, Leo, Capricorn) it would bring loss of livestock. More generally, the Sixth house indicates illness and enmity, the Eighth defeat and frustration, and the Twelfth heavy expenses and losses.
- If the Lord of the year separates from a malefic, the lord of the natal Ascendant being itself a malefic or containing a malefic in the annual chart, then there will be danger (or perhaps even death), even when the Year Lord also has Kamboola yoga with a benefic. A similar, though not quite so extreme, conclusion may be inferred if any of the other four planets eligible for Lord of the year finds itself in the same situation.

- If a malefic as Year Lord conjuncts the Sun in a four-legged sign in the Sixth, Eighth or Twelfth there will be enmity and quarrels with servants (i.e., with one's employees).
- If the Lord of the year is afflicted and defeated by Mars, there will be trouble with one's relatives or possible military service accompanied by great fear.
- If the Sun as Lord of the year falls in the Twelfth house there will be eye troubles and stomach ailments.
- If the Moon as Lord of the Year is afflicted in the Sixth there will be diseases arising from an imbalance of kapha.
- If Mars as Lord of the year is retrograde in the sixth the native will suffer from jaundice or diseases due to impurity of the blood.
- If Mars as Lord of the Year occupies a friendly house and forms Kamboola Yoga with planets which are exalted or in their own signs, then the native will gain "elephants, horses, vehicles, etc." (cars, boats and planes being the modern equivalents) .If Mars is Lord of the year, afflicted, and conjunct Saturn in the Twelfth, then there will be anguish of mind and loss of vehicles.
- If Mars, as Lord of the year, is devoid of strength and defeated by another malefic, there will be danger of injury due to some weapon. If Mars in the above condition is in a fire sign (Aries, Leo, Sagittarius) , there is danger from fire; if in dwipada signs (Gemini, Virgo, Libra, Sagittarius) one's death may be caused by "a cruel person"; in the Tenth house the danger comes from people in authority or from one's enemies (competitors); if in the Fourth house there is reason to fear danger from one's mother, maternal uncles or father.
- If Mercury as Lord of the year is retrograde and afflicted in the Sixth there will be diseases arising from an

imbalance of vata or trouble with the nervous system. If Mercury should become Lord of the year while devoid of strength, and if the natal sign of Mars appears as the annual chart's Ascendant, it will not be a good year.

- If Saturn is Lord of the year and devoid of strength it causes depression and a loss in status, especially in the Tenth house, where it brings frustration and failure in work.

The Houses

First House Combinations

- If the lord of the Ascendant in the Solar Return chart is endowed with full strength, then the native will be healthy, will gain wealth, and will experience other fortunate events during the year. If the Ascendant lord is of medium strength, then the good results will be less intense. But if the Ascendant lord is devoid of strength there will be sorrow, mental anguish, and chronic health problems.
- If the Ascendant lord and the lord of the Ascendant's hadda are in the Seventh, Eighth or Twelfth conjoined with or aspected by a malefic, there will be serious illness during their dasha periods. But if they are aspected by one or more benefics, there will be no untoward results.
- When a malefic occupies the annual First house and no benefic either aspects or occupies that house as well, then there will be quarrels and "unwholesome food"; the native will be the victim of deception.

In general, we may say that if the First house is occupied by the Sun, Mars, Saturn or a waning Moon then the native will suffer from fevers and loss of wealth. If Mercury, Jupiter or Venus are in the First, then the native's health will be good; there will be luster in his face, gain in wealth, and other good things. A First house occupied solely by malefics, and lacking even the aspect of benefics, will shape a native who is easily fooled by tricksters and con men, who wastes his time in fruitless discussions, and who eats tamasic food.[1]

If Jupiter becomes Lord of the year and occupies the First house while receiving afflictions from a malefic, there is "fear from the king" (i.e., the possibility of persecution by or trouble with the government) .

Sixth House Combinations

If the Lord of the year is retrograde, conjoined with malefics and placed in the Sixth house, health problems will arise relative to the nature of the planet:

Sun: an imbalance of pitta or, if in the Twelfth rather than the sixth, diseases of the .eyes.

Moon: disorders of kapha.

Mars: disorders of the blood.

Mercury: vata disorders.

Jupiter: vata disorders and disorders arising from an excess of pleasure (these problematical indications are overcome if Jupiter forms Kamboola Yoga with the Moon.

Venus: pitta disorders, unless Venus is also aspected by the ruler of the Ascendant, in which case it causes kapha disorders.

Saturn: high fever due to gout, rheumatism, enlargement of the spleen and so on.

- If there is Itthashal between the lord of the Solar Return's Ascendant, the Lord of the year and the lord of the Sixth house, then there will be health problems due to the dhatu or attributes of the planet ruling the Ascendant.
- If a benefic planet rules the Sixth house and is posited

1. Tamaic fool is "non-spiritual" food; for instance, a diet of junk food or a diet heavily dependent upon meat, oninions, garlic and beet roots.

therein, the native's spouse will experience health problems.

- If Mars rules the natal Sixth and is posited in the annual sixth there will be health problems of some sort; the problem will be acute if Mars applies to a malefic or mild if it applies to a benefic.

Eighth House Combinations

If the lord of the natal Ascendant is conjunct a malefic in the annual chart's Eighth house and Muntha is conjunct with Saturn, death may occur. If Mars also casts an inimical aspect upon the Ascendant lord, the cause of the death will be suicide.

- If the Ascendant lord is in the Eighth or the Eighth lord in the Ascendant, and if either of these is aspected by Mars while Mercury and Jupiter are also combust, either illness or accident will occur in the course of the year.
- If the lords of the First and the Eighth are conjoined with and/or aspected by malefics (especially in the Eighth house itself) , the native will be in "fear of death".
- If the lords of the First and the Eighth are conjunct with Muntha in the Fourth, Eighth or Twelfth houses, disease occurs due to an imbalance of the dosha (humor or constitution) signified by the lord of the Eighth.
- If the Lord of the year is conjunct Mars in the Eighth, death may occur. If the Lord of the year, lord of the Solar Return's Ascendant, or dispositor of Muntha should happen to be the lord of the Eighth house or in Itthashal with the lord of the Eighth, death may occur

during that part of the year when the dasha of a maraka[1] is in force.[2]

- Mars in the Eighth causes danger from fire, injuries involving weapons, or trouble with the government. If Mars is in the Tenth there may be some danger of "falling from a horse" (in modern terms, an auto accident) or diseases involving impurities in the blood. Mars in the Eighth in Aries, Taurus, Leo or Sagittarius causes injury from a sword (or, in contemporary terms, a stabbing of some kind). If the lord of the natal Ascendant is combust in the Eighth house of the Solar Return chart there will be enmity and disease. A conjunction of Mars and the Sun in the Eighth house causes auto accidents; this is especially true if Saturn is also involved in the conjunction (the same results may occur if the three planets are conjunct in the Tenth). If the Solar Return occurs during the day while Mars is conjunct the Sun, then there is also "fear from the king" (i.e., the native may suffer at the hands of those in positions of authority) .
- If Jupiter as Lord of the year falls in the Second or the Eighth, the native's wealth is destroyed. If it occupies the Eighth house natally and is not a candidate for Lord of the year, there will be disharmony with one's spouse, though an aspect from Venus will assure success and harmony in the end. If Jupiter is in a Mars-ruled sign both natally and annually, a candidate for Lord of the year, and is separating from and/or defeated by malefics, there will be unavoidable quarrels with others.

---

1. A maraka is defined as a planet which may cause death. Traditionally, the lords of the Second and Seventh house are the principal marakas. (See *Astrology & You* by the Authors).
2. Before predicting death, due consideration should be given to the native's general life-span as determined by way of the Maharishi Gemini's system. See our *Predictive Astrology of the Hindus,* op.cit., pp. 236-8.

- If Saturn rules the natal Eighth (i.e., if the natal Ascendant is either Gemini or Cancer) and applies to the lord of the Solar Return Ascendant with an inimical aspect, it may cause death at the very beginning of the year. If it occupies the Eighth and applies to the lord of the Eighth, this is also an indicator of death. But if it applies to a benefic, no evil combination involving Saturn will cause the native any real harm.

The following combinations are based upon the sensitive points:

If the lord of the Punya Saham is in the Eighth position from the Punya-Saham itself, and if the lord of the natal Eighth house is conjunct both the Punya Saham and a malefic, then there will be "trobules equal to death".

If the sign in the natal Eighth is occupied by its own lord in the annual chart, or if the annual Eighth house is occupied by both the Punya Saham and its own lord, death may occur.

Twelfth House Combinations

If a strong Moon becomes Lord of the Year and occupies the Twelfth, the native will spend a great deal of money in civic imporvements.

Mars and the Moon conjunct in the Twelfth cause great uneasiness; in the Tenth there will be "destruction of horses" (i.e., loss of livestock or difficulties in transportation).

CHAPTER X

WEALTH, LOVE AND FAMILY

This chapter is divided in three sections. The first section deals with Wealth and Prosperity; the second section deals with Love and Marriage; and in the third section, we have the *'Kutumb'*, i.e., Family. This section of family is devoted to Siblings (brothers and sisters), parents (father and mother), and Children (sons and daughters).

Section I

WEALTH AND PROSPERITY

General

'Money is necessary even for the survival of Religion'. Without money most things come to standstill. In the general consideration, Jupiter and other benefic are assigned with importance. Jupiter is the most important planet. One who is born with Jupiter in the second house in the birth chart will always be flux with money most of the times but particularly so when Jupiter comes back in the 2nd, 11th or 8th house in the Solar Return chart. Most benefic are good in the 2nd house.

Any benefic planet which occupies the natal Ascendant and the annual Second house confers wealth. This planet as well as Jupiter may be taken as a significator of wealth. Note that if the significator of wealth and the lord of the Second are both weakened in the annual chart, then the native will lose his wealth and he will be cheated by his business partners.

Combinations with Jupiter

As the principal significator of wealth, Jupiter is the planet most commonly associated with financial gains. Many combinations for wealth, therefore, are based upon the position of Jupiter.

- If Jupiter rules the natal First and occupies the annual First, Third or Fourth there will be financial gain and great happiness.
- If Jupiter rules the Second house of the birth chart (i.e., if Scorpio or Aquarius is rising) and if, in the Solar Return chart, it either appears in the Second house or has Itthashal with the lord of the Solar Return's Ascendant, then there will be wealth throughout the year. But if Jupiter has Israf with a malefic there will be financial loss and depletion of one's savings.
- Jupiter in the annual Second house, conjoined with or aspected by benefics, confers wealth and position, especially if it aspects Muntha's sign in both the natal and annual charts. This principle applies to Venus as well. But if there is Israf between the lords of the First and the Second, the combination is cancelled and there wil be loss of wealth.
- If annual Jupiter occupies one of the houses he rules natally and has Itthashal with the lord of the annual First then there will be happiness pertaining to that house. For example: If Leo is the natal Ascendant, then Jupiter is lord of the natal fifth. If Cancer rises in the annual chart and Jupiter is in the Fifth in Scorpio, having Itthashal with the Moon (ruler of the First), then the native may have a son (Fifth house) or, if unmarried, experience other Fifth house benefits, as through gambling, speculation, etc.
- If the sign occupied by Jupiter in the birth chart should happen to appear as the Ascendant in the Solar Return

chart, if its ruler is benefic,and if that ruler either aspects or occupies that particular sign, then there will be rulership and gain of wealth. But if Jupiter occupies the Eighth along with malefics, there will be "losses through the government" (for example, the native may have tax problems).

- If Jupiter is in the Second or Eighth afflicted by malefics the native will have to pay a financial pentalty.
- If Jupiter is eligible to become Lord of the year and occupies the Seventh house, there will be gain through trade and commerce, or through lending money.

Jupiter's influence as Lord of the year itself is detailed under "Combinations with the Lord of the year" later in this chapter.

Combinations with Mercury

As the natural significator of the Eleventh house, Mercury to some degree rules over "gains" or income. Hence, a number of combinations involving wealth focus on this planet.

- Mercury conjunct Muntha in the First house gives wealth from teaching, writing, etc. If the combination also features benefics in conjunction with the Point of wealth, there will be gain of "hidden wealth" (i.e., wealth from under the earth, usually signifying mining or minerals in a modern context). But if the combination is aspected by malefics, no such gains occur.
- When Mercury is conjunct Muntha in the Sixth, Eighth, or Twelfth, any gains will come from menial jobs or. types of work. Mercury combust or aspected. by malefics cancels any possibility of gain from writing.
- If Mercury occupies the hadda of Mars and is afflicted by malefics there will be loss of wealth. The problem will be mitigated by any aspects from benefics.

Other Combinations

- If Jupiter, Venus or Saturn happen to be exàlted and to have Itthashal with a benefic, then there will be gain of wealth.
- If Mercury and Venus are in Israf and Jupiter is in the Third house, there will be a rise in status and the acquisition of wealth due to wise conduct on the part of the native.
- If Saturn occupies the Second, then one's work and its fruits will be destroyed and any gains will be extremely limited. But if Saturn is exalted, in its own sign, or conjunct with Jupiter in the Second and aspected by benefics, then wealth and happiness will come from one's siblings. But if the combination is aspected by malefics, then there will be loss and misery from the same quarter. Note that the Second house is the twelfth (loss) from the Third (siblings) .
- If the lords of the Second house and the house containing the Point of Wealth are both strong and receive friendly aspects from benefics, there will be financial gain. If the aspects are inimical there will still be some gain, but only through effort.
- If the Moon and Saturn are conjunct in the Twelfth house while benefics occupy the Sixth there will be loss of wealth. If the Moon also separates from a malefic, mental distress will follow the loss. But if the Sixth house planet separates from a benefic rather than a malefic, the unfavorable results are canceled. Similarly, benefics aspecting the Moon suggest that the native, despite his losses, will be free of mental turmoil.
- If the Moon, Mercury and Venus are in their own haddas while all the malefics occupy the Third or Eleventh houses (whether severally or jointly) , the native will earn wealth and reputation due to his own efforts.

- If the lords of the Second and Ninth are strong and in the First house without the aspect of of malefics, then other unfavorable financial configurations are nullified and the native will experience a substantial increase in money and reputation.
- If the lords of the Second and Ninth are weak and malefics occupy the First house there will be loss of wealth.

Natal-Annual Combinations

- If the lord of the natal Ascendant, the lord of the annual Ascendant, and the dispositor of Muntha are all strong, posited in the Second or Eleventh, in angles or trines (jointly or severally) there will be happiness and the acquisition of wealth.
- If the lord of the natal Second house and the natal planet most concerned with the accumulation of wealth (i.e., benefics in the First, Second or Eleventh or benefics which aspect the Second, the Eleventh or Jupiter) are all weak, and/or combust and occupying evil houses in the Solar Return, then there will be financial scandal and loss of wealth. Conversely, if these planets are strong, well placed and well aspected in the Solar Return, then there will be gain of money. Though this principle is stated here simply in regard to wealth and its significators, it is a general one and may be applied to the affairs and significators of all other houses.
- If benefics occupy the natal First and then appear in the annual Second, there will be gain of wealth.
- The Sun in the natal First and the annual Second indicates gain of money and wealth.
- If Mercury rules the natal Sixth (i.e., if Aries or Capricorn is the natal Ascendant) and also occupies the Solar Return's Sixth house, then there will be only a little gain during the course of the year.

Combinations with the Lord of the Year

- If any planet as Lord of the year is exalted or occupying its own sign in the Tenth, there will be gains through the areas of life signified by that planet.

The Sun

- If the Sun, endowed with strength, becomes Lord of the year and occupies the Eleventh house, it confers the "friendship of the king and his ministers" (i.e., fruitful contacts with those in positions of authority).

The Moon

- If a strong Moon is Lord of the year and placed in the Sixth, Eighth or Twelfth, then there will be expenditures on auspicious projects such as improving one's real estate. The same is true if the Moon rules the annual Ascendant and occupies these houses.

Mars

- If Mars as Lord of the year is in his own sign and forming Kamboola Yoga with planets which are also in their own signs there will be acquisition of real estate, vehicles, and money in general.

Mercury

- If Mercury is strong as Lord of the year, as well as conjunct Muntha in the First house and either conjunct or well aspected by other benefics, then there will be gains through reading, writing, or other Mercury activities.
- If Mercury as Lord of the year is posited in the Sixth, Eighth or Twelfth and conjunct a malefic, then the native may resort to dishonesty in business or wind up in a very menial job. Mercury combust or aspected by malefics prevents any gain from reading or writing.

- If Mercury is Lord of the year, conjoined with or aspected by a benefic, and occupying the Second house, there will be gain from trade and commerce.

Note: This is a combination quoted from a medieval text. Please remember that in actual practice a planet will seldom become Lord of the year unless it aspects the Ascendant. Thus, it is unlikely that Mercury will be Lord of the year in the Second.

We would prefer to modify this dictum to say that if Mercury is Lord of the year, strong and well placed, and aspecting the Second or Eleventh, he will show the good results mentioned above. The same is true if Mercury rules the annual Ascendant and is placed in the Second with good aspects.

Jupiter

If Jupiter happens to rule the Second house in the natal chart and then to become Lord of the year in the Solar Return chart, then its position by house will indicate the *source* from which wealth is gained (or lost) during the year. For example:

First House: the native earns through his own effort.

Second: he gains from financing and money markets.

Third: from siblings.

Fourth: from one's parents, friends, or from real estate.

Fifth: from children, education, or speculation.

Sixth: there will be losses due to the actions of enemies or competitors, but gains from maternal relatives.

Seventh: gains from one's spouse.

Eighth: money comes through an inheritance, insurance or because of a death, or, according to the medieval classics, from "treasures hidden underground".

Ninth: from travels or through religious people.

Tenth: through "kings" or from the government.

Eleventh: from "the royal family".

Twelfth: there will be losses due to debts and heavy expenditures.

Note: Here again the classical texts postulate a Year Lord which, contrary to the standard definitions, does not aspect the Ascendant. It is unlikely that Jupiter as Year Lord will be found in the Second, Sixth, Eighth or Twelfth.

- If Jupiter as Lord of the year should happen to aspect the Second house, then the native will gain wealth without any effort. In fact, when Jupiter is the Lord of the year it will benefit any house it aspects in the natal chart. Whatever Jupiter's rulership may be, it will bring good fortune to its own houses when placed in the First house of the Solar Return chart and involved in Itthashal with the ruler of the Solar Return's First house. For instance: Let us say that Leo is the natal Ascendant and that Jupiter therefore rules the Fifth. Let us say that the Ascendant for the Solar Return chart is Cancer, and that Jupiter is exalted therein, occupying the First, and that it also applies to Moon. During the year the native's wife will conceive or give birth to a child, or else there will be great happiness from already existing children.
- If Jupiter as Lord of the year occupies the First but suffers from the affliction of malefics, then there will be apprehension or loss through the medium of the government.
- If Jupiter as Lord of the year occupies the Third or Ninth there will be money gained through diplomacy or general cleverness.
- If Jupiter as Lord of the year occupies the Second or Eighth and is aspected by malefics there will be loss of wealth. (Note: Again, this judgment postulates a Year Lord which does not aspect the Ascendant, and we feel that this dictum is more appropriate to Jupiter as lord of the First house.)
- Jupiter as Lord of the year or candidate for the same, if positioned in the Seventh, brings acquisition of wealth due to one's innate practicality.

Venus

- If Venus as Lord of the year is weak, inimically aspected by malefics, and occupies a biped sign (Gemini, Virgo, Libra or Sagittarius) in the Sixth there will be "loss of servants" or, in a modern context, trouble with one's employees. If Venus is in a quadruped sign (Aries, Taurus, Leo or Capricorn), then, according to the old texts, "loss of horses" is signified. The same principles applied here may be applied to any other planet in a similar situations.
- If Venus is Lord of the year and occupies the Second house, it confers wealth. But if there is Israf (separation) between the lords of the First and the Second, then that which is gained will also be lost. (See notes in the previous sections regarding Year Lords which do not aspect the Ascendant.)

Saturn

- If Saturn (or Jupiter) as Lord of the year is exalted or occupies its own sign in the Tenth house, then there will be good health and gain of money.

The Houses

Second House Combinations

- If the lords of the First and Second apply to each other with a friendly aspect, sudden gains of wealth will occur. But if there is separation between these two planets, wealth is destroyed and there is danger of treachery.
- If Mercury is strong in the Second house, there will be gain of money from writing or due to the kinds of knowledge and effort governed by Mercury — journalism, publicity, trade, mediation, etc.
- If Mars is strong in the Second house, there will be wealth, increase in fame and sudden gain or good luck leading to happiness.

- If Mars is strong and in the Second house then the native will gain wealth, fame, luster and sudden happiness during the year.
- If the ruler of the Point of Wealth and the ruler of the Second house (in strength) are both aspected by benefics with a friendly aspect, then gain of money occurs easily. But an inimical aspect, even from benefics, means that money will only be gained through sustained effort. If Mercury, Jupiter, and Venus all aspect or occupy the Second house and/or the Sign where the Point of Wealth is, then great wealth and status will be gained.

Eleventh House Combinations

Any planet in the Eleventh house, whether malefic or benefic, will yield excellent gains of money if strong. Weak planets in the Eleventh bring only mildly favourable results.

If there is an application between the lords of the First and Eleventh, there will be gains and fame within one's own circle.

Section II

LOVE AND MARRIAGE*

General

Man is a Social animal. He needs friends and society to interact with and who else could be more important than a wife. A wife is no different than a women friend with whom one has an intimate relationship, mental, spiritual, emotional or physical. The only extra thing is that a wife has is the Sanctity of Law and Religion and as such she occupies the highest position. There are 8 types of marriages according to the Scriptures.

The parameter of marriage changes with the times, country and society . Religious marriages or 'Brahma Vivah' has been acknowledged as the highest form of union. Most books mention 'wife' but when examining the horoscope of a

* For an exciting understanding see '*The Astrological Secrets of Friendship, Love and Marriage*' by Authors.

woman then the word 'wife' should be substituted with 'husband'.

All the ancient texts are written from the man's point of view, and hence all the delineations regard one's "wife". However, the same basic factors which govern a man's life are equally applicable to a woman's horoscope. Here we have preferred the neutral term "spouse" —and the modern Westerner may even choose to substitute a term such as "significant other".

Also, most of these delineations speak of "marriage during the year". This judgment obviously requires some adjustment to individual circumstances. For very young children, nothing at all, may transpire. For the young and active, there may be a love affair. For those who are already married, some kind of benefit may accrue to the spouse or to a business partner.

The question may be asked: Can such indications refer to extra-marital relationships or affairs? The answer is yes. But to avoid causing more harm than good, the wise astrologer never initiates such a topic, and leaves it alone unless asked a direct question.

- If the Point of Marriage in the Solar Return is aspected by its own lord and by Venus then there will be marriage (or the beginning of a major relationship) during the year.
- If the Point of Marriage is aspected by both Mars and Venus then there will be "gain of a spouse".
- If a strong Venus rules the Seventh and occupies the Ascendant, then there will be happiness in regard to one's spouse; if it also receives an aspect from Jupiter, the situation is even better, and if it receives an aspect from Mars when that planet is a candidate for Lord of the Year, there will be mutual happiness between marriage partners.
- If Muntha is aspected by Jupiter while Muntha's dispositor is eligible to become Lord of the year, there will be marriage during the year.

- If both the Seventh house lord and the lord (i.e., dispositor) of the house containing the Point of the Spouse are afflicted through combustion, retrogradation, or inimical aspects, then there will be illness or trouble for one's spouse.
- If the lord of the Ascendant is devoid of strength, combust, and conjoined with malefics, there will be quarrels with one's spouse.
- If the Sun or its dispositor is one of the candidates for Lord of the year there will be uneasiness and agitation of mind for or because of the native's spouse.

Natal-Annual Combinations

- If the lord of the natal Ascendant is strong and occupies the annual Seventh then there will be happiness through one's spouse.
- If the lord of the Ascendant's hadda or the dispositor of the annual Point of Marriage occupies the natal sign of Venus in an angle or trine in the Solar Return, there will be happiness through one's spouse or through marriage.
- If the lord of the natal Seventh becomes the dispositor of the annual Point of Marriage there will be marriage during the year or happiness through one's spouse.
- If the lord of the natal Seventh, the Lord of the year and Muntha's dispositor fall in the annual Tenth or Seventh (severally or together) , there will be marriage or happiness through one's spouse.
- If a strong Mars occupies the sign of natal Venus there will be marriage and/or conjugal happiness.
- If Venus rules the natal Seventh (i.e., Aries or Scorpio is the natal Ascendant) and falls in the annual Seventh, strong and having Itthashal with the lord of the annual First, then there will be marriage or gain through a relationship.
- If the Moon is afflicted (combust or conjoined with

and/or aspected by malefics) and posited in the sign of natal Venus then there will be very little sexual intercourse during the course of the year.

Combinations with the Lord of the Year

- If Mars as Lord of the year is aspected by Venus or if Venus as Lord of the year is aspected by Mars there will be marriage or gain of a relationship.
- If Venus is the Lord of the year and placed in the Seventh house
  a. there is love with a much younger partner (or a person married to someone else) when Venus is aspected by Mercury.
  b. there is love with a much older partner (also married to someone else) if Venus is aspected by Saturn
  c. marriage and childbirth will bring happiness within a very short time if Venus is aspected by Jupiter.
- If Venus is Lord of the Year, and if her natal sign occupies the Seventh house of the annual chart with the lord of the natal Ascendant placed therein, there will be amorous pleasure, whether through marriage or otherwise.
- If Venus is the Lord of the year and conjunct with or aspected by the lord of the natal Seventh, there will be happiness with regard to one's spouse. The same result occurs if Jupiter in the annual chart occupies the same sign as natal Venus in either an angular or trine house: or, again, if the ruler of the annual Ascendant's hadda and the ruler of the Point of Marriage both occupy the same sign as natal Venus in an angular or trine house.
- If a strong Venus as Lord of the year falls in the Seventh, then there will be happiness as regards one's spouse or mate. If such a Venus is aspected by Jupiter, there is great happiness indeed: if aspected by a Mars

which is eligible for Lord of the year then the sexual side of the relationship will be very intense.

The Houses

Seventh House Combinations

- If there is Itthashal between the lords of the First and the Seventh, then there will be gain of a spouse.
- If Muntha is conjunct the Sun and/or Mars in the Seventh house while the Point of the Spouse is conjunct a malefic then there will be trouble to (or from) one's spouse and children. This is especially true if Muntha and the Point of the Spouse both receive inimical aspects from malefics.

Section III

KUTUMB (FAMILY)

A. General

The entire section 3 has been divided into (A) General, (B) Natal-Annual combinations, (C) Combination with the year lord, and (D) The Houses-in which we have dealt with the effects of the 3rd, 4th, and 5th houses. In each of these sub-division viz., A, B, C, and D, Siblings, parents and children, has been separately dealt with so that it would become easier for the readers.

Siblings

The following configurations suggest the illness of a sibling or some other form of "separation" from a sibling:

- The lord of the sign which contains the Point of siblings is conjunct a malefic and not aspected by the lord of the Third.
- The lord of the Third and the dispositor of the Point of siblings are both combust.

- If the Point of Brothers is occupied by malefics, there will be sorrow due to or on account of one's siblings.
- If the lords of the Third house and the Point of Brothers are combust, "destruction of brothers" will take place (i.e., one's siblings may suffer misfortune).
- If the Lord of the year or the ruler of the Solar Return's Ascendant is placed in the seventh from the Third (i.e., in the Ninth), there will be arguments between siblings.
- If Venus is a candidate for Lord of the year, as well as being placed in Cancer in both the natal and Solar Return charts, and if the Moon is strong as well, then there will be the birth of a brother.

Parents

The student must remember that a Solar Return is likely to be erected for adults who have already lost their parents. In this case, the combinations given here are more likely to be applicable to real estate. In fact, this may be true even when the parents are living.

- If the sensitive point for either the mother or father should have Itthashal with the Ascendant lord or fall in the Fourth house then there will be happiness with respect to the parent indicated. But if either of these sensitive points have Itthashal with the lord of the Eighth or with a natural malefic then the indicated parent may experience fear and suffering.
- A conjunction of Saturn and the Sun in the birth chart will bring the native into enmity with the father and cause him to suffer insults from other people generally. If Saturn conjuncts the Moon, then the native's quarrels and enmity will be with the mother. These natal configurations will come into prominence in the native's life when they are repeated in the Solar Return chart, i.e., when the annual chart contains a conjunction of the Sun or Moon with Saturn.

Children

The period in one's life when one is likely to bear a child is obviously limited from the onset of puberty until late in one's forties. Many Solar Returns will involve children or older people. Remember that these Fifth house combinations may well indicate that the native's child will prosper (rather than being born), that a student will do well in his studies and examinations, and so on.

Though there are exceptions, we may state that as a general rule the male planets (Sun, Mars and Jupiter) signify male children. The female planets (Moon, Mercury, Venus, and Saturn) signify daughters.

- If the Fifth house and/or the sensitive point for Sons or Daughters happens to be strong in terms of position, aspects and lordship, or if the sensitive point for either Sons or Daughters should in itself be strong and placed in the Fifth house, then there will be the birth of a child or great happiness with respect to a child. [NOTE: This combination, like many others, is dependent upon the planets involved being *strong* — in terms of their house position, their aspects, and the condition of their lords. It follows that unfavorable results will be likely if those planets are weak. This is a general guideline, applicable to everything in this book, and the maxims of the old masters are intended to stimulate the student's own intellectual process rather than serve as cut-and-dried absolutes. Only by working with the material can the student acquire the necessary flexibility and balance.]
- A strong Mercury conjunct Mars in a benefic's sign in the Fifth or Eleventh brings much happiness in regard to one's child. If Mercury is weak, however, the child may suffer.

B. Natal-Annual Combinations

Siblings

Siblings benefit if the lord of the native's natal Third house is well placed and conjoined with or aspected by benefics in the Solar Return.

If the lords of the natal and annual Third house are themselves both posited in the Third in their respective charts and aspected by benefics then the native will derive great satisfaction from siblings.

- If the lord of either the natal or annual Ascendant (or, according to one source, the Lord of the year) is posited in the Third house while Mercury or Venus is strong, there will be happiness with respect to one's siblings.

Parents

- If the lord of the Fourth is weak in the natal chart, while that planet as well as the lord of the annual Fourth are both weak in the Solar Return, there will be trouble for the parents. If the sensitive points for either the mother or father are also conjunct or aspected by malefics, combust, or in the Fourth house from Muntha, there may even be the death of a parent.
- If the sign which occupies the natal Fourth as well as the natal sign in which the Fourth house lord is located should both be occupied by Mars and Saturn in the Solar Return, then the native's parents may suffer.
- If Saturn is in the sign occupied by the natal Moon the mother may become ill.

Children

Let the student take note: the combinations given below cover so many planets that it will be very common to find one of these combinations in any gven Solar Return. In ancient times, families were indeed much larger than they are now! In a contemporary context, these combinations may indicate the welfare or prosperity of a child rather than actual birth. They may also indicate that any of the other matters ruled by the Fifth house (gambling, speculation, romance, spiritual observance) may flourish.

- Note Jupiter's natal sign. If that sign occupies the Fifth house of the Solar Return and is strong, then there will be happiness with regard to children. The same is true if Jupiter's natal sign rises in the annual chart, though here the judgment more specifically indicates "birth of a son".
- Note the natal sign of Mercury or Venus. If this sign rises in the annual chart, the birth of a child is indicated.
- If the natal sign occupied by Saturn or Mars appears in the First or Fifth of the Solar Return and is well aspected by a benefic, then there will be the birth of a son.
- If Venus is lord of the natal Fifth and posited in the annual Fifth while having Itthashal with the lord of the First there will be the birth of a child or else very favorable relationships with one's children.
- If Saturn's natal sign occupies the annual Fifth and is aspected by other malefics one's children will suffer.

C. Combinations with the Year Lord

Siblings

- If the Lord of the year and the lord of the Third house make separating aspects with each other, then there will be anxiety or worry regarding one's siblings, or perhaps the illness of a sibling.
- If the Sun or Venus is Lord of the year and neither conjoined with nor aspected by malefics, there will be mutual happiness between siblings. But if they are devoid of strength (in terms of Panchavargyabala) and aspected by malefics, there will be opposition between siblings.

- If Venus as Lord of the year is combust the Sun and side by side with a weak Jupiter in the Third, or if the Sun itself as Year Lord is conjunct a weak Jupiter in the Third, then there will be enmity between siblings.

Parents

- If the Sun is Lord of the year, endowed with strength, and in the Fourth, it brings gain of property and happiness in the family. But if it is aspected by or conjoined with malefics, it causes suffering to the father, whereas the Moon in similar condition will affect the mother.

Children

- If any planet as Lord of the year is in the Fifth house and aspected by benefics there will be much happiness with regard to one's children.
- If the Sun, Mars, Mercury or Venus should happen to be the Lord of the year and posited in either the Fifth or Eleventh house, then one's children will bring to the native a great deal of family contentment and peace of mind. But if any of the planets as year Lord in the houses noted above should also happen to be afflicted by malefics, then there will be sorrow and unhappiness on account of one's children.
- If Jupiter as Lord of the year occupies the Fifth or Eleventh, the same favorable judgments apply, but in greater measure.

D. The Houses

Third House Combinations
(Siblings)

Note: The Third house combinations given throughout this chapter all specifically involve siblings. Nevertheless, the student should remember that the Third house governs other matters as well, and that any Third house combinations given here may at times be applicable to those issues as well.

- If the lord of the Third house has Itthashal with either the Lord of the year or the lord of the Solar Return's Ascendant, and if Jupiter is in the Third, there will be happiness with one's siblings.
- If the lord of the Third house has Israf with a malefic there will be either separation from or quarrels with one's siblings.
- If the lord of the Third house is a candidate for Lord of the year, and if it is either placed in or makes an applying aspect to the Third house, there will be mutual happiness between siblings.
- If a malefic lies in the Third house while the Third is neither aspected by its own lord nor by the lord of the sign which contains the Point of siblings, there will be some form of separation (illness, travel, etc.) from a sibling.
- If Mercury and Venus are strong in both the natal and annual charts, and if they are conjunct in the Third house along with a strong Jupiter, they confer happiness regarding one's relatives.
- If Mars is in one of Saturn's signs (Capricorn or Aquarius) or Mercury in a sign of Mars (Aries or Scorpio) , conjoined with or aspected by benefics while occupying the Third house, there will be mutual love between siblings. Mars in the Third house in Saturn's natal sign, if combust and devoid of strength, increases "sinful activities".
- If Mars is in the Third, unaspected by the Lord of the Third or the lord of the Sahmesh, there will be sorrow on account of one's siblings.
- If Saturn is in the Third in a sign ruled by Mars (Aries or scorpio) and conjoined with or aspected by benefics, or if Mercury is in the Third in a Mars sign under similar circumstances, there will be great happiness among siblings.
- Saturn in the Third in a Mars sign (but without the benefic aspects noted above) brings illness to a sibling.

- If the Moon and Mars are conjunct in the Third house and unrelieved by the conjunction or aspect of Jupiter, there will be quarrels with one's siblings. The same result may occur if:
- Mars is in Gemini or Virgo in the Third house (a younger, sibling is indicated here)
- Jupiter is weak in the Third house
- Saturn is in Aries or Scorpio in the Third

Fourth House Combinations (Parents)

In Tajik, the father is generally symbolized by the Tenth house and the mother by the Fourth. Chandeshwar, an old master, disagrees and lists both parents as signified by the Fourth house. Another master, Yadava, states that in order to discriminate between the father and mother we must scrutinize the Sun and Moon as well as the Fourth house. Also, there are sensitive points for both the mother and the father, which can help to clarify which parent actually appears in any given delineation.

- If the lord of the Fourth occupies the Fourth there will be happiness with respect to one's parents. The same result will occur if the lord of the Fourth is strong and has Itthashal with the lord of the First.
- If the lord of the Solar Return's Ascendant applies to the lords of the Fourth house and of the Points of the Mother and Father, then there will be happiness with respect to one's parents. But if it applies to the lord of the Eighth house and separates from malefics, then there may be danger to one's parents or they themselves may have reason for apprehension during the course of the year.
- If the lord of the natal Fourth is devoid of strength in both the natal and annual charts, it indicates that the parents of the native will suffer. If the problem is further compounded by the Point of the Mother receiving afflictions from malefics while in the fourth

house from Muntha, or by the lords of the Points of Father and Mother in combustion, then there will be "destruction" of the parents.

- If the Sun or Moon should be conjunct a malefic in the Fourth house there will be illness or trouble for the father (Sun) or mother (Moon) .
- If the lords of both the natal and annual Fourth house are conjunct Mars and Saturn and bereft of conjunction with or aspects from benefics, the native's parents will experience sorrow.

Fifth House Combinations
(Children)

- Itthashal between the lords of the First and the Fifth denotes the birth of a child.
- The Moon, Jupiter or Venus exalted in the Fifth house signifies the birth of a child.
- If the Point of Sons is in the Fifth house and aspected by benefics, there will be happiness with regard to one's children. And if the Punya Saham, aspected by benefics, is strong in the Fifth along with the lords of the First and Fifth, the result is the same.
- If Mercury and Mars conjoin in a benefic's sign in the Fifth or Eleventh, or if either of these planets as Lord of the year should occupy the Fifth, then there will be happiness in respect to one's children. But if Mercury and Mars are weak, then there may be hard times for one's children during the year in question.
- Other combinations which are unfavorable for Fifth house matters are the occupation of the annual Fifth by Saturn's natal sign, aspected by malefics, or the presence of a retrograde Mars in the annual Fifth (this placement is said to be dangerous to one's son) .

If the Moon, Jupiter or Venus occupies its sign of exaltation in the Fifth house, then the birth of a son will take place.

CHAPTER XI

THE WORLDLY GAME

In this chapter the matters related with the 10th house viz., Power, Position, Status etc. has been dealt with. We have also undertaken matters related to the 'Trik' (the 6th, 8th, and 12th houses) i.e., conflicts and quarrels, and thirdly all houses which indicate Travels. Distant Travels come under the purview of the 7th, 12th, and 9th houses and short trips fall under the 3rd house. The above matters are segregated in 4 sections, (A) General, (B) Natal-Annual Combinations, (C) Combination with the Lord of the Year, and (D) The Houses.

A. General

Power and Position

- If there is Itthashal between the Lord of the Year, the lord of the First, and the lord of the Tenth, the native will enjoy elevation of rank and obtain a high position.
- If malefics occupy the Third, Sixth and Eleventh (one or more of these houses) and benefics are in the angles and/or trines, then the effects of any other unfavorable combinations are cancelled and the native will enjoy good health, happiness, wealth, and a rise in status or renown.
- If the lords of the First and Tenth are both strong, well-placed and in Itthashal with each other, there will be a rise in status or position.
- If there is Itthashal between the lords of the First and Eleventh there will be gain of money and an increase in one's respectability among the community.

- If Muntha occupies the Third or Ninth in a benefic's sign then there will be "acts of religious merit". But if Muntha occupies a malefic's sign in one of these houses there will be "sinful conduct". (One must also examine any planets which may be conjoining or aspecting Muntha.)
- If Muntha is in the Ascendant or the Tenth house, and if either of these houses constitutes the Sun's natal sign, it confers "happiness of a kingdom". But if the Sun itself is debilitated or conjoined with malefics, it causes "imprisonment on account of the king" (i.e. political persecution of some sort) or, at worst, death.
- If the lords of the Ninth and Tenth houses are combust, debilitated, or posited in evil houses (Sixth, Eighth or Twelfth) , one's spiritual concerns as well as one's career will suffer.
- "Loss of religious merit" (i.e. falling away from the spiritual path) results if the lord of the Ninth is combust.
- "Loss of position or failure in endeavor" results if the lord of the Tenth is combust (although one should look to other combinations for confirmation on this dictum).

Because the Sun is the significator of fame and position, it is the single most important planet for assessing issues of worldly renown.

- The Sun conjunct Muntha in the First or Tenth brings promotion and happiness.
- If the Sun is in Libra conjunct malefics the native may suffer at the hands of the government.
- If Mars and the Sun are conjunct in a diurnal annual chart the native has reason to fear trouble from the government.
- If the Sun, Jupiter and Venus are in mutual Itthashal there will be a rise in status, position, renown, and financial prosperity.
- Mercury afflicted by malefics makes for a troublesome journey. And if *natal* Mercury fulfills all the conditions

relevant to candidacy for lordship over the year as well as falling in one of Saturn's signs in the annual chart while conjoining a malefic, travel is undertaken due to quarrels with an enemy.

- Jupiter as a candidate for Lord of the Year, if conjunct a malefic in one of Saturn's signs, signifies a long journey. We may also say that, in general, Jupiter aspected by malefics indicates a troublesome journey.
- Jupiter rising in conjunction with Mercury or Mars brings fame and military victories.
- If Jupiter or the Seventh house lord are in the First house, unaspected by malefics, and enjoying friendly aspects from benefics, then the native will overcome all obstacles and gain money, happiness, and status. During Jupiter's dasha there will be the chance for government favor.
- If Saturn is in the Seventh the native will be abused or reprimanded; he is likely to become involved in a scandal.

Conflicts and Quarrels

- The Sun in the Sixth, Eighth or Twelfth, afflicted by malefics and placed in a quadruped sign (Aries, Taurus, Leo, the latter half of Sagttarius and the first half of Capricorn), provokes quarrels with "servants or subordinates" (employees in a modern context) .
- If the lord of the First is weak, combust and conjunct a malefic, there will be quarrels with one's spouse or lovers or because of them.
- If the Sun is in the Second and Mars in the Twelfth there will be trouble and hardships due to competition.

Travels

- There will be sudden traveling if the lords of the First form an itthashal with the lord of the 9th or 3rd. If the light is translated from the First house lord to that of the Ninth, then the journey will be worrisome.

- If there is Itthashal between the First house and the Lord of the Year or the dispositor of Muntha, a similar (worrisome) situation takes place.
- If Mars is in the ninth position from Jupiter, there will be auspicious travels leading to success.
- When Muntha is in the Seventh house and the Moon strong in the Ninth, one will travel abroad. But if the Moon is aspected by malefics, the journey will be troublesome.
- The Moon, when posited in the seventh house from Muntha in its own sign or in exaltation (i.e. Cancer or Taurus) will bring foreign travel. But if it is aspected by malefics there will be trouble on the journey.

B. Natal-Annual Combinations

Power and position

- Note the sign of the Tenth house lord in the birth chart. If this sign occupies a favorable house in the annual chart, and if its own lord is placed there in conjunction with or aspected by benefics, then there will be a rise in status. But if the Tenth lord's natal sign falls in an evil house in the annual chart, tenanted by weak malefics and receiving inimical aspects from malefics, then one's professional status will suffer.
- If the lord of the natal Tenth is strong in the birth chart but weak in the Solar Return, there will be a setback in one's career.
- If the lord of the natal First or Ninth occupies the Tenth house in both the natal chart and the Solar Return while conjunction with or receiving aspects from benefics in the Solar Return, there will be a rise in position.
- If the Sun rules the natal Tenth, occupies the annual Tenth, and has Itthashal with the lord of the annual Ascendant, then there will be a rise in status according to the strength of the planets.

- If a strong Moon occupies the annual Tenth in the natal sign of Mars, it causes a beneficial change in one's position or place.
- If Mars is combust and conjoined with or aspected by malefics while occupying the sign of natal Saturn in the Third or Ninth house of the annual chart, there will be unethical conduct and a consequent loss of prestige.
- Mars in the annual Tenth house, aspecting Muntha and occupying Saturn's natal sign, indicates problems with the government and loss of wealth due to the native's own misconduct.

Conflicts and Quarrels

- If Jupiter occupies the natal Eighth and fails to become eligible for Lord of the Year, there will be quarrels during that year. But if such a Jupiter also receives an aspect from Venus in the Solar Return chart, the native will be victorious against all his adversaries or competitors.

The following group of combinations is much more powerful if the ruler of the natal Ascendant becomes a candidate for Lord of the Year.

- If the Moon becomes eligible for lordship over the year and rules the natal First house, then falls in the same sign in the Solar Return which Saturn occupied in the natal chart while at the same time suffering affliction from malefics, there will be quarrels.
- If the Moon rules the natal Ascendant, occupies the natal sign of Mercury(in the annual chart), and suffers affliction from malefics, the native will go abroad as the result of a quarrel.
- If Jupiter rules the natal Ascendant and occupies (in the annual chart) the sign tenanted by natal Mars, there will be quarrels.

Travels

- If either the Moon or Jupiter occupies Saturn's natal sign in the Ninth house of the Solar Return chart, there will be a long journey.
- If Mars occupies Jupiter's natal sign in the Ninth house of the Solar Return there will be gainful traveling, augmentation of one's wealth, and an "increase in the number of servants" (i.e. employees) .
- If Mars is in the First house in the sign occupied by natal Mercury and aspected by the lord of the Ascendant, one's travels will bring joy. If Mars in strength occupies its own natal house and aspects the Ascendant, the same results may be expected.
- If Mars occupies the annual Ninth house and is in his own sign in the birth chart as well as the Solar Return, there will be "beneficial travel".
- If Mercury rules the natal Ascendant and occupies Saturn's natal sign while suffering conjunction (in the annual chart) with a malefic, then the native will be forced to travel due to quarrels with his enemies.

C. Combinations with the Lord of the Year

Power and position

- If the Lord of the Year is strong (i.e. if it obtains more than 10 Panchavargyabala units) and in the Tenth, there will be a rise in status and renown along with gain of wealth and comforts. In fact, such a Lord of the Year in any of the other angular houses will bring a similar gain in comforts and property, though perhaps without the gain in status.
- If the Lord of the Year occupies the same sign as the Point of Political Authority and has Itthashal with the Sun a very "exalted" position is attained.
- If the Sun as Lord of the Year is strong in the Fourth house, the native will regain a job or position he had previously relinquished, or recover former property.

- If the Sun in exaltation or in Leo becomes Lord of the Year and occupies the Tenth house, there will be gains from the king.
- If the Sun as Lord of the Year is strong in the Eleventh, there will be friendship with highly placed people, especially politicians or people in the government.
- If Mars in exaltation or in its own sign becomes Lord of the Year and occupies the Tenth there will be gains from one's own valor and courage.

Mercury in exaltation or its own sign as Lord of the Year in the Tenth brings gains through Ayurveda (medicine), Jyotish (astrology), poetry or sculpture.

Jupiter or Saturn in exaltation or their own signs, occupying the Tenth house as Lord of the Year, bring good health and gain of money.

- If Saturn or the Sun is Lord of the Year and occupies the Third or Ninth there will be "religious performances" during the year. (In the content of Western society, we might say that the native will be active in his or her church.) But if Saturn is combust or either Saturn or the Sun is afflicted by malefics, the native's "speech is blasphemous and he indulges in sinful conduct."
- If Mars is Lord of the Year and conjunct Saturn in the Tenth, then the classical texts affirm that there will be "loss of horses".

Travels

Any time the Lord of the Year is strong, not conjoined with a malefic, and placed in an angular house, there will be travel. (Note: We believe that the possibilities for travel increase if the sign is a cardinal one.) If Mars is in this condition and the lord of the Tenth house is strong, then the native may lead an army or travel on a military expedition. If Mars or Mercury as Year Lord is conjunct Jupiter and free of combustion, then the native will be victorious in his military endeavors. (Note: This judgment was far more applicable in medieval times, when each chieftain or lord maintained his own army.)

The following combinations specify the effects of various planets when they occupy the Third or Ninth house as Lord of the Year. Note that if the planet in question is either weak or afflicted, one's travels will be neither comfortable nor conducive to gain.

Sun: If the Sun as Lord of the Year occupies the Third or Ninth and has Kamboola Yoga with another planet, there will be happiness during travel. The Sun in the same houses, if ineligible to become Lord of the Year, signifies that the native travels on another's errand.

Mars: If a strong Mars as Lord of the Year occupies the Third or Ninth and remains free of conjunction with or aspects from malefics, then one's travels will be long and beneficial and money will be earned thereby. If it is weak and posited in the Ninth there will be foreign travel, though there will also be some sorrow concerning being separated from one's relatives.

Mercury: If Mercury as Lord of the Year occupies the Third or Ninth there will be travel or pilgrimage, but if Mercury is retrograde there will be a great deal of inconvenience and/or loss in one's travels.

Jupiter: If Jupiter is strong as Lord of the Year and occupies the Third or Ninth, one will travel "on pilgrimage".

Venus: If Venus as Lord of the Year occupies the Third or Ninth there will be happiness and success in travel. But if Venus is combust or retrograde there will be troubles, losses and defeat in travel.

Saturn: If Saturn becomes or aspires to become Lord of the Year, its position in the Ninth (or Third) increases one's religious fervor. But if Saturn is combust or debilitated, the native "abuses religion" and indulges in "sinful deeds".

D. The Houses

Power and Position (Tenth House Combinations)

- A strong Sun in Leo in the Tenth brings government patronage and the chance to obtain a good professional position.
- If the Sun rules the natal Tenth, occupies the annual Tenth, and applies to the Ascendant lord, it gives "gain of kingdom" according to its strength.
- The Sun in the Tenth in Saturn's natal sign brings punishment from the government on account of one's misdeeds as well as loss of wealth, but Jupiter in the same situation brings gain of wealth in a "pure" and systematic manner.
- If the lord of the Tenth and the dispositor of the Point of Action are conjoined with or aspected by malefics while one or more malefics occupy or aspect the Tenth house itself, then there will be frustration and failure in one's work.

Conflicts and Quarrels (Sixth House Combinations)

- Malefics in the Sixth house, especially if they are strong, help one to annihilate one's enemies.
- If the lords of the First and Sixth houses apply to each other with a friendly aspect, there may be a compromise with the opposing party in a litigation.
- Benefics in the Sixth house cause trouble and enmity, especially if they are weak.

Travel (Ninth House Combinations)

- If the lord of the Ascendant applies to the lord of the Third or Ninth, the journey one desires will take place. (The same inference should be drawn if there is Itthashal between the Ascendant lord and Year Lord or between the Ascendant lord and Muntha's dispositor.) If the lord of the Ascendant and the lord of the Ninth both apply to each other, the journey will be excellent and free of worries.

- If Mars is in a Jupiter sign (Sagittarius or pisces) in the Ninth house, one's travels will bring prosperity.
- Jupiter in the Ninth confers "the company of kings" and "gain of wealth" when one journeys abroad.
- If Saturn occupies the Ninth house but fails to become a candidate for Lord of the Year, traveling will prove to be harmful and inauspicious.

This concludes our study of Solar Returns. Let the careful student remember to exercise his knowledge of Jyotish in general, and thus always correlate the transits of the planets with the indications of the Solar Return.

CHAPTER XII

HORARY ASTROLOGY

We have mentioned Horary Astrology at many places in the book. However we would like to add that the principles of the Solar Return Chart are the same as the principles of Horory Astrology. However, these are not identical twins and certain differences do exist. We have so far covered up the various matters related to the Solar Return Chart.

However what happens if there is no horoscope or the time of birth is not known? In that case as well as when pin-point replies are needed then and there, the Horary Chart is exactly the thing that is needed. The chart is based on the time of calculation when a querent asks a question or when one goes to meet an Astrologer. The method of calculation will be the same as it is for the Solar Return chart. We have in this chapter given some interesting questions which are generally being asked from Astrologers. The readers can think up or better write down a question, note the time of it, and calculate the chart on their own and get the reply to arrive at right decisions.

We now give below some of the questions and how they should be dealt with:

Special Horary Questions

1. Buy & Sell

In the horary chart, the lord of the Ascendant is buyer and Lord of the 11th house is the seller. If some one ask a question, "when should I buy a particular thing?". In this case if the Ist house is comparatively stronger then the 11th house then the buyer will benefit.

If the question is "when should I sell?" In this matter if the 11th house is the stronger of the two then he should be advised to sell.

2. Rumours

If the question is concerning a rumour. Then benefic planets in angles, and Moon, ascendant and the ascendant lord all the three of them are conjoined with or aspected by benefics then the rumour should be taken as *true* and good. However if malefics are in the above positions then the rumour is true and scandalous. If the Ascendant Lord is retrograde or about to become retrograde then the rumour is not true.

3. Question Related to Gains

If the lord of the 1st and 8th houses are in the 8th house and in the same decanate, then the native will have definite gains. Similar judgement should be arrived at for all the 12 houses, from the Dreshkana (Decanate), irrespective of the other yogas.

If in a horary chart, the Ascendant has more benefic sub divisions, then irrespective of other houses and planets, good results should be predicted. The lords of the 1st and 11th, both indicate gains and so their yoga is always beneficial. If in the above yoga, Moon also joins in then excellent results should be predicted. This is so because without support from the Moon full realization of other yogas can not be attained.

If there is an application between the lords of the 1st and the 10th houses then improvement in work and status should be predicted. It is also an indication of good time in the Company of one's father.

If there is a yoga involving the lord of Ascendant (or lord of the Prasana Horoscope) on one side and on the other side the lord of the 9th house, then increase in spiritual life as well as a wonderful and unique times should be predicted.

Similar judgement should be made for other houses when the lords of that house is in a yoga with the lord of the Ascendant.

If the lord of the 1st house is in the 6th house, then one's own soul becomes one's enemy (or enmity with one's own son); if in the horary chart, the lord of the Ascendant is all alone (not even aspected by any planet) then it can cause death and anguish; in the 12th house it causes constant losses and the native is the cause of his own downfall.

4. Mental or Silent Question

A. We will point out the method as to how the old masters used to decipher the question of the visitor without any words being uttered.

(a) If the Lord of the horary chart or Moon is
   i. in own Navansha and
   ii. posited in the 1st, 5th or 9th house and
   iii. aspects its own Navansha, then the question is related to metals':

(b) If it aspects navansha other than its own and condition (i) and (ii) above are fulfilled then the question would be related to a living being.

(c) If the lord of the Ascendant or Moon
   i. is in a navansha other than its own
   ii. also aspect navansha other than its own.
   iii. is situated in 1st or 9th house then the question is related to a root.

(d) If the Ascendant falls in an odd sign (1, 3, 5, 7, 9, 11); then (i) the question is related to metals if the navansha is the 1st, 4th, 7th) ; (ii) to living beings if the 2nd, 5th and 8th Navansha is rising; or (iii) to root if the 3rd, 6th or 9th Navansha rises.

(e) If the Ascendant is an even sign (2, 4, 6, 8, 10 or 12) then the question is related to a:

i. living being if the 1st, 4th and 7th Navansha rises
ii. root if the 2nd, 5th or 8th Navansha is rising, or
iii. Metals if the 3rd, 6th or 9th Navansha rises.

This is in short the interpretation of a silent question.

B. *According to Bhattotphal*
Sun or Mars endowed with strength in an angle indicate, question related to Metals; Mercury or Saturn in such position related to Root; and Moon, Jupiter, or Venus in the position mentioned above, indicates the question to be related to a 'living being'.

C. If Mars or Sun is posited in or aspects the Ascendant which is Aries, Scorpio or Leo, then the question relates to 'Metals'.
If Mercury or Saturn both associated with the Ascendant which is Gemini, Aquarius or Virgo then the question relates to 'root'; and if Moon Jupiter or Venus aspect or posited in the Ascendant which is Taurus, Libra, Capricorn, Pisces, Sagittarius or Cancer then the question is related to a Living Being.

D. In an elaborate Astrological book "Gyan Prakash", it is stated that whichever is stronger out of the lords of the 1st or 11th house, the position of Moon in a house as counted from that lord, will indicate the question related to that house viz., if conjoined with the lord (of 1st or 11th) then the question is related to self, in the 2nd house wealth, in the 6th house disease or related to job etc.
Another method is that the position of the Ascendant lord from the Moon, which is endowed with full strength, will give an indication as to the house to which the question is related to.

5. *What should be Judged from which House*

i. If a question relates to self, body, mental anxiety etc. then planets posited in the 1st house should be considered.

ii. Planets in the 3rd house will be considered if the question relates to brother / sister, kinsmen.
iii. Planets in the 5th house should be taken into account for question related to sons, education, and sudden gains.
iv. From the 4th house, all questions pertaining to mother to be considered.
v. From the 6th house, matters related to enemies.
vi. From the 7th house all matters and questions related to wife.
vii. From the 8th house, conjugal bliss, relationship with spouse, inheritance should be considered.
viii. From the 9th house, questions related to religion and fortunes should be deciphered.
ix. From the 10th, all questions regarding father, promotion, and status should be judged.
x. Interpretation regarding friends and enemies will be judged according to the strength of the friends and enemies of the lord of Navansha (of the Ascendant).

A. Questions related to servants, animals:

If the lord of the Ascendant and Moon are in the 6th house and they (or one of them at least) form an application with the lord of the 6th than gains of servants and animals should be judged.

In this case lord of the 1st and Ascendant represent the native and the lord of the 7th and 7th house, the giver. An application in between the two of them indicates gains.

Q. Whether this girl is of good character?

In these types of questions if the three viz., Moon, Ascendant and the lord of the Ascendant are in fixed house than the girl is of good character. If all the three are in moveable signs than her character should be judged to be fickle; if they are in dual signs than only a little bit of fickleness due to rumours.

B. If both the Moon and Mars are in moveable and dual signs than she has secret alliance with other than her husband.

If both the Saturn and Moon are in the Ascendant* than she has other relationship which will also come to light.

If Mars and Saturn are in angles, or Venus is in Scorpio and is aspected by Moon, or Venus is in Scorpio as also in the decanate of Scorpio, then she is definitely not pure.

Q. If a question is related to the character of a woman.

a. If Moon and the lord of the Ascendant are within 2 degree orb and applies to Mars than the woman in question is involved with a man other than her husband in her place of residence.
b. If Mars is also in Aries or Scorpio in the above application than she visits the house of the man involved.
c. If Moon and the lord of the Ascendant are in 2° orbs and applies to Sun than she is involved with a person who is a Government Servant/ official.
d. If in the above case they apply to an afflicted Mercury than she is in love with a Scribe (Writer, author, Journalist).
e. If Venus is in own sign, and Moon and the lord of the Ascendant (in the same degree) apply to it, than she is in love with another woman. When these combinations take place than only a woman should be judged.
f. If Moon or the Ascendant lord separates from Mars than she is involved with some one other than her husband.

The aspect of different planets will put a stop to the relationships. If Jupiter aspects than by her son or due to the fear of the son.

---

* Ascendant in this chapter should be read as the Ascendant in a horary chart unless otherwise stated.

If Sun aspects than due to punishment from the rulers

If Venus aspects than due to fear of other woman residing in the neighbourhood.

If Venus and Mercury from one sign aspect then the woman will abandon the relationship on account of being humiliated.

Many times questions are asked related to the theft of wealth and other articles.

a. If there is an exchange between the lords of the 1st and 7th or they are posited in the 7th house and from an application then lost wealth will be recovered.
b. If lords of the 7th and Ascendant are placed in the Ascendant and are in application than the thief returns the stolen wealth.
c. If Sun is in the 1st house or Sun and Moon are in the 7th house and Moon is combust than the lost money is not recovered.

The location of the thief

d. If the lords of the Ascendant and 10th houses apply, then it should be understood that the thief has left the city .
e. If Moon and the lord of the 7th house are both combust than the thief is apprehended together with the stolen wealth.
f. If the lord of the 7th house is in an angle than the thief is in the city. In any other house, then the thief is out of town.
g. If the lord of the 7th house, applies to the lord of the 3rd or the 9th house than the thief will be found in another city. In this case by going to another city, the money will be recovered.
h. If the lords of the first and 10th are applying than the stolen wealth will be recovered by the police or a Government Agency.

i. If Moon is posited in the Ascendant or 10th house and is also applying with a benefic than the stolen material will be recovered.
j. If the Sun and other benefic aspect the Ascendant and Moon in a friendly manner forms a benefic aspect (sextile or trine), then the recovery should be surmised.

Where the lost wealth or article can be found?

a. If there is an exchange between the lords of the 1st and 7th or if they apply to each other than the lost money will be found in the house itself.
b. If Moon is in the 1st, 10th, 7th or 4th house than the lost money is in the East, South, West or North direction respectively.
c. If Moon is not in angle but within 45 degrees of the nearest angle then the direction of wealth should be taken to be in the direction of that angle as mentioned in (b).
d. According to the nature of the element of the Ascendant viz., Fire, Earth, Air or Water the money should be understood to be in the East, South, West or North.
e. In all questions related to theft:
   i. Seventh house represents the thief.
   ii. Fourth indicates the place of wealth
   iii. Ascendant represents the wealth and the Moon signifies the native (the person asking the question).
f. Calculate the 'Pars-fortuna' (Punya Saham) of the horary chart and if it is not afflicted by malefic then the thief is a new thief who did not commit theft before.
   If however the lord of the 7th house is unaspected by malefic than the thief is a professional who has committed theft earlier.
   If Mars applies to the lord of the 7th house than the thief has been convicted before.

g. The age of the thief should be judged according to the planet in the Ascendant. Venus indicate a young person; Mercury - a child; Jupiter - a middle aged; Mars - a grownup person; Saturn - an older or old person; Sun - a very old person.

If there is no planet in the Ascendant then the location of Sun between 1 and 10 - indicate a child; between 10 and 7 - a young person; between 7th and 4th then a middle aged person; and between 4th and I then a very old, aged person should be understood.

The gender of the thief will be known according to the lord of the 7th house. If it is a male than the thief will be a man otherwise a woman.

The above matter related to the Horary Chart should be analysed with care and no hasty judgement should be drawn. The background of the person, country and times should be considered appropriately.

Sometimes a Question is asked if *I move to another city would I gain* ?

In this type of questions, if the lord of the 2nd is retrograde than it is better not to move or change. Success will not come. If the 2nd lord is fast in motion (above average) than the change will be for a long duration and without any accomplishment.

If lord of the 2nd is in the 3rd or 9th house than the work is accomplished at an early date and so change should be undertaken which will be of a short duration.

If the lord of the 2nd is posited in the Ascendant, 10th or 11th house then good result will ensue due to moving over to another city. However if the 2nd lord with a malefic is in the 7th house than obstacles will come on the way and if these are (7th lord and a malefic) in the 4th house than quarrels will take place due to change.

Similar results should be judged if the question relates to moving over to a new place of residence.

1. If the lord of sign in which the lord of the Ascendant is posited goes to the trik i.e., 6th, 8th, or 12th house than frustration in the work should be judged.
2. Sometimes a question is asked *can I trust my employee?*

In this type of question if the lords of the 1st and 7th houses apply to each other and also get support from the Moon viz., Kambool Yoga then the employee could be trusted. If there is an application between the two from a friendly positions (sextile, trine) then also the employee should be judged to be trustworthy.

Q. Will I lose my job?

In this, the lords of the 1st and 10th houses should be in one sign and a slow moving planet should be in angle, then there would be no loss of job and it would continue. If however the slow moving planet is retrograde or is about to become retrograde then the job will be terminated.

If there is Kamboola yoga then gain of a new job or regaining of the same work should be judged.

An Israf between the lords of the 1st on one side and the lord of the 10th or 6th house on the other side indicate loss of job due to being asked to resign by the employer or due to leaving it for personal reasons, respectively.

Q. Will I travel?

In this question look if benefics are in the 4th or 10th houses, then travel plans will be cancelled. If however Malefics are posited in the 4th or the 10th house then the answer is *Yes.*

Q. Shall I be able to marry a particular person ?

The reply to this question will be in the affirmative, if the lord of Ascendant or Moon (if a woman then Sun instead of the Moon), is in Itthashal (application) with the lord of the 7th house, who should be powerful and dignified in benefic Vargas, and should occupy the 1st, the 10th or the 11th house.

If the above application is from a friendly house and no other planet is creating frustration or the Significators do not become retrograde before the application is completed then good results should be expected.

An inimical aspect viz., square or opposition will also indicate success but with efforts (difficulties).

Q. What part the person will be whom I marry?

If the lord of the 7th house is in the 9th then the perosn will marry a stranger. If the lord of the 1st and 7th houses are in one house, sign or in one quarter then one marries near to one's own residence (near birth place).

Consider the sign of the 7th house, and the quarter of the Heaven, the lord of the 7th house is in, then judge according to the majority of indications. The sign should be preferred compared to the quarter of the heaven.

Q. Whether this child is mine?

In such cases observe the lord of the Ascendant and Moon (significators of the querrent); then observe the sign of the 11th house and its lord which signify the child (or conception). If these significators aspect one another by sextile and trines with reception or not then the child (or conception) is legitimate. If the lord of the Ascendant or Moon are in the 5th house then also the child is a legitimate child.

However if Saturn, Mars or Mercury behold the lord of the 5th house or 5th house with inimical aspect, there is some suspicion as to the fatherhood.

Q. Should I enter into partnership?

In this case if good planets are in the 1st and 7th house, the partnership will take place and will last.

If the lord of the second house is stronger than the lord of the 8th house then the querent will benefit more or vice versa.

Q. Will I be successful in my litigation?

If Jupiter and Sun goes to the 7th house then success should be judged. The lord of the Ascendant or Moon should apply to the lord of the 7th by sextile or trine then out of court settlement will take place.

Q. What work should I do?

Consider the lords of the Ascendant and 10th house, the Moon as well as the placement of Mars and Venus. Calculate the strength of the planets (Panchvargyabala). The strongest planet and its sign will indicate the type of work one should be engaged in.

The placement of the strongest planet indicates the work one should undertake. These will vary according as the planet goes to different signs (mentioned below). The indication will be strongest if the signifying planet is also in the 10th house.

Aries

Cattle-dealer; Connected with Vehicle manufacturing; Veterinary doctor, dealer of horses etc.

Taurus

Gardening; Work connected with flowers, dealers in Grains; Women's Clothing, Tailors, Assistants.

Gemini

Writer, Clerks, Professor, Bailiff; or a Painter, Surveyor; Astronomer, Astrologer.

Cancer

Success in various types of occupation, Work connected with Sea, Navy, Water, all types of liquids, Caretaker, Politician, a dealer of animals; Travelling and with Travel Industry.

Leo

Driver, Trainer of horses, Watchmaker, Huntsman, any trade connected with fire, own work or business is better.

Virgo

Good Secretary; a middlemen; Cook, dealer in food; Connected with hotel industry; accountant; printer, publisher, a good Astrologer, an excellent politician, actor.

Libra

Poet, Orator, Judge, Lawyer; Singer, Musician, Manufacturer of Silk.

Scorpio

A good Surgeon, Medicine dealer, Chemist, a Butcher, a Detective, Electrician, Founder, A Goldsmith or dealer in arms and ammunition.

Sagittarius

Pandit, Padri, Spiritual person or a Sportsman, a good Player. A cook.

Capricorn

Farmer, dealer in wool, a leader, money lender.

Aquarius

Head of a charitable institution, Computer genius, Carpenter, Painter, Success in work connected with import-export.

Pisces

Good Jester, Singer, Playboy, brewer, fishmonger.

The judgement regarding the type of work should be taken after blending all the factors together.

APPENDIX

Calculation of the House Divisions

The system of *House Division* followed in the *Tajik* is that of Shripati or Keshava. This is the same as the Western system known as Porphyry's, except for the fact that Hindu astrology defines a *cusp* as the *midpoint* of a house rather than its border or boundary, as in the West. *Tajik*, in distinction to other branches of Hindu astrology, lays a great emphasis on house positions, house boundaries, and the placement of planets in houses.

In order to illustrate the calculation of house according to the Shripati system we shall use a different example chart. In this example the Ascendant or Lagna is 6 degrees 54'0" Cancer (3S–06–54–00), and the Meridian or Midheaven is 29° degrees 27' 0" Pisces (11S–29°-27'–00'). The formula for finding the house cusps and midpoints is:

a. Subtract the longitude of the Midheaven from that of the Ascendant
b. Divide the remainder by 6
c. Add this quotient to the longitude of the Midheaven
d. Add this quotient again to the total until the degree of the Ascendant is reached

Using our example chart, the procedure would be as follows:

a. 03S–06°–54'–00"
   <u>11S–29°–27'–00"</u>
   03 –07°–27'–00"=97°–27'–00"
b. (97°–27'–00") divided by 6=16°–14'–30" c and d)

X Cusp (M.C.)   11–29°–27'–00"
                     <u>16–14–30</u>

Midpoint	00–15–41–30
	16–14–30
XI Cusp	01–01–56–00
	16–14–30
Midpoint	01–18–10–30
	16–14–30
XII Cusp	02–04–25–00
	16–14–30
Midpoint	02–20–39–30
	16–14–30
Ascendant	03–06–54–00

Now add six signs to each of the values above in order to derive the cusps and midpoints for the Fourth, Fifth, and Sixth house.

Subtract our basic quotient (16–14–30) form 30 degrees (13–45–30) and add this to the Ascendant so as to derive the midpoint of the First house, then the cusps and midpoints for the Second and Third houses.

Then add six signs to each of those values in order to derive the cusps and midpoints for the Seventh, Eighth, and Ninth houses.

	I	MP	II	MP	III	MP	IV	MP
Sign	3	3	4	4	5	5	5	6
Degrees	6	20	4	18	1	15	29	15
Minutes	54	39	25	10	56	41	27	41
Seconds	00	30	00	30	00	30	00	30.

	V	MP	VI	MP	VII	MP	VIII	MP
Sign	7	7	8	8	9	9	10	10
Degrees	1	18	4	20	6	20	4	18
Minutes	56	10	25	39	54	39	25	10
Seconds	00	30	00	30	00	30	00	30

	IX	MP	X	MP	XI	MP	XII	MP
Sign	11	11	11	00	01	01	02	02
Degrees	01	15	29	15	01	18	04	20
Minutes	56	41	27	41	56	10	25	39
Seconds	00	30	00	30	00	30	00	30

The following Table is adopted from the Lahiri's Ephemeris. It gives an easy method to work out the balance of the Mahadasha from the longitude of the Moon. In the first column, longitude of Moon is given. In the rows above, the names of the Zodiacal Signs to which the column below pertains to, are indicated. By combining the two we shall get the balance of Dasha at birth. For example if Moon is in Cancer at 3°–40' and then we look to the first column at 3° —40' and then we look to the 5th column under Cancer, and it gives us the balance of Saturn as 18 years 6 months 9 days at birth. In subsequent pages (3rd to 9th page) the Antardashas of Planets are given in Tabular form.

Table of Balance of Vimshottari Dasha and Antar-dasha

Balance of Vimshottari Dasha by Longitude of Moon

Long. of Moon		*Moon in Aries Leo, Sagittarius*				*Moon in Taurus Virgo, Cap.*				*Moon in Gemini Libra, Aquarius*				*Moon in Cancer Scorpio, Pisces*			
°	'		Y	M	D		Y	M	D		Y	M	D		Y	M	D
0	0	Ketu	7	0	0	Sun	4	6	0	Mars	3	6	0	Jup.	4	0	0
0	20		6	9	27		4	4	6		3	3	27		3	7	6
0	40		6	7	24		4	2	12		3	1	24		3	2	12
1	0		6	5	21		4	0	18		2	11	21		2	9	18
1	20		6	3	18		3	10	24		2	9	18		2	4	24
1	40		6	1	15		3	9	0		2	7	15		2	0	0
2	0		5	11	12		3	7	6		2	5	12		1	7	6
2	20		5	9	9		3	5	12		2	3	9		1	2	12
2	40		5	7	6		3	3	18		2	1	6		0	9	18
3	0		5	5	3		3	1	24		1	11	3		0	4	24
3	20		5	3	0		3	0	0		1	9	0	Saturn	19	0	0
3	40		5	0	27		2	10	6		1	6	27		18	6	9
4	0		4	10	24		2	8	12		1	4	24		18	0	18
4	20		4	8	21		2	6	18		1	2	21		17	6	27
4	40		4	6	18		2	4	24		1	0	18		17	1	6
5	0		4	4	15		2	3	0		0	10	15		16	7	15
5	20		4	2	12		2	1	6		0	8	12		16	1	24
5	40		4	0	9		1	11	12		0	6	9		15	8	3
6	0		3	10	6		1	9	18		0	4	6		15	2	12
6	20		3	8	3		1	7	24		0	2	3		14	8	21

Long. of Moon		*Moon in Aries Leo, Sagittarius*				*Moon in Taurus Virgo, Cap.*				*Moon in Gemini Libra, Aquarius*				*Moon in Cancer Scorpio, Pisces*			
°	'		Y	M	D		Y	M	D		Y	M	D		Y	M	D
6	40		3	6	0		1	6	0	Rahu	18	0	0		14	3	0
7	0		3	3	27		1	4	6		17	6	18		13	9	9
7	20		3	1	24		1	2	12		17	1	6		13	3	18
7	40		2	11	21		1	0	18		16	7	24		12	9	27
8	0		2	9	18		0	10	24		16	2	12		12	4	6
8	20		2	7	15		0	9	0		15	9	0		11	10	15
8	40		2	5	12		0	7	6		15	3	18		11	4	24
9	0		2	3	9		0	5	12		14	10	6		10	11	3
9	20		2	1	6		0	3	18		14	4	24		10	5	12
9	40		1	11	3		0	1	24		13	11	12		9	11	21
10	0		1	9	0	Moon	10	0	0		13	6	0		9	6	0
10	20		1	6	27		9	9	0		13	0	18		9	0	9
10	40		1	4	24		9	6	0		12	7	6		8	6	18
11	0		1	2	21		9	3	0		12	1	24		8	0	27
11	20		1	0	18		9	0	0		11	8	12		7	7	6
11	40		0	10	15		8	9	0		11	3	0		7	1	15
12	0		0	8	12		8	6	0		10	9	18		6	7	24
12	20		0	6	9		8	3	0		10	4	6		6	2	3
12	40		0	4	6		8	0	0		9	10	24		5	8	12
13	0		0	2	3		7	9	0		9	5	12		5	2	21
13	20	Venus	20	0	0		7	6	0		9	0	0		4	9	0
13	40		19	6	0		7	3	0		8	6	18		4	3	9
14	0		19	0	0		7	0	0		8	1	6		3	9	18
14	20		18	6	0		6	9	0		7	7	24		3	3	27
14	40		18	0	0		6	6	0		7	2	12		2	10	6
15	0		17	6	0		6	3	0		6	9	0		2	4	15
15	20		17	0	0		6	0	0		6	3	18		1	10	24
15	40		16	6	0		5	9	0		5	10	6		1	5	3
16	0		16	0	0		5	6	0		5	4	24		0	11	12
16	20		15	6	0		5	3	0		4	11	12		0	5	21
16	40		15	0	0		5	0	0		4	6	0	Merc.	17	0	0
17	0		14	6	0		4	9	0		4	0	18		16	6	27
17	20		14	0	0		4	6	0		3	7	6		16	1	24
17	40		13	6	0		4	3	0		3	1	24		15	8	21
18	0		13	0	0		4	0	0		2	8	12		15	3	18
18	20		12	6	0		3	9	0		2	3	0		14	10	15
18	40		12	0	0		3	6	0		1	9	18		14	5	12
19	0		11	6	0		3	3	0		1	4	6		14	0	9

Long. of Moon		*Moon in Aries Leo, Sagittarius*				*Moon in Taurus Virgo, Cap.*				*Moon in Gemini Libra, Aquarius*				*Moon in Cancer Scorpio, Pisces*			
°			Y	M	D		Y	M	D		Y	M	D		Y	M	D
19	0	Venus	11	6	0	Moon	3	3	0	Rahu	1	4	6	Merc.	14	0	9
19	20		11	0	0		3	0	0		0	10	24		13	7	6
19	40		10	6	0		2	9	0		0	5	12		13	2	3
20	0		10	0	0		2	6	0	Jupiter	16	0	0		12	9	0
20	20		9	6	0		2	3	0		15	7	6		12	3	27
20	40		9	0	0		2	0	0		15	2	12		11	10	24
21	0		8	6	0		1	9	0		14	9	18		11	5	21
21	20		8	0	0		1	6	0		14	4	24		11	0	18
21	40		7	6	0		1	3	0		14	0	0		10	7	15
22	0		7	0	0		1	0	0		13	7	6		10	2	12
22	20		6	6	0		0	9	0		13	2	12		9	9	9
22	40		6	0	0		0	6	0		12	9	18		9	4	6
23	0		5	6	0		0	3	0		12	4	24		8	11	3
23	20		5	0	0	Mars	7	0	0		12	0	0		8	6	0
23	40		4	6	0		6	9	27		11	7	6		8	0	27
24	0		4	0	0		6	7	24		11	2	12		7	7	24
24	20		3	6	0		6	5	21		10	9	18		7	2	21
24	40		3	0	0		6	3	18		10	4	24		6	9	18
25	0		2	6	0		6	1	15		10	0	0		6	4	15
25	20		2	0	0		5	11	12		9	7	6		5	11	12
25	40		1	6	0		5	9	9		9	2	12		5	6	9
26	0		1	0	0		5	7	6		8	9	18		5	1	6
26	20		0	6	0		5	5	3		8	4	24		4	8	3
26	40	Sun	6	0	0		5	3	0		8	0	0		4	3	0
27	0		5	10	6		5	0	27		7	7	6		3	9	27
27	20		5	8	12		4	10	24		7	2	12		3	4	24
27	40		5	6	18		4	8	21		6	9	18		2	11	21
28	0		5	4	24		4	6	18		6	4	24		2	6	18
28	20		5	3	0		4	4	15		6	0	0		2	1	15
28	40		5	1	6		4	2	12		5	7	6		1	8	12
29	0		4	11	12		4	0	9		5	2	12		1	3	9
29	20		4	9	18		3	10	6		4	9	18		0	10	6
29	40		4	7	24		3	8	3		4	4	24		0	5	3
30	0		4	6	0		3	6	0		4	0	0		0	0	0

Proportional Parts for Dasha of Planets

(To be subtracted from the balance of *dasha* for increase by minutes of the longitude of Moon)

	Ketu (7y)	*Venus (20y)*	*Sun (6y)*	*Moon (10y)*	*Mars (7y)*	*Rahu (18y)*	*Jupiter (16y)*	*Saturn (19y)*	*Merc. (17y)*	
	m d	*m d*	*m d*	*m d*	*m d*	*m d*	*m d*	*m d*	*m d*	
1	0 3	0 9	0 3	0 5	0 3	0 8	0 7	0 9	0 8	1
2	0 6	0 18	0 5	0 9	0 6	0 16	0 14	0 17	0 15	2
3	0 9	0 27	0 8	0 14	0 9	0 24	0 22	0 26	0 23	3
4	0 13	1 6	0 11	0 18	0 13	1 2	0 29	1 4	1 1	4
5	0 16	1 15	0 14	0 23	0 16	1 11	1 6	1 13	1 8	5
6	0 19	1 24	0 16	0 27	0 19	1 19	1 13	1 21	1 16	6
7	0 22	2 3	0 19	1 2	0 22	1 27	1 20	2 0	1 24	7
8	0 25	2 12	0 22	1 6	0 25	2 5	1 28	2 8	2 1	8
9	0 28	2 21	0 24	1 11	0 28	2 13	2 5	2 17	2 9	9
10	1 1	3 0	0 27	1 15	1 1	2 21	2 12	2 26	2 17	10
15	1 17	4 15	1 11	2 8	1 17	4 2	3 18	4 8	3 25	15
20	2 3	6 0	1 24	3 0	2 3	5 12	4 24	5 21	5 3	20

VIMSHOTTARI DASHA—SUB-SUB PERIODS

Sun—Sub-Periods—6 Years

Sun—Inter-Periods

SUN—Sun	m	d	h	*SUN—Moon*	m	d	h	*SUN—Mars*	m	d	h
Sun	0	5	10	Moon	0	15	0	Mars	0	7	8
Moon	0	9	0	Mars	0	10	12	Rahu	0	18	22
Mars	0	6	7	Rahu	0	27	0	Jupiter	0	16	19
Rahu	0	16	5	Jupiter	0	24	0	Saturn	0	19	23
Jupiter	0	14	10	Saturn	0	28	12	Mercury	0	17	21
Saturn	0	17	2	Mercury	0	25	12	Ketu	0	7	8
Mercury	0	15	7	Ketu	0	10	12	Venus	0	21	0
Ketu	0	6	7	Venus	1	0	0	Sun	0	6	7
Venus	0	18	0	Sun	0	9	0	Moon	0	10	12
Total	**3**	**18**	**0**	**Total**	**6**	**0**	**0**	**Total**	**4**	**6**	**0**

SUN—Rahu	m	d	h	*SUN—Jupiter*	m	d	h	*SUN—Saturn*	m	d	h
Rahu	1	18	14	Jupiter	1	8	10	Saturn	1	24	3
Jupiter	1	13	5	Saturn	1	15	14	Mercury	1	18	11
Saturn	1	21	7	Mercury	1	10	19	Ketu	0	19	23
Mercury	1	15	22	Ketu	0	16	19	Venus	1	27	0
Ketu	0	18	21	Venus	1	18	0	Sun	0	17	2
Venus	1	24	0	Sun	0	14	10	Moon	0	28	12
Sun	0	16	5	Moon	0	24	0	Mars	0	19	23
Moon	0	27	0	Mars	0	16	19	Rahu	1	21	7
Mars	0	18	22	Rahu	1	13	5	Jupiter	1	15	15
Total	**10**	**24**	**0**	**Total**	**9**	**18**	**0**	**Total**	**11**	**12**	**0**

SUN—Mercury	m	d	h	*SUN—Ketu*	m	d	h	*SUN—Venus*	m	d	h
Mercury	1	13	8	Ketu	0	7	8	Venus	2	0	0
Ketu	0	17	20	Venus	0	21	0	Sun	0	18	0
Venus	1	21	0	Sun	0	6	7	Moon	1	0	0
Sun	0	15	7	Moon	0	10	12	Mars	0	21	0
Moon	0	25	12	Mars	0	7	8	Rahu	1	24	0
Mars	0	17	21	Rahu	0	18	22	Jupiter	1	18	0
Rahu	1	15	22	Jupiter	0	16	20	Saturn	1	27	0
Jupiter	1	10	19	Saturn	0	19	23	Mercury	1	21	0
Saturn	1	18	11	Mercury	0	17	20	Ketu	0	21	0
Total	**10**	**6**	**0**	**Total**	**4**	**6**	**0**	**Total**	**12**	**0**	**0**

Moon—Sub-Periods—10 Years

Moon—Inter-Periods

MOON—Moon	m	d	h	*MOON—Mars*	m	d	h	*MOON—Rahu*	m	d	h
Moon	0	25	0	Mars	0	12	6	Rahu	2	21	0
Mars	0	17	12	Rahu	1	1	12	Jupiter	2	12	0
Rahu	1	15	0	Jupiter	0	28	0	Saturn	2	25	12
Jupiter	1	10	0	Saturn	1	3	6	Mercury	2	16	12
Saturn	1	17	12	Mercury	0	29	18	Ketu	1	1	12
Mercury	1	12	12	Ketu	0	12	6	Venus	3	0	12
Ketu	0	17	12	Venus	1	5	0	Sun	0	27	0
Venus	1	20	0	Sun	0	10	12	Moon	1	15	0
Sun	0	15	0	Moon	0	17	12	Mars	1	1	0
Total	**10**	**0**	**0**	**Total**	**7**	**0**	**0**	**Total**	**18**	**0**	**0**

MOON—Jupiter	m	d	h	*Moon—Saturn*	m	d	h	*Moon—Mercury*	m	d	h
Jupiter	2	4	0	Saturn	3	0	6	Mercury	2	12	18
Saturn	2	16	0	Mercury	2	20	18	Ketu	0	29	18
Mercury	2	8	0	Ketu	1	3	6	Venus	2	25	0
Ketu	0	28	0	Venus	3	5	0	Sun	0	25	0
Venus	2	20	0	Sun	0	28	12	Moon	1	12	12
Sun	0	24	0	Moon	1	17	12	Mars	0	29	18
Moon	1	10	0	Mars	1	3	6	Rahu	2	16	12
Mars	0	28	0	Rahu	2	25	12	Jupiter	2	8	0
Rahu	2	12	0	Jupiter	2	16	0	Saturn	2	20	18
Total	**16**	**0**	**0**	**Total**	**19**	**0**	**0**	**Total**	**17**	**0**	**0**

MOON—Ketu	m	d	h	*Moon—Venus*	m	d	h	*Moon—Sun*	m	d	h
Ketu	0	12	6	Venus	3	10	10	Sun	0	9	0
Venus	1	5	0	Sun	1	0	0	Moon	0	15	0
Sun	0	10	12	Moon	1	20	0	Mars	0	10	12
Moon	0	17	12	Mars	1	5	0	Rahu	0	27	0
Mars	0	12	6	Rahu	3	0	0	Jupiter	0	24	0
Rahu	1	1	12	Jupiter	2	20	0	Saturn	0	28	12
Jupiter	0	28	0	Saturn	3	5	0	Mercury	0	25	12
Saturn	1	3	6	Mercury	2	25	0	Ketu	0	10	12
Mercury	0	29	18	Ketu	1	5	0	Venus	1	0	0
Total	**7**	**0**	**0**	**Total**	**20**	**0**	**0**	**Total**	**6**	**0**	**0**

Mars—Sub-Periods—7 Years

Mars—Inter-Periods

MARS—Mars	m	d	h	*MARS—Rahu*	m	d	h	*MARS—Jupiter*	m	d	h
Mars	0	8	13.8	Rahu	1	26	16.8	Jupitar	1	14	19.2
Rahu	0	22	1.2	Jupiter	1	20	9.6	Saturn	1	23	4.8
Jupiter	0	19	14.4	Saturn	1	29	20.4	Mercury	1	17	14.4
Saturn	0	23	6.6	Mercury	1	23	13.2	Ketu	0	19	14.4
Mercury	0	20	19.8	Ketu	0	22	1.2	Venus	1	26	0.0
Ketu	0	8	13.8	Venus	2	3	0.0	Sun	0	16	19.2
Venus	0	24	12.0	Sun	0	18	21.6	Moon	0	28	0.0
Sun	0	7	8.4	Moon	1	1	12.0	Mars	0	19	14.4
Moon	0	12	6.0	Mars	0	22	1.2	Rahu	1	20	9.6
Total	**4**	**27**	**0.0**	**Total**	**12**	**18**	**0.0**	**Total**	**11**	**6**	**0.0**

MARS—Saturn	m	d	h
Saturn	2	3	4.2
Mercury	1	26	12.6
Ketu	0	23	6.6
Venus	2	6	12.0
Sun	0	19	22.8
Moon	1	3	6.0
Mars	0	23	6.6
Rahu	1	29	20.4
Jupiter	1	23	4.8
Total	**13**	**9**	**0.0**

MARS—Mercury	m	d	h
Mercury	1	20	13.8
Ketu	0	20	19.8
Venus	1	29	12.0
Sun	0	17	20.4
Moon	0	29	18.0
Mars	0	20	19.8
Rahu	1	23	13.2
Jupiter	1	17	14.4
Saturn	1	26	12.6
Total	**11**	**17**	**0.0**

MARS—Ketu	m	d	h
Ketu	0	8	13.8
Venus	0	24	12.0
Sun	0	7	8.4
Moon	0	12	6.0
Mars	0	8	13.8
Rahu	0	22	1.2
Jupiter	0	19	14.4
Saturn	0	23	6.6
Mercury	0	20	19.8
Total	**4**	**27**	**0.0**

MARS—Venus	m	d	h
Venus	2	10	0
Sun	0	21	0
Moon	1	5	0
Mars	0	24	12
Rahu	2	3	0
Jupiter	1	26	0
Saturn	2	6	12
Mercury	1	29	12
Ketu	0	24	12
Total	**14**	**0**	**0**

MARS—Sun	m	d	h
Sun	0	6	7.2
Moon	0	10	12.0
Mars	0	7	8.4
Rahu	0	18	21.6
Jupiter	0	16	19.2
Saturn	0	19	22.8
Mercury	0	17	20.4
Ketu	0	7	8.4
Venus	0	21	0.0
Total	**4**	**6**	**0.0**

MARS—Moon	m	d	h
Moon	0	17	12
Mars	0	12	6
Rahu	1	1	12
Jupiter	0	28	0
Saturn	1	3	6
Mercury	0	29	18
Ketu	0	12	6
Venus	1	5	0
Sun	0	10	12
Total	**7**	**0**	**0**

Rahu—Sub-Periods—18 Years

Rahu—Inter-Periods

RAHU—Rahu	m	d	h
Rahu	4	25	19.2
Jupiter	4	9	14.4
Saturn	5	3	21.6
Mercury	4	17	16.8
Ketu	1	26	16.8
Venus	5	12	0.0
Sun	1	18	14.4
Moon	2	21	0.0
Mars	1	26	16.8
Total	**32**	**12**	**0.0**

RAHU—Jupiter	m	d	h
Jupiter	3	25	4.8
Saturn	4	16	19.2
Mercury	4	2	9.6
Ketu	1	20	9.6
Venus	4	24	0.0
Sun	1	13	4.0
Moon	2	12	0.8
Mars	1	20	9.6
Rahu	4	9	14.4
Total	**28**	**24**	**0.0**

RAHU—Saturn	m	d	h
Saturn	5	12	10.8
Mercury	4	25	8.4
Ketu	1	29	20.4
Venus	5	21	0.0
Sun	1	21	7.2
Moon	2	25	12.0
Mars	1	29	20.4
Rahu	5	3	21.6
Jupiter	4	16	19.2
Total	**34**	**6**	**0.0**

RAHU—Mercury	m	d	h
Mercury	4	10	1.2
Ketu	1	23	13.2
Venus	5	3	0.0
Sun	1	15	21.6
Moon	2	16	12.0
Mars	1	23	13.2
Rahu	4	17	16.8
Jupiter	4	2	9.6
Saturn	4	25	8.4
Total	**30**	**18**	**0.0**

RAHU—Ketu	m	d	h
Ketu	0	22	1.2
Venus	2	3	0.0
Sun	0	18	21.6
Moon	1	1	12.0
Mars	0	22	1.2
Rahu	1	26	16.8
Jupiter	1	20	9.6
Saturn	1	29	20.4
Mercury	1	23	13.2
Total	**12**	**18**	**0.0**

RAHU—Venus	m	d	h
Venus	6	0	0
Sun	1	24	0
Moon	3	0	0
Mars	2	3	0
Rahu	5	12	0
Jupiter	4	24	0
Saturn	5	21	0
Mercury	5	3	0
Ketu	2	3	0
Total	**36**	**0**	**0**

RAHU—Sun	m	d	h
Sun	0	16	4.8
Moon	0	27	0.0
Mars	0	18	21.6
Rahu	1	18	14.4
Jupiter	1	13	4.8
Saturn	1	21	7.2
Mercury	1	15	21.6
Ketu	0	18	21.6
Venus	1	24	0.0
Total	**10**	**24**	**0.0**

RAHU—Moon	m	d	h
Moon	1	15	0
Mars	1	1	12
Rahu	2	21	0
Jupiter	2	12	0
Saturn	2	25	12
Mercury	2	16	12
Ketu	1	1	12
Venus	3	0	0
Sun	0	27	0
Total	**18**	**0**	**0**

RAHU—Mars	m	d	h
Mars	0	22	1.2
Rahu	1	26	16.8
Jupiter	1	20	9.6
Saturn	1	29	20.4
Mercury	1	23	13.2
Ketu	0	22	1.2
Venus	2	3	0.0
Sun	0	18	21.6
Moon	1	1	12.0
Total	**12**	**18**	**0.0**

Jupiter—Sub-Periods—16 Years

Jupiter—Inter-Periods

JUPITER—Jupiter	m	d	h
Jupiter	3	12	9.6
Saturn	4	1	14.4
Mercury	3	18	19.2
Ketu	1	14	19.2
Venus	4	8	0.0
Sun	1	8	9.6
Moon	2	4	0.0
Mars	1	14	19.2
Rahu	3	25	4.8
Total	**25**	**18**	**0.0**

JUPITER—Saturn	m	d	h
Saturn	4	24	9.6
Mercury	4	9	4.8
Ketu	1	23	4.8
Venus	5	2	0.0
Sun	1	15	14.4
Moon	2	16	0.0
Mars	1	23	4.8
Rahu	4	16	19.2
Jupiter	4	1	14.4
Total	**30**	**12**	**0.0**

JUPITER—Mercury	m	d	h
Mercury	3	25	14.4
Ketu	1	17	14.4
Venus	4	16	0.0
Sun	1	10	19.2
Moon	2	8	0.0
Mars	1	17	14.4
Rahu	4	2	9.6
Jupiter	3	18	19.2
Saturn	4	9	4.8
Total	**27**	**6**	**0.0**

JUPITER—Ketu	m	d	h
Ketu	0	19	14.4
Venus	1	26	0.0
Sun	0	16	19.2
Moon	0	28	0.0
Mars	0	19	14.4
Rahu	1	20	9.6
Jupiter	1	14	19.2
Saturn	1	23	4.8
Mercury	1	17	14.4
Total	**11**	**6**	**0.0**

JUPITER—Venus	m	d	h
Venus	5	10	0
Sun	1	18	0
Moon	2	20	0
Mars	1	26	0
Rahu	4	24	0
Jupiter	4	8	0
Saturn	5	2	0
Mercury	4	16	0
Ketu	1	26	0
Total	**32**	**0**	**0**

JUPITER—Sun	m	d	h
Sun	0	14	9.6
Moon	0	24	0.0
Mars	0	16	19.2
Rahu	1	13	4.8
Jupiter	1	8	9.6
Saturn	1	15	14.4
Mercury	1	10	19.2
Ketu	0	16	19.2
Venus	1	18	0.0
Total	**9**	**18**	**0.0**

JUPITER—Moon	m	d	h
Moon	1	10	0
Mars	0	28	0
Rahu	2	12	0
Jupiter	2	4	0
Saturn	2	16	0
Mercury	2	8	0
Ketu	0	28	0
Venus	2	20	0
Sun	0	24	0
Total	**16**	**0**	**0**

JUPITER—Mars	m	d	h
Mars	0	19	14.4
Rahu	1	20	9.6
Jupiter	1	14	19.2
Saturn	1	23	4.8
Mercury	1	17	14.4
Ketu	0	19	14.4
Venus	1	26	0.0
Sun	0	16	19.2
Moon	0	28	0.0
Total	**11**	**6**	**0.0**

JUPITER—Rahu	m	d	h
Rahu	4	9	14.4
Jupiter	3	25	4.8
Saturn	4	16	19.2
Mercury	4	2	9.6
Ketu	1	20	9.6
Venus	4	24	0.0
Sun	1	13	4.8
Moon	2	12	0.0
Mars	1	20	9.6
Total	**28**	**24**	**0.0**

Saturn—Sub-Periods—19 Years

Saturn—Inter-Periods

SATURN—Saturn	m	d	h
Saturn	5	21	11.4
Mercury	5	3	10.2
Ketu	2	3	4.2
Venus	6	0	12.0
Sun	1	24	3.6
Moon	3	0	6.0
Mars	2	3	4.2
Rahu	5	12	10.8
Jupiter	4	24	9.6
Total	**36**	**3**	**0.0**

SATURN—Mercury	m	d	h
Mercury	4	17	6.6
Ketu	1	26	12.6
Venus	5	11	12.0
Sun	1	18	10.8
Moon	2	20	18.0
Mars	1	26	12.6
Rahu	4	25	8.4
Jupiter	4	9	4.8
Saturn	5	3	10.2
Total	**32**	**9**	**0.0**

SATURN—Ketu	m	d	h
Ketu	0	23	6.6
Venus	2	6	12.0
Sun	0	19	22.8
Moon	1	3	6.0
Mars	0	23	6.6
Rahu	1	29	20.6
Jupiter	1	23	4.8
Saturn	2	3	4.1
Mercury	1	26	12.5
Total	**13**	**9**	**0.0**

SATURN—Venus	m	d	h
Venus	6	10	0
Sun	1	27	0
Moon	3	5	0
Mars	2	6	12
Rahu	5	21	0
Jupiter	5	2	0
Saturn	6	0	12
Mercury	5	11	12
Ketu	2	6	12
Total	**38**	**0**	**0**

SATURN—Sun	m	d	h
Sun	0	17	2.4
Moon	0	28	12.0
Mars	0	19	22.8
Rahu	1	21	7.2
Jupiter	1	15	14.4
Saturn	1	24	3.6
Mercury	1	18	10.8
Ketu	0	19	22.8
Venus	1	27	0.0
Total	**11**	**12**	**0.0**

SATURN—Moon	m	d	h
Moon	1	17	12
Mars	1	3	6
Rahu	2	25	12
Jupiter	2	16	0
Saturn	3	0	6
Mercury	2	20	18
Ketu	1	3	6
Venus	3	5	0
Sun	0	28	12
Total	**19**	**0**	**0**

SATURN—Mars	m	d	h
Mars	0	23	6.6
Rahu	1	29	20.4
Jupiter	1	23	4.8
Saturn	2	3	4.2
Mercury	1	26	12.6
Ketu	0	23	6.6
Venus	2	6	12.0
Sun	0	19	22.8
Moon	1	3	6.0
Total	**13**	**9**	**0.0**

SATURN—Rahu	m	d	h
Rahu	5	3	21.6
Jupiter	4	16	19.2
Saturn	5	12	10.8
Mercury	4	25	8.4
Ketu	1	29	20.4
Venus	5	21	0.0
Sun	1	21	7.2
Moon	2	25	12.0
Mars	1	29	20.4
Total	**34**	**6**	**0.0**

SATURN—Jupiter	m	d	h
Jupiter	4	1	14.4
Saturn	4	24	9.6
Mercury	4	9	4.8
Ketu	1	23	4.8
Venus	5	2	0.0
Sun	1	15	14.4
Moon	2	16	0.0
Mars	1	23	4.8
Rahu	4	16	19.2
Total	**30**	**12**	**0.0**

Mercury—Sub-Periods—17 Years

Mercury—Inter-Periods

MERCURY—Mercury	m	d	h
Mercury	4	2	19.8
Ketu	1	20	13.8
Venus	4	24	12.0
Sun	1	13	8.4
Moon	2	12	6.0
Mars	1	20	13.8
Rahu	4	10	1.2
Jupiter	3	25	14.4
Saturn	4	17	6.6
Total	**28**	**27**	**0.0**

MERCURY—Ketu	m	d	h
Ketu	0	20	19.8
Venus	1	29	12.0
Sun	0	17	20.4
Moon	0	29	18.0
Mars	0	20	19.8
Rahu	1	23	13.2
Jupiter	1	17	14.4
Saturn	1	26	12.6
Mercury	1	20	13.8
Total	**11**	**27**	**0.0**

MERCURY—Venus	m	d	h
Venus	5	20	0
Sun	1	21	0
Moon	2	25	0
Mars	1	29	12
Rahu	5	3	0
Jupiter	4	16	0
Saturn	5	11	12
Mercury	4	24	12
Ketu	1	29	12
Total	**34**	**0**	**0**

MERCURY—Sun	m	d	h
Sun	0	15	7.2
Moon	0	25	12.0
Mars	0	17	20.4
Rahu	1	15	21.6
Jupiter	1	10	19.2
Saturn	1	18	10.8
Mercury	1	13	8.4
Ketu	0	17	20.4
Venus	1	21	0.0
Total	**10**	**6**	**0.0**

MERCURY—Moon	m	d	h
Moon	1	12	12
Mars	0	29	18
Rahu	2	16	12
Jupiter	2	8	0
Saturn	2	20	18
Mercury	2	12	6
Ketu	0	29	18
Venus	2	25	0
Sun	0	25	12
Total	**17**	**0**	**0**

MERCURY—Mars	m	d	h
Mars	0	20	19.8
Rahu	1	23	13.2
Jupiter	1	17	14.4
Saturn	1	26	12.6
Mercury	1	20	13.8
Ketu	0	20	19.8
Venus	1	29	12.0
Sun	0	17	20.4
Moon	0	29	18.0
Total	**11**	**27**	**0.0**

MERCURY—Rahu	m	d	h
Rahu	4	17	16.8
Jupiter	4	2	9.6
Saturn	4	25	8.4
Mercury	4	10	1.2
Ketu	1	23	13.2
Venus	5	3	0.0
Sun	1	15	21.6
Moon	2	16	12.0
Mars	1	23	13.2
Total	**30**	**18**	**0.0**

MERCURY—Jupiter	m	d	h
Jupiter	3	18	19.2
Saturn	4	9	4.8
Mercury	3	25	14.4
Ketu	1	17	14.4
Venus	4	16	0.0
Sun	1	10	19.2
Moon	2	8	0.0
Mars	1	17	14.4
Rahu	4	2	9.6
Total	**27**	**6**	**0.0**

MERCURY—Saturn	m	d	h
Saturn	5	3	10.2
Mercury	4	17	6.6
Ketu	1	26	12.6
Venus	5	11	12.0
Sun	1	18	10.8
Moon	2	20	18.0
Mars	1	26	12.6
Rahu	4	25	8.4
Jupiter	4	9	4.8
Total	**32**	**9**	**0.0**

Ketu—Sub-Periods—7 Years

Ketu—Inter-Periods

KETU—Ketu	m	d	h
Ketu	0	8	13.8
Venus	0	24	12.0
Sun	0	7	8.4
Moon	0	12	6.0
Mars	0	8	13.8
Rahu	0	22	1.2
Jupiter	0	19	14.4
Saturn	0	23	6.6
Mercury	0	20	19.8
Total	**4**	**27**	**0.0**

KETU—Venus	m	d	h
Venus	2	10	0
Sun	0	21	0
Moon	1	5	0
Mars	0	24	12
Rahu	2	3	0
Jupiter	1	26	0
Saturn	2	6	12
Mercury	1	29	12
Ketu	0	24	12
Total	**14**	**0**	**0**

KETU—Sun	m	d	h
Sun	0	6	7.2
Moon	0	10	12.0
Mars	0	7	8.4
Rahu	0	18	21.6
Jupiter	0	16	19.2
Saturn	0	19	22.8
Mercury	0	17	20.4
Ketu	0	7	8.4
Venus	0	21	0.0
Total	**4**	**6**	**0.0**

KETU—Moon	m	d	h
Moon	0	17	12.0
Mars	0	12	6.0
Rahu	1	1	12.0
Jupiter	0	28	0.0
Saturn	1	3	6.0
Mercury	0	29	18.8
Ketu	0	12	6.0
Venus	1	5	0.0
Sun	0	10	12.0
Total	**7**	**0**	**0.0**

KETU—Mars	m	d	h
Mars	0	8	13.8
Rahu	0	22	1.2
Jupiter	0	19	14.4
Saturn	0	23	6.6
Mercury	0	20	19.8
Ketu	0	8	13.8
Venus	0	24	12.0
Sun	0	7	8.4
Moon	0	12	6.0
Total	**4**	**27**	**0.0**

KETU—Rahu	m	d	h
Rahu	1	26	16.8
Jupiter	1	20	9.6
Saturn	1	29	20.4
Mercury	1	23	13.2
Ketu	0	22	1.2
Venus	2	3	0.0
Sun	0	18	21.6
Moon	1	1	12.0
Mars	0	22	1.2
Total	**12**	**18**	**0.0**

KETU—Jupiter	m	d	h
Jupiter	1	14	19.2
Saturn	1	23	4.8
Mercury	1	17	14.4
Ketu	0	19	14.4
Venus	1	26	0.0
Sun	0	16	19.2
Moon	0	28	0.0
Mars	0	19	14.4
Rahu	1	20	9.6
Total	**11**	**6**	**0.0**

KETU—Saturn	m	d	h
Saturn	2	3	4.2
Mercury	1	26	12.6
Ketu	0	23	6.6
Venus	2	6	12.0
Sun	0	19	22.8
Moon	1	3	6.0
Mars	0	23	6.6
Rahu	1	29	20.4
Jupiter	1	23	4.8
Total	**13**	**9**	**0.0**

KETU—Mercury	m	d	h
Mercury	1	20	13.8
Ketu	0	20	19.8
Venus	1	29	12.0
Sun	0	17	20.4
Moon	0	29	18.0
Mars	0	20	19.8
Rahu	1	23	13.2
Jupiter	1	17	14.4
Saturn	1	26	12.6
Total	**11**	**27**	**0.0**

Venus—Sub-Periods—20 Years

Venus—Inter-Periods

VENUS—Venus	m.	d	h
Venus	6	20	0
Sun	2	0	0
Moon	3	10	0
Mars	2	10	0
Rahu	6	0	0
Jupiter	5	10	0
Saturn	6	10	0
Mercury	5	20	0
Ketu	2	10	0
Total	**40**	**0**	**0**

VENUS—Sun	m	d	h
Sun	0	18	0
Moon	1	0	0
Mars	0	21	0
Rahu	1	24	0
Jupiter	1	18	0
Saturn	1	27	0
Mercury	1	21	0
Ketu	0	21	0
Venus	2	0	0
Total	**12**	**0**	**0**

VENUS—Moon	m	d	h
Moon	1	20	0
Mars	1	5	0
Rahu	3	0	0
Jupiter	2	20	0
Saturn	3	5	0
Mercury	2	25	0
Ketu	1	5	0
Venus	3	10	0
Sun	1	0	0
Total	**20**	**0**	**0**

VENUS—Mars	m	d	h
Mars	0	24	12
Rahu	2	3	0
Jupiter	1	26	0
Saturn	2	6	12
Mercury	1	29	12
Ketu	0	24	12
Venus	2	10	0
Sun	0	21	0
Moon	1	5	0
Total	**14**	**0**	**0**

VENUS—Rahu	m	d	h
Rahu	5	12	0
Jupiter	4	24	0
Saturn	5	21	0
Mercury	5	3	0
Ketu	2	3	0
Venus	6	0	0
Sun	1	24	0
Moon	3	0	0
Mars	2	3	0
Total	**36**	**0**	**0**

VENUS—Jupiter	m	d	h
Jupiter	4	8	0
Saturn	5	2	0
Mercury	4	16	0
Ketu	1	26	0
Venus	5	10	0
Sun	1	18	0
Moon	2	20	0
Mars	1	26	0
Rahu	4	24	0
Total	**32**	**0**	**0**

VENUS—Saturn	m	d	h
Saturn	6	0	12
Mercury	5	11	12
Ketu	2	6	12
Venus	6	10	0
Sun	1	27	0
Moon	3	5	0
Mars	2	6	12
Rahu	5	21	0
Jupiter	5	2	0
Total	**38**	**0**	**0**

VENUS—Mercury	m	d	h
Mercury	4	24	12
Ketu	1	29	12
Venus	5	20	0
Sun	1	21	0
Moon	2	25	0
Mars	1	29	12
Rahu	5	3	0
Jupiter	4	16	0
Saturn	5	11	12
Total	**34**	**0**	**0**

VENUS—Ketu	m	d	h
Ketu	0	24	12
Venus	2	10	0
Sun	0	21	0
Moon	1	5	0
Mars	0	24	12
Rahu	2	3	0
Jupiter	1	26	0
Saturn	2	6	12
Mercury	1	29	12
Total	**14**	**0**	**0**

GLOSSARY

Aspects : Sextile (3rd-11th) and Trine (5th-9th) are friendly or benefic aspects; Square (4th-10th) and opposition (1st-7th) are inimical aspects. Conjunctions can be both-depends upon the planets. Value aspects are given in Table VI.

Attributes of Planets : For attributes viz., nature, gender, direction, appearance, temperament, Hue, Colour etc. See Tables IV and V

Combust : When a planet is within 15 degrees of the sun then it is called Combust and its effect becomes malefic. Venus and Mercury do not lose their effect by combustion. Another important point is that if a planet comes with in 7 minutes of Sun (inside the penumbra of Sun) then it becomes a benefic and shows wonderful results.

Dufalikuttha : It is a variation of Itthashal Yoga. If a slower moving planet instead of the faster moving planet, is in its own or exaltation sign, then it is called Dufalikuttha Yoga.

Dutthothambir : When (i) both the planets in question are weak (ii) one of the above planet apply to a third planet which is stronger (iii) or two other planets are strong and one of these apply to the lord of the Ascendant or the significator. This yoga indicates accomplishment through a third party.

Duraffa : This is just the opposite of the Kuttha Yoga. When all the planets are weak then it is called Duraffa Yoga-Indication is that the year under consideration would be loaded with problems.

Drekkana Strength : Drekkana is the same as decanate. A sign divided into three parts of 10° each. See Table XI for the Drekkana. Total ten points are allotted to it.

Directional Strength : It is an important factor in the Solar Return. Planets in certain houses have full directional strength viz., Mercury and Jupiter in the 1st house; Moon and Venus in the 4th house; Saturn in the 7th house; Sun and Mars in the 10th house. Directional strength proportionately decreases according as the distance from the cusp of the houses where they have full i.e., 100 percent strength.

Exaltation Strength : Twenty points are allotted to this. See Table IX for exact degree of exaltation of each planet.

Friends-Enemies : For Friendships between planets see Table VII. The temporary friendship in the Solar Return are planets in the 3rd, 5th, 9h and 11th from each other are friends. Planets in the 4th, 7th and 10th from each other are enemies. Planets in the same sign can be either friends or enemies. The remaining planets are neutrals.

Gair Kamboola : When (i) the Ascendant lord and the Significator apply with in orb and (ii) Moon is void of course in the last degree of a sign but within orb of a planet of a Planet (A) which is posited in the next sign, (iii) Planet (A) is in its own or exaltation sign or is very powerful then it is called Gair Kambool Yoga. 'Gair' in Persian means an unknown person, not related, and this yoga indicates accomplishment through an unknown or outside agency.

Hadda Strength : See Table X for Hadda Rulership. Total 15 points are allotted to it.

Houses : There are 12 houses. The matters to be judged are given on pages (65 to 75) of Ch. II.

Hinansha-Patyansha : Another type of Dasha for the year, very useful. The Ascendant and the seven planets (excluding Rahu and Ketu) are written down in Ascending order irrespective of their signs. The difference in their degrees i.e; between (2 and 1), (3 and 2), and so on gives the duration of the dahsas (See Table XX).

Horary Astrology : It is an amazing branch of Astrology. A chart is erected for the time a query is made or when a querent goes to an Astrologer. The Astrologer erects a Chart for that time and this chart tells us about the past, present and future. This is based on the principle that a querent takes with him the essence of his stars when he meets an Astrologer. The Horary Astrology is also useful when there is no horoscope or no recording of the birth time.

Israf : It is called 'separation'. When two planets are in orb and the faster moving planet separates from the slower moving planet then it is called Israff. This yoga causes frustration.

Itthashal : Application between two planets when they are in orb and the faster moving planet applies to the slower one and completes the degree of the slower planet before the other planet changes sign, then it is called 'Itthashal'. This yoga, is an indication of successful completion of the work.

Ikkabal : All planets in angular and succeedent houses indicate Ikkaabal yoga. This is a good yoga.

Induvar : All planets in the cadent houses create Induvar yoga. This is not a good yoga.

Joys of Planets : Planets strong and well placed in own sign, exaltation sign, in particular houses are said to be joyously placed and they are deemed to be strong (see pages 54, 55 ch I) .

Khallasar : This yoga means 'Khallas' i.e., finished, no accomplishment. When Moon is void of course without any of the features mentioned above in the Gair Kamboola Yoga then it is called Khallasar yoga.

Kambool Yoga : If Itthashal exists and simultaneously Moon also applies to either of the two planets than the Itthashal Yoga becomes many times stronger. There would be 16 types of Kambool Yoga which would depend upon the strength of the Moon and the Planets.

Kuttha Yoga : If all planets are strong then this is called Kuttha Yoga and it indicates a remarkable year for success.

Mudda Dasha : The major periods of each planet in the Vimshottari Mahadasha is divided by 120 (which is the total duration of it) and we get the Mudda Dashas for the year. For example 20 years of Venus divided by 120 [(20 × 12) months ÷ 120]=2 months. See Table XVIII for the beginning of Dasha.

Manau Yoga : If a planet (A) within orb with planet (B) to which it applies but before the application is over, a third planet (C) or another planet which is nearer completes an aspect with the planet (B), then frustration of the work should be judged. This is Manau yoga.

Nakta Yoga : Two planets not in aspect or not in orbs, receiving light from a third planet which is in aspect or in orb with both the planets then it is called Nakta Yoga. This is an indication of realization through a third party.

Navamsha : A house is divided in 9 parts. Each part is of 3 degrees 20 minutes. Total five points are allotted to it. A planet strong in Navansha is deemed to be very strong both in the Natal Chart as well as in the Solar Return Chart. (see sub division). ch I.

Orb : Planets within 8° of each other on either side are said to be in orb. For Sun it is 15° and for Moon 12°.This is called Deeptansha in Sanskrit. In astrology it stands for degrees around which a planet is more effective For example if we say that a planet has 8 to 15 degrees of orb, it means that if we draw a circle (to be more precise, a sphere) with a radius of 8 to 15 degrees taking the planet in question as the centre, it will indicate the area inside which a planet would be more effective. As the circumference come closer and closer to the center the effectiveness increases. Orbs are needed to see if the Sixteen Yogas will be effective or not.

Panchavargyabala : Panch means five-bala means Strength. The word means five types of strengths viz., Exaltation strength, Rashi Strength, Hadda Strength, Drekkana Strength and Navansha Strength. The strength of planets is calculated and then added. After adding them together they are divided by 4 (for illustration see Table XII) to arrive at the proper strength. This strength is called the Panchavargyabala. It gives an idea as to how the Mudda Dasha of that planet will be and (2) to decide as to which planet will be the Varshesh viz., Lord of the Year.

Planets : All nine planets viz., Sun, Moon, Mars, Mercury, Jupiter, Venus, Saturn, Rahu and Ketu are used in the Solar Return Charts. Uranus, Neptune and Pluto's light did not come to Earth at the time of Tajik and Vedic Astrology so these are not used.

Rashi Strength : Total thirty points are allotted to it. See page 89 chapter III.

Radda yoga : This Persian word means cancellation, rejection. This will be when a planet (A) applying to another Planet is so weak by being combust, debilitated, in an enemy's sign or being retrograde or in the same degree as a malefic, that it is incapable of transferring any light to the other planet, then it should be taken as frustration.

The Solar Return Chart : Or Varshaphal; when the Sun in its revolution comes back to the same sign, degree, minutes, and seconds which it occupies at birth then the chart erected for that time is called the Solar Return Chart. Technically speaking the Sun is stationery and it is the earth which rotates and so in its rotation when it completes exactly one revolution then it is in easier language called that the Sun has come back to the position that it occupied at birth. This chart is like viewing the events of the year with a magnifying glass.

Surya Siddhanta : A monumental work on Hindu Astronomy (in Sanskrit), dating back to more than two thousand years ago. It states that a Solar Revolution takes 365 days 15 Ghatis 31 Palas and 30 Vipalas. (Ghatis, Palas, and Vipalas are the system of keeping time.

Subdivisions : 'Vargas' are used in the Natal and the Varsha charts. In the Varsha lagna the sub-divisions are somewhat different. The emphasis is mostly laid on the 'Navansha' which is the ninth divisions of a sign. Each division consists of 3° and 20' each-(See Table) the 12 divisions are Graha, Hora, Dreshkana, Chaturthansha, Panchmansha, Dwadashansha, Shashthansha, Saptamansha, Ashtamansha, Navansha, Dashmansha and Ekadashansha. See Sub-Divisions in Ch. I and Table III and Appendix.

Sign of the Zodiac : The same twelve signs viz., Aries, Taurus, Gemini, Cancer, Leo, Virgo, Libra, Scorpio, Sagittarius, Capricorn, Aquarius, Pisces.

Sensitive Points : These are called Saham in Sanskrit. Each one of these points are calculated for a specific matter viz., wealth, brother, friends, etc. they are related to different departments of life. This is arrived at by the addition and subtraction of the longitudes of various planets. This gives an insight into the crux of an issue. Out of these the most important is the Punya Saham also called 'Pars Fortunae' in English. These sahams are analysed in the in the nativity as well as in the Horary Charts and the Solar return charts. See Table XIV .

Tajik : As regards Zodiacal sign, these are the same twelve as in the Natal Chart. Tajik is an Arabic word. Some difference do exists in the gender of the planets viz., Sun, Mars and Jupiter are male whereas Moon, Mercury, Venus and Saturn are female. There is no planet of neutral gender in it. The planets in the Tajik System aspect mutually as in the Western System viz., Conjunctions, Square, Sextile, trine and opposition.

Trirashipati : See Table VIII.

Timing of Events : In the Solar Return, timing is arrived at by (a) Mudda Dasha or (b) by

Hinansha Patyanasha Dasha or (c) by the sixteen yoga.

The Lord of the Year : Also called Varsheh; Strength of the planet after calculating the five types of strength i.e., Panchavagayabala, the lord of the year is decided. The eligible planets are; Lord of the Ascendant in birth chart, lord of the Ascendant in Solar Return Chart; the dispositer of Muntha; The lord of the Sun-sign if the year commences during the day otherwise the lord of Moon sign (if the birth is at night). The fifth planet entitled to be the lord of the year is the Trirashipati. See Table VIII for the rulers (Trirashipati).One of the above five and only if he also aspects the Ascendant can be Varshesh i.e. Lord of the Year.

Tambira Yoga : This yoga indicates belated success. This takes place when (1) the two planets are not in aspect to each other (2) Either of the above two is strong and placed at the end of a sign (with in orb or conjunction) with a third planet, which is in a stronger position in the next sign, then it is called Tambir yoga.

Tripataki Chakra : The erection of this figure combines, the birth Chart, the number of years elapsed and the Solar Return Chart. The Vedh of Moon gives a clear indication as to how the entire year would be.

Vedha : Obstruction. It is calculated in different manners in the nativity and the Solar Return Chart.

Vedic	:	Of the Vedas, Astrology or Jyotish originates in the Vedas and so it is called the Vedic. It is the same as the Hindu System or as practised in India viz., Nirayan System.
Yamaya Yoga	:	If no aspect exists between the lord of Ascendant and a significator and a third planet slower in motion than one of the two above, is situated in a degree which is more than the degree of one planet and less than the degree of the other planet then it is called yamaya Yoga. This is an indication of accomplishment through the help of an agency.

INDEX

Q

R

S

T

U

V